ISLAMIC HISTORY

A.D. 600–750 (A.H. 132)

A NEW INTERPRETATION

To Bessie and Neil Tamim Shaban

ISLAMIC HISTORY

A.D. 600–750 (A.H. 132)

A NEW INTERPRETATION

M. A. SHABAN

Lecturer in Arabic,
School of Oriental and African Studies,
University of London

CAMBRIDGE
AT THE UNIVERSITY PRESS
1971

Published by the Syndics of the Cambridge University Press
Bentley House, 200 Euston Road, London NW1 2DB
American Branch: 32 East 57th Street, New York, N.Y.10022

Library of Congress Catalogue Card Number: 79–145604

ISBN: 0 521 08137 8

Printed in Great Britain
at the University Printing House, Cambridge
(Brooke Crutchley, University Printer)

CONTENTS

MAPS

ACKNOWLEDGEMENTS

It is my pleasant duty to express my gratitude to many friends and colleagues. Mr William Q. Hunter, a former student and good friend, generously gave time and effort to help re-write a good part of the first draft of this work; many of the better phrases in this book are the product of his elegant style. Professor Ira Lapidus read an early draft and kindly made some useful suggestions. I shall always be indebted to Professor C. F. Beckingham, who read the typescript at various stages of development, for his continual encouragement and invaluable advice. I am also grateful to Professor T. M. Johnstone who read the proofs with meticulous care, correcting many a mistake and smoothing the rough edges of this work.

My special thanks go to Mrs Dawn Hubbard who typed and re-typed the manuscript with a skill and patience which made my task of re-writing almost a pleasant one. I also thank Mrs Helga Ramsay who assisted in the re-typing of the manuscript. My debt to my wife, for all her help, is immeasurable.

Thanks are due to the Cambridge University Press for publishing the book. I am greatly indebted to the editorial staff and the printers for the considerable patience they have shown and the great care they have taken in the production of this book.

PREFACE

This work presents a new interpretation of early Islamic history in the light of a detailed scrutiny of the sources available. This interpretation not only uses newly discovered material but also, and perhaps to a greater extent, re-examines and re-interprets material which has been known to us for many decades. Indeed, the latter proved most rewarding in my study *The 'Abbāsid Revolution*, and in this volume I follow basically the same approach, applying it to the whole Arab empire instead of only to the province of Khurāsān.

For the purposes of this work, a systematic attempt has been made to follow, as closely as possible, the establishment of an Islamic regime in Arabia and its sudden expansion into an empire. Special attention has been given to the way the Arab tribesmen were settled in the various provinces, their relationship with the conquered peoples, their varying interests, activities and rivalries, their relations with the central government and the attempts of the latter to establish its authority over the vast conquered territories. At the same time, an effort has been made to spare the reader the elaborate details of each particular situation and to present instead a concerted analysis of the constantly changing conditions all over the empire.

The events of this period have too often been explained on the basis of imaginary tribal jealousies or irrational personal conflicts. Such explanations completely neglect the logical interests of the Arabs and severely underrate their normal human capability to adjust to new circumstances. Admittedly this is never easy to do and it takes time, but the Arabs, who were able to adapt themselves to the harsh life of the Arabian Peninsula, could certainly adapt themselves to a more comfortable life elsewhere. The history of the period studied in this volume is, in fact, the history of the problems of this adaptation with all its implications. The Arab statesmen, in spite of their occasional shortcomings, were responsible leaders primarily concerned with the success of their policies, the preservation of their empire and the welfare of their followers in the circumstances of their times. The political behaviour of these leaders and their changes of policy must be understood in this light as logical steps in pursuit of their objectives rather than as whimsical actions based on personal hatred or fanatical delusions.

There is no doubt that Arabic sources contain enough reliable material to provide a good deal more than a broad outline of the history of this period. It has been my concern to find, understand and analyse such material in the light of the general character of each source and in relation to the material collected from other sources. In this respect, considerable care has been taken to ascertain the exact meaning and to define the precise use of important terms used by the compilers of the sources and the authorities they quote. In most cases such definition has helped to explain the specific interests and activities of the groups and peoples concerned. This basic understanding is vital to the proper use of these sources and without it one can be led into a wilderness of incomprehensible phenomena.

Footnotes have been deliberately kept to a minimum and only major sources are cited in support of points of fact and interpretation. No attempt has been made to discuss the arguments of other scholars of this period. Such discussion would only have confused the issues and seriously disrupted the sequence of arguments put forward in this volume. However, it is my hope that this work will be challenging to students and scholars alike and may stimulate further research on the subject.

I also hope that it will not be long before the appearance of my next work which deals with the history of the ʻAbbāsid period until the Turkish Saljūq invasion.

M. A. S.

Cambridge
February, 1971

I

THE ISLAMIC REVOLUTION IN ITS ENVIRONMENT

It is difficult to write objectively about the rise of Islam or, for that matter, of any other religion. Leaving aside personal convictions, the historian is usually confronted with a great deal of obscurity about the origins of the religion concerned. If any details about the early development of the religion survive, they are, in most cases, highly coloured and often exaggerated, so that it is difficult to distinguish fact from myth. Islam is more fortunate than Christianity in so far as we have more information, at least about its founder. Yet the material we have about the condition of Arabia at this time is so tantalizingly fragmentary that it does not allow us fully to understand the history of this period. Much has been written about the life and career of Muḥammad, and every detail has been adequately scrutinized and fully analysed to the extent that we are now generally assured about the basic facts of his activities. Nevertheless, these facts by themselves do not explain all these activities nor do they make it any easier to understand his motives. Of course any explanation is subject to the interpretation of these activities and it is only natural that historians should differ in such interpretation. The problem is that because of the scarcity of material about the rest of Arabia, these interpretations are mostly conjectures rather than adequately documented historical analyses. Thus E. A. Belyaev was relying on the arguments of Friedrich Engels rather than on our sources when he wrote, "thus Islam arose in Arabia, a new ideology reflecting considerable changes in Arab society, namely inequality in property, slavery and development of exchanges. The rise of this new ideology was due to the formation of a slave-holding regime within a decaying primitive-communal society".[1] Undoubtedly it was a new ideology and undoubtedly there were considerable changes in Arab society, but the rest of the argument

[1] E. A. Belyaev, *Arabs, Islam and the Arab Caliphate*, tr. Adolphe Gourevitch, London, 1969, p. 115.

is not supported by any shadow of evidence in our sources. On the other hand W. Montgomery Watt writes, "the essential situation out of which Islam emerged was the contrast and conflict between the Meccan nomadic outlook and attitudes and the new material (or economic) environment in which they found themselves". Watt continues to say, "With (the) breakdown of morality and failure of public opinion was connected a deterioration in the religious life of the Meccans. The traditional morality of the desert had become irrelevant in Mecca."[1] There is much to commend Watt's argument, but unfortunately he limited himself mainly to study and discussion of Makka and Madīna. He did not pay enough attention to investigating conditions in Arabia as a whole. Such investigation is essential if we are to understand conditions in Makka and the activities of Muḥammad in both Makka and Madīna. But this is a very difficult task and, in all fairness, the insufficiency of research in this respect is mainly the fault of previous scholarship. Fortunately more attention is now being paid to these problems and it is to our advantage that we have the badly needed work of such scholars as M. J. Kister.[2] A picture is now emerging of highly complex relationships in Arabia prior to the rise of Islam. These relationships linked the inhabitants of Makka with the inhabitants of most of the rest of Arabia, both nomad and settled, in expanding trade. This was international trade on a large scale which involved the two great powers of the time, the Sāsānian and Byzantine empires. Naturally their interests had far-reaching effects in Arabia itself. The Sāsānians were more inclined than the Byzantines to use force to safeguard their interest in this trade. Although they occupied Yaman *c.* A.D. 570–5 and established their control on both sides of the Persian Gulf, the rest of Arabia eluded their domination. They tried to make use of their vassals, the kings of Ḥīra, on their south-west frontiers to subjugate by force the tribesmen of the central Arab plateau, but this policy only served to disclose the weakness of the kingdom of Ḥīra and the result was its fall. It was no coincidence that the fall of Ḥīra was concurrent with the rise of Makka to new wealth and power.

The Byzantines were perhaps more realistic in their Arabian

[1] W. Montgomery Watt, *Muḥammad, Prophet and Statesman*, London, 1961, pp. 48–51.

[2] References are made below to Kister's well-documented articles; with some modification his explanations of hitherto unexplained phenomena and his exhaustive references to the sources provide the basis for this present interpretation.

policy. While they themselves refrained from any military adventures in Arabia, they witnessed and probably encouraged the attempt of their co-religionists the Abyssinians to conquer Yaman about A.D. 525 and then to attack Makka itself soon afterwards in order to establish control over the Yaman–Syria route. After the failure of this venture the Byzantines satisfied themselves with diplomatic manœuvres aimed at extending their sphere of influence southwards, if not at establishing a vassal regime in Makka like that of the kingdom of Ghassān in southern Syria. When this did not succeed they were only too happy to treat with the Makkans in order to guarantee the flow of trade.

It is impossible to think of Makka in terms other than trade; its only *raison d'être* was trade. It was first established as a local trading centre around a religious shrine. As a sanctuary, the visitors there were assured the safety of their lives and were required to suspend their feuds as long as they remained. To guarantee their safety *en route*, an elaborate system of sacred months, pilgrimage and religious rites was established with the concurrence of the surrounding tribesmen. The success of this system resulted in the expansion of trade, and this in turn led to the establishment of new market places. The notion of the sacred territory, *ḥaram*, was extended to cover those markets which were also held in the sacred months in co-ordination with the pilgrimage.[1] Thus from the very beginning religion was inseparable from trade and the success of one only helped to enhance the success of the other. In such circumstances and in spite of the fact that each clan had its own deity it was inevitable that the Makkan sanctuary should hold a certain pre-eminence for the tribesmen benefiting from the Makkan trade system. To signify this the clans adhering to this system used to place symbols of their deities in the Kaʿba, the shrine of Makka. It was also inevitable that the Makkan deities should hold a higher status in this house of gods. Allah was certainly one of the Makkan deities, probably one of the earliest, although by the time of Muḥammad he was surpassed in status by other deities. In the first half of the sixth century, Makka was prospering and its local trade was dependent on its religious prestige, but this was in itself part of its trade system.

[1] This notion is adequately emphasized by R. B. Serjeant, "*Ḥaram* and *Ḥawṭah*, The Sacred Enclave in Arabia", *Mélanges Taha Husain*, Cairo, 1962, pp. 41–58.

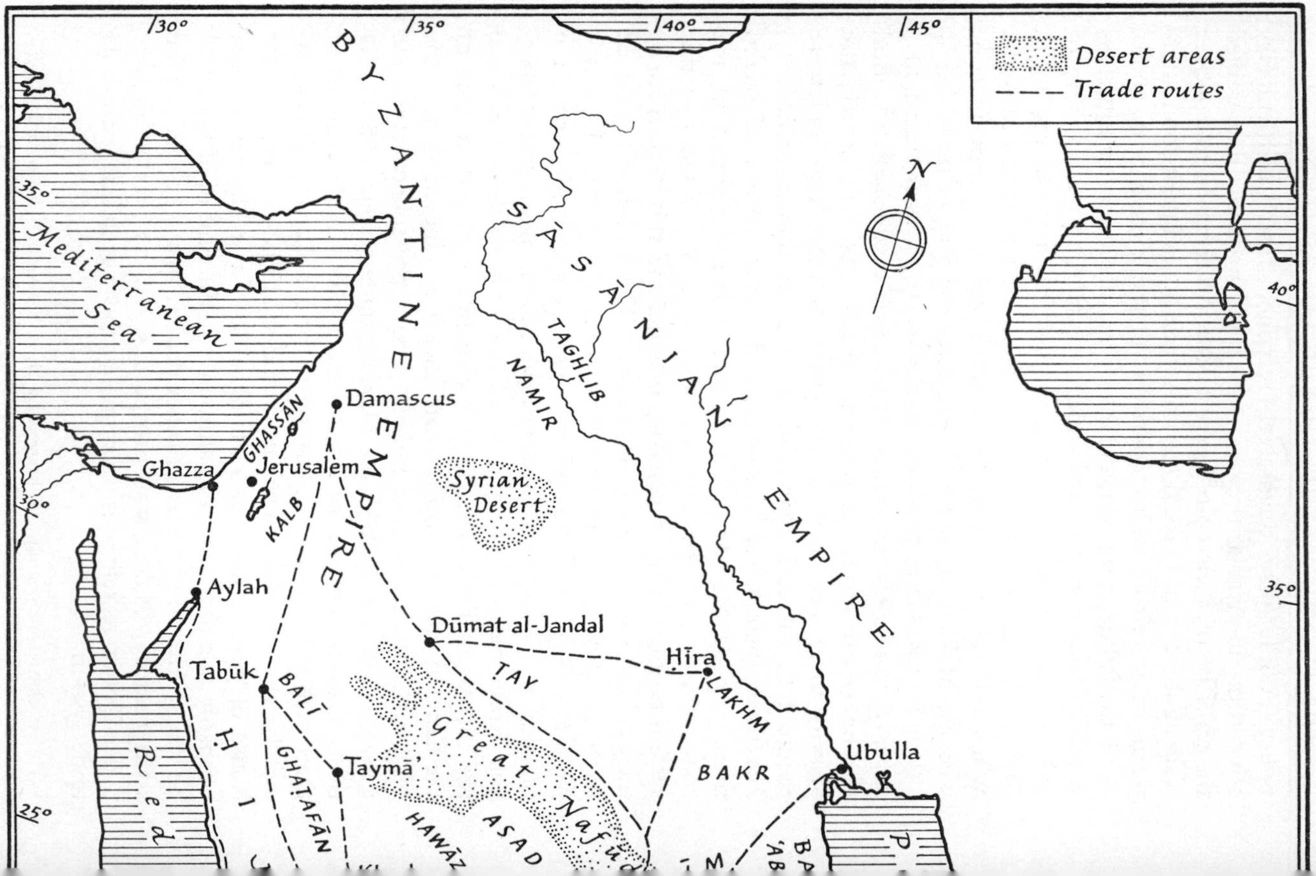
Desert areas
Trade routes
BYZANTINE EMPIRE
SĀSĀNIAN EMPIRE
Mediterranean Sea
Syrian Desert
Great Nafūd
Red
Damascus
Jerusalem
Ghazza
Aylah
Tabūk
Taymā'
Dūmat al-Jandal
Ḥīra
Ubulla
GHASSĀN
KALB
TAGHLIB
NAMIR
TAY
LAKHM
BAKR
BALĪ
GHAṬAFĀN
ASAD
HAWĀZ
'AB
BA
P
N
30°
35°
40°
45°
25°

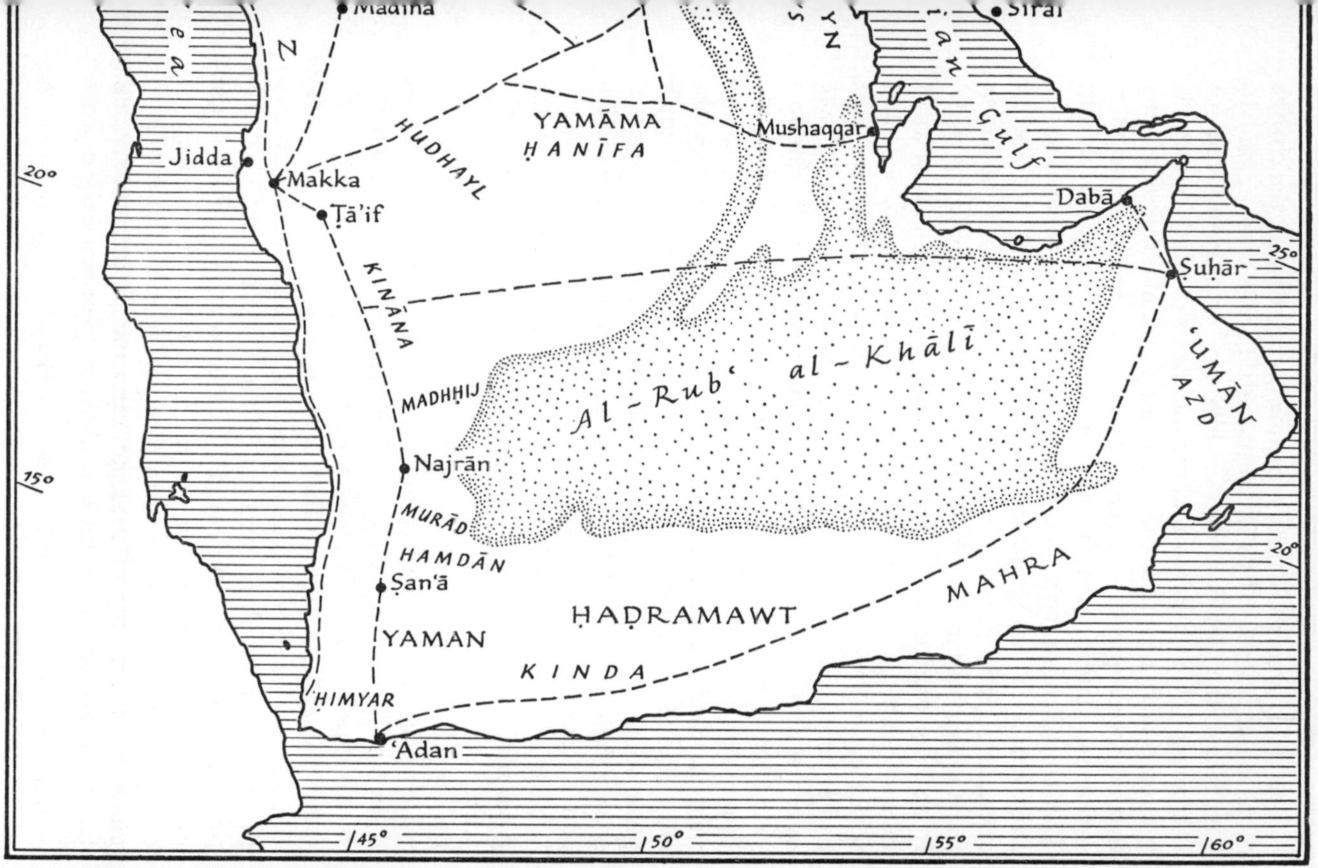

1 The Arabian Peninsula at the rise of Islam, illustrating trade routes, desert areas and tribal distribution

The real change in Makka's fortunes occurred with the change of its trade from local to international. This is now proved to have been the achievement of Hāshim, great-grandfather of Muḥammad, who lived around the middle of the sixth century. It is a remarkable tribute to the astuteness of the Makkan merchants that they were quick to perceive the vacuum created in the international commerce of their time, let alone to step swiftly into it. The struggle of the two great powers to dominate the trade routes and centres in Arabia was coming to a standstill. Makka, an expanding trade centre, situated on the crossroads of major trade routes, was in a most fortunate position to handle this trade. It had the expertise, the contacts and apparently a surplus of internal trade which could be channelled to foreign markets and which could very well supply the necessary capital. Above all it had an existing system which could be easily expanded to take over the greater volume of international trade, and Hāshim provided the conditions for this expansion. He secured from the Byzantine emperor a safe conduct for the merchants of Makka and their merchandise when they visited Syria. The emperor was probably glad to grant such a charter, at no cost to himself, which promised to extend his influence at least with some leading personages in Arabia. Similar charters were also secured from the Persian and Abyssinian rulers.[1]

Now, Hāshim turned to the more difficult side of the deal, the Arab side. The security of the caravans of Makka depended on the attitude of various clans, some of whom were not participants in the local Makkan system. To these Hāshim submitted a proposal which gave them a market for their products and a profit for their merchandise at no cost to themselves. Makkan merchants would simply take such goods with them to Syria and, on their return, would pay back to their would-be partners their capital and all their profits. In return these tribesmen would guarantee the safety of Makkan caravans in their territories. This was probably the original form of *īlāf*, pact of security, which was the most widely applied. Other forms of *īlāf* involved a payment of tax by the tribesmen wishing to take part in trade but unable to guarantee the safety of Makkan caravans in their territories. Hāshim collected these taxes to enable him to organize the defence

[1] M. J. Kister, "Mecca and Tamīm", *Journal of Economic and Social History of the Orient*, 1965, pp. 116–17.

of the caravans.[1] As for those clans which were already participating in the local trade of Makka and thus recognized its sanctuary and its sacred months and were committed to defend them, the situation was much simpler. The expansion of Makkan trade would give them more reason to abide by these agreements. They emerged as the *ḥums*, a word which denotes ideas of courage, strictness in religion and also dedication to a sanctuary. Thus Makka itself was proclaimed *dār* (abode) *al-ḥums*, and the Kaʿba was *al-ḥamsā'*. This alliance, the *ḥums*, included Quraysh, the inhabitants of Makka, and many other clans which lived in different areas of Arabia and had no common tribal origins. More significant is that these clans were in control of many trade routes across the peninsula.[2] They also referred to themselves as *ahl* (the people of) Allah.[3] Adherence to the *ḥums* was thus equivalent to and embodied the recognition of this one deity, who was possibly the personal god of Hāshim and his immediate family.[4]

To cement the alliances of the *ḥums* Quraysh granted the other clans a share in its dominance in accordance with their strength and services to the "Commonwealth of Makka". Kister has proved beyond any doubt the close relationship between Quraysh and clans of Tamīm who were "even included in the body politic of Makka".[5] Quraysh granted leaders of these clans some control of the markets in its own territory and even authority in performing the rites of the pilgrimage. Another plausible suggestion by Kister is that some of Tamīm participated in an inter-tribal militia to guard Makka itself and its markets.[6] Of course such sharing in responsibility would entail sharing in the profits of the whole enterprise. It is also reasonable to assume that Quraysh would require the participant clans to pay their share in the expense of maintaining the system. This almost egalitarian association was the basis of the rise of Makka to new wealth and power, shared by their allies.

In Makka itself it was again Hāshim who introduced another revolutionary measure. This was to give the poor some share in the profits as payment for their work or, probably, against investment of small sums for poor relatives.[7] Therefore it was a joint

[1] *Ibid.*, pp. 117–20. [2] *Ibid.*, pp. 132–8. [3] *Ibid.*, p. 139.

[4] The occurrence of the name ʿAbdullah among his descendants before Islam is significant, and also that the name did not occur among his ancestors.

[5] Kister, "Mecca and Tamīm", p. 131, for more details.

[6] *Ibid.*, p. 143. [7] *Ibid.*, p. 123.

enterprise with co-operation between all concerned. This co-operation, added to the elaborate network of highly organized alliances and agreements, succeeded well and certainly increased the prosperity of all participants. In fact it was too successful to last and endure the pressures of competition for a larger share in the expanding trade. By the time Muḥammad appeared on the scene, there was a tendency in Makka for wealth to be concentrated in fewer hands to the exclusion of poorer clans. It has been suggested that the formation of limited alliances, *ḥilf*, within the clans of Quraysh was in fact an attempt to monopolize trade in one direction or the other.[1]

Outside Makka, the member clans of the commonwealth also scrambled for an increase of their rewards or a decrease of their dues to Quraysh. The causes of many wars like the Wicked War can be traced to the attempts of some of the clans along the trade routes to increase their own control over territories belonging to other clans.[2] Moreover, the expansion of trade encouraged the growth of several market towns, increasing the wealth and strength of their settled communities to the disadvantage of the nomadic clans around them. In consequence, a state of tension existed between the settled and nomadic clans though they may have belonged to the same tribal groups.[3] Undoubtedly these increasing tensions within the system represented a threat to the trade network and the far-sighted Qurayshites must have realized the dangers inherent in such an explosive situation. Nevertheless, nobody came forward with any suggestion as to how the balance of the alliance might be restored or to warn against the inevitable disaster to Makka and its trade; nobody, that is, but Muḥammad.

He was an active participant in this trade and he cannot have been blind to the fact that not only Quraysh's livelihood but that of many others depended on its prosperity. He cannot have advocated the destruction of Makkan trade, he can only have suggested means to maintain and strengthen it. As a party to the *ḥums* alliance he must have realized the imminent breakdown and he

[1] W. Montgomery Watt, *Muḥammad at Mecca*, Oxford, 1953, p. 15.
[2] *Ibid.*, p. 14; M. J. Kister, "Al-Ḥīra", *Arabica*, vol. 15, 1968, p. 154.
[3] The tendency of the settled communities to control the nomads around them was not only clear in Makka, Madīna and Ṭā'if, but also in Dūmat al-Jandal and al-Ḥajr, and was clearly a major objective of Musaylima, the prophet of Ḥanīfa.

suggested a more equitable basis for its maintenance.[1] Makka enjoyed a privileged religious sanctity which was closely connected with its commercial activities. Any attempt to reform or revolt against the existing system would have to be directed against both trade and religion. Muḥammad's religious convictions and his sincere belief in his divinely inspired mission are self-evident and this is not the place to pass a theological judgement on his prophethood or the religion he founded. From a historian's point of view his revolution and his statesmanship should be explained and understood in the light of their environment. In Makka this meant trade. To attempt a study of Muḥammad's activities in Makka and Arabia without taking trade into consideration is equivalent to studying contemporary Kuwayt or Arabia without paying attention to oil. In all his preachings Muḥammad never encouraged his followers to neglect their worldly affairs. He only preached moderation reminding them that they should work for success in this world as much as for salvation in the other. That Islam itself encourages trade and considers it a highly honourable occupation needs no proof. What needs explaining is Muḥammad's plans for the continuation and prosperity of trade in his time.

At first Muḥammad decided to lead a revolt from within the system itself. He consistently preached that Quraysh should put its own house in order. The pursuit of excessive wealth, the deprivation of the weak and the neglect of the poor in Makka were all evil. The salvation of his fellow Qurayshites was to consist in taking care of their poor relatives, in watching over the well-being of their orphans and in being generous to the poor amongst them. This Co-operation between rich and poor is the basic tenet of all Muḥammad's preaching just as Love is for that of Jesus Christ. Having established this Co-operation within Makka itself, it would be easy to apply it to all members of the commonwealth. However, this demanded from the richer Qurayshites a certain sacrifice which they could not accept. Although his early followers included some rich men like 'Uthmān b. 'Affān, few Makkans were ready to heed his warnings, and his attempt at a revolution from within was doomed to failure. For thirteen years he persisted in preaching to his fellow Qurayshites, in spite of great difficulties. Economic warfare ensued between his followers and the rest of Quraysh. His rich enemies instituted an economic

[1] Kister, "Mecca and Tamīm", p. 139, especially nn. 9 and 10.

boycott of his clan. He tried, by sending some of his followers to Abyssinia, to establish independent trade relations there, but Quraysh was quick to foil his attempt.[1]

Finally, Muḥammad began to look for outside support with which to challenge Makka. Significantly he turned first to Thaqīf of Ṭā'if, the junior partners in the Makkan trade. He must have realized that his teachings were likely to be more acceptable to settled communities. Still, his choice of Ṭā'if was surprising unless it is to be seen as a desperate move. He could not have seriously expected the Thaqīfites to challenge Quraysh on his behalf. In the event his journey to Ṭā'if ended in his being chased by the town rabble who flung stones at him. Again in desperation he tried to find support among the clans which had come to Makka for trade in the pilgrimage season, but to no avail. Nobody felt strong enough to challenge the powerful Quraysh and its allies.

Meanwhile Muḥammad's situation in Makka was deteriorating very fast and even his life was not safe. He had no alternative but to leave. Rescue came from the most unexpected direction, Madīna. It must be noted that the Madīnans were not active participants in the Makkan trade or alliances. Moreover, Madīna had its own peculiar problems. Its population was not homogeneous and tension existed between its Jewish and non-Jewish communities. The latter, the Aws and the Khazraj, were competing for the domination of the town and its resources, most of which were in Jewish hands. In the light of the close connections between the Madīnan Jews and other Jewish communities in Arabia it is not unreasonable to suggest that a Jewish trade network existed there at the time.[2] This would explain the absence of any large-scale operations between Makka and Madīna. The Madīnans were certainly aware of the situation in Makka and the opposition to Muḥammad there, yet they chose to assume the potentially dangerous attitude of hostility towards Makka. Furthermore, it was to give protection to a Qurayshite against Quraysh itself that they invited Muḥammad to Madīna. To add to the complexity of the situation they gave him a privileged position as arbitrator amongst themselves.

It was in fact only a very small minority of Madīnans who were

[1] Watt, *Muḥammad at Mecca*, pp. 114–15.

[2] These connections extended as far north as with Adhra'āt in Syria, and at least as far as Najrān in the south.

converted to the new religion at this time. However, this small minority was able to persuade their fellow Madīnans to adopt a course of action which could incur the wrath of the powerful Quraysh. We must also remember that in Madīna itself this venture was greeted unenthusiastically by the Jews and openly opposed by others. We are impelled, therefore, to look further for the reason behind such unexpected behaviour by the Madīnans.

The overriding factor in Arab politics at the time was Makkan trade and there is no reason to think that the Madīnans did not take it into consideration, particularly when Makka itself was involved. It is significant that the Madīnans accepted not only Muḥammad but also some seventy of his Makkan followers and undertook to provide for them. They were thus securing adequate Makkan expertise and paying for it. As an active participant in Makkan trade for the greater part of his life, Muḥammad had established his reputation as "the trustworthy", *al-amīn*, by managing the interests of richer Qurayshites. He was very successful at it and it compensated for his own lack of capital in early life.[1] Moreover he was personally involved in the Makkan alliance system and was well informed about its workings. In addition to his commercial expertise his organizational abilities were invaluable assets even in Makka itself.[2] The Madīnans must have appreciated these qualities and must have arranged with Muḥammad that he should have enough authority in Madīna to organize a Madīnan commonwealth. The long, hard bargaining which preceded his move to Madīna and which finally culminated in the so-called "constitution of Madīna" laid the foundation of the new commonwealth known to us as *umma*. It included every group who would accept the basis for co-operation in the new enterprise, and the agreement was concluded between all these groups of Madīnans and all the Qurayshites who joined Muḥammad in Madīna. Most significant is that the members of the new commonwealth did not have to accept the new religion; they only had to accept the special authority of Muḥammad. They were used to accepting the authority of arbitrators as was established in Arab tradition, but Muḥammad had more responsibility than merely adjudicating in minor disputes and accordingly he demanded

[1] Khadīja, his first wife, was one of his first clients before their marriage.

[2] His solution to the problem of removing the Black Stone is too well known to be repeated.

and was allowed greater authority. The Jews, the most prosperous members of the *umma*, were persuaded and adhered to the agreement, probably grudgingly. Most important, this new *umma* had built-in provisions for continuous growth, as it allowed the inclusion of any group which would accept the basis of its co-operation and the authority of Muḥammad. Although the "constitution" did not refer to any trade agreement, probably because it was taken for granted by the contractors, it made stipulations for treaties with outside groups. Muḥammad's declaration of Madīna as a *ḥaram* was a strong indication of the establishment of a new centre for trade.[1]

Of course these activities near Makka were closely watched by Quraysh and they probably would have been tolerated had the new rivals confined themselves to normal commercial practices. But in Arabia raiding of trade caravans was a recognized hazard, and although every possible arrangement was made to ensure security, raiding was traditional unless special agreements were reached with people along the trade routes. No such agreement existed between Makka and Madīna before Muḥammad's arrival, and when he started attacking Makkan caravans this served as a declaration of his wish to reach such an agreement as well as a real threat to their trade and their whole position. The Makkans realized that Muḥammad's terms for an agreement would be unacceptable and the limited economic conflict soon deteriorated into actual war. The Makkans were determined to eliminate any threat to their economic power, which quickly suffered as the Madīnans raided the route to their most important markets in the north.

This new situation created new tensions inside and outside Madīna. In the newly formed *umma* these rose very high. First, those who had not initially approved of the scheme found their conviction strengthened by the outbreak of war against Makka, which was a powerful disruptive factor to the very flow of the trade they were aiming to capture. Second, many Madīnans were not convinced that they could withstand a full-scale attack by the Makkans and their allies. Third, the Jews of Madīna saw that the breakdown of relations with the Makkans would certainly affect the already prosperous trade which involved allies of Makka

[1] W. Montgomery Watt, *Muḥammad at Medina*, Oxford, 1956, pp. 221–5, for a translation of this "constitution".

like Ṭā'if, where they had an active Jewish trading-post.[1] On the other hand Muḥammad saw that by disrupting Makkan trade he was inadvertently strengthening the Jewish trade network. In fact he soon realized that the inclusion of the Jews of Madīna in the *umma* was incompatible with its basic interests and they had to be dropped. Significantly the first to go were Banū Qaynuqā' who were those most involved in trade in Madīna.[2] But when they joined their fellow Jews in the north of Ḥijāz the Jewish trade did not cease and furthermore they openly sided with Muḥammad's enemies.

Finally Muḥammad had to take the most drastic action in his whole career to break once and for all the Jewish link at Madīna. The last Jewish clan remaining there was massacred to a man and their fate was a powerful lesson to Muḥammad's enemies in and outside Madīna.

Meanwhile, the Makkan trade practically ceased and the Makkans concentrated their efforts on defeating Muḥammad so that they could resume in safety. They mobilized all their allies and mounted the biggest attack so far on Madīna. The failure of this ultimate effort at the Battle of the Ditch was the real victory of Muḥammad. Makka's prestige began to wane and it was only a matter of time before it accepted Muḥammad's terms. Nevertheless, Muḥammad himself was aware of the great value of the Makkans' contacts and of their particular skill. In order to use such potential in the resumption of disrupted trade, it was essential that Makka should fall to him intact and that the Makkans should not be humiliated. His attempts to win over his weakened opponents were successful and they were magnanimously accepted as respected members of the *umma*.

The surrender of Makka was certainly a great victory for Muḥammad but it was not the end of his problems. He very soon found himself in the ironic situation of having to defend Quraysh against those who had formerly been its staunch allies. Alarmed by the fall of Makka they decided to mount their last effort to save themselves, but the final victory rested with Muḥammad and Quraysh, his new allies.[3] As soon as the news of this victory

[1] Al-Balādhurī, Aḥmad b. Yaḥyā, *Futūḥ al-Buldān*, ed. M. J. de Goeje, Leiden, 1866, p. 56.

[2] For this conflict see M. J. Kister, "The Market of the Prophet", *Journal of Economic and Social History of the Orient*, 1965, pp. 272–6.

[3] Watt, *Muḥammad at Medina*, pp. 70–7.

spread in Arabia, delegations from all the powerful tribes began to arrive at Madīna to reach agreements with Muḥammad. It is not surprising that at this point his terms became harder. At the beginning, acceptance of Islam was not a necessary condition for belonging to the *umma*, but now not only had they to accept Islam but also to agree to the payment of tax, *zakāt*, to Muḥammad. This tax was no more than a revival of the old tax which some tribes had had to pay in order to participate in the Makkan trade.[1] Ḥanīfa was the only significant tribe which refused both terms, but no action was taken against them in spite of the fact that they had their own rival prophet.[2]

The hostilities in Arabia had completely stopped trade and it was Muḥammad's responsibility to take measures to restore it. Now he had to convince the foreign powers that he was in control of and able to secure the trade routes. Accordingly he sent expeditions along the northern route to impress the Byzantine authorities and the Arab tribes on the Syrian borders with his strength. However nothing in particular came out of this show of strength before Muḥammad's death. Moreover, the appearance of new rival prophets in Central Arabia and Yaman was an indication of continuing instability in the area and was indeed an ominous sign of more serious troubles to come. Although Muḥammad, in less than ten years, had succeeded in setting up the necessary mechanism for a great trade centre which could have surpassed the previous centres of Arabia, he did not have enough time to exploit his success. Nevertheless the system he established and the new energies he unleashed in Arabia were destined to go far beyond what he could possibly have imagined. The inevitable economic recession resulting from his activities impelled the Arabs to utilize these energies in raiding neighbouring territories and, not long after his death, in unintentionally acquiring an empire.

In all his activities Muḥammad was no innovator and he repeatedly emphasized this point. Even his religion was not new. He insisted that it had always been there and it was no different from that of previous prophets beginning with Abraham. He was only calling for the restoration of the proper application of the

1 See above p. 6.

2 This big tribal group continued to be stubborn in its opposition to Quraysh not only in the wars of *ridda* but even as late as the time of the revolt of Ibn al-Zubayr. See below pp. 20, 96.

principles of the eternal truth. This restoration would ensure justice and salvation for all his followers. Justice for all based on Co-operation by all was the best guarantee for peace and prosperity. In terms of human values this was not an innovation. Indeed Hāshim had laid the foundations of Makkan prosperity on similar co-operative principles, though at various levels between the different groups of participants. This very discrepancy was the basic weakness of the Makkan commonwealth and it opened the door to the abuses which ultimately threatened the system. Muḥammad's real innovation was the strict application of the principles of Co-operation among all members of the new commonwealth (*umma*) in all their activities. Muḥammad the Prophet established a religion embodying Co-operation in all its tenets. Muḥammad the Leader established a community based on Co-operation in all human relations. Again there was nothing inherently novel in this social organization. It was definitely Arab, based on Arab traditions and shaped in Arab forms. The real innovation simply lay in Muḥammad's organizational genius. Using Arab forms and accepted tradition he changed the emphasis in such a way as to allow his principles of Co-operation to work to their best advantage. Thus the clan continued to be the basic social unit but was almost completely enveloped in the suprastructure of the *umma*. The pacts of *īlāf* and the alliances of *ḥums* with all their trade and religious implications were scornfully set aside in favour of Islam, "Pax Islamica", where all adherents belonged to the same organization on an equal footing. Muḥammad did not establish a state, nor did he unite the Arabs. He took over an existing established regime and modified it, introducing as few changes as possible. But with a superb sense of direction he never lost sight of his ultimate goal. His subtle changes had a far-reaching cumulative effect, which accounts not only for the victory of his moderate revolution but also for the successful establishment of a world religion.

2

THE EMERGENCE OF ABŪ BAKR

Although Muḥammad died fairly suddenly after a brief illness, he had been visibly in failing health for at least three months. At sixty-three he was an old man, by the standards of the time, and he knew that the end was near. Nevertheless he made no pronouncement on the question of how the *umma* should continue after him. The famous Shīʿite tradition that he designated his cousin ʿAlī as his successor at Ghadīr Khum should not be taken seriously. Such an event is inherently improbable considering the Arabs' traditional reluctance to entrust young and untried men with great responsibility. Furthermore, at no point do our sources show the Madīnan community behaving as if they had heard of this designation. Nor was Muḥammad's appointment of Abū Bakr to lead the prayers during his illness of any importance, for on previous occasions when he was absent he had often delegated this task and indeed the actual affairs of Madīna to nonentities. One can only conclude that Muḥammad intended that his followers should settle, on their own, the problem of his succession, if indeed there was to be any successor at all. This fits in very well with his deep understanding of his times and it was the only practical course for him to take.

Muḥammad's unprecedented power had developed gradually, and his success in Madīna was the ultimate factor in his rise to the position of undisputed leadership. When he was first brought to Madīna he was little more than the leader of the "clan" of the *muhājirūn*, i.e. the Makkan immigrants who were far outnumbered by the native Madīnan clans. His prophethood was recognized by only a minority in Madīna but his authority as arbitrator–organizer was accepted by the majority. It is a tribute to his qualities of leadership that he was able to utilize the limited powers of these various functions to their mutual enhancement. When he was finally recognized as the Prophet by all, he was also recognized as leader by all. But like everything else in his career his leadership was Arab in nature. It was deeply rooted in Arab tradition in the sense that leaders emerged and were recognized as they proved their abilities. Abū Sufyān emerged, without having any particular office there, as the leader of Makka against Muḥammad through the same tradition. It would be wrong to ascribe to Arab leaders at that time any real authority over their followers. Arab society then was not authoritarian, on the contrary it was highly individualistic and in such circumstances the powers of the leader were those of persuasion rather than of command. Of course, Muḥammad's power as leader was significantly supplemented by his religious powers, but his often repeated call for some semblance of obedience from his followers is a clear indication of his difficulties in this respect. He made it abundantly clear that there would not be a successor to him as the Prophet of God, and in true Arab tradition he left the door open for a new leader to emerge. This proves his own farsightedness and also the fact that his followers had learnt the lesson of applying Arab tradition to their new circumstances. We do not know whether their leaders discussed what they should do after Muḥammad's death, but if they did, which is possible, their decision can only have been a confirmation of their belief in their tradition, and the conviction that the problem would solve itself when the sad moment came. On the other hand one must remember that Islam was still very new and far from established. The protagonists of these years could all remember pre-Islamic times and a return to former arrangements was still very possible. The pre-Islamic network of authority in Madīna and elsewhere had not been abolished but only supplemented by a nascent supra-tribal authority. There were already signs that some of the tribes allied to the Madīnan commonwealth were getting restless and attempting to restore their freedom of action. There was also no reason why Makka should not again be ruled by its *mala*', council of clan leaders. Above all Madīna itself could have reverted to a state of internal tribal war, which Muḥammad had barely kept in check.

Evidently the clans of Khazraj of Madīna were aware of this possibility, for on the very afternoon of Muḥammad's death they met by themselves to decide on the question of leadership, probably wanting to advance as leader of a Madīnan-dominated regime their own leader, Sa'd b. 'Abāda.[1] This meeting consti-

[1] He was the only leader who persistently rejected the leadership of Abū Bakr and 'Umar and at the first opportunity left Madīna altogether for Syria where he died. Significantly his son Qays was the last one to give up fighting for the cause of 'Alī more than a quarter of a century later.

tuted a grave threat to the fragile unity of Madīna itself, for it might well have reopened the hostilities between the Khazraj and their fellow-Madīnans, the Aws. What is more it indicated a fairly natural Madīnan distrust of the Qurayshites, equally dangerous to the coherence of the *umma*.

This situation alarmed the Muslim community of Madīna to the extent that the succession problem was settled on the very day of Muḥammad's death and was even given priority over his burial. The urgent meeting of the Khazraj was a clear portent of what would happen to the *umma* should it lose that supra-tribal leadership Muḥammad had provided. This immediately settled the question of the nature of the succession – only the individual who was to succeed remained to be decided. The issue narrowed down to finding the candidate most acceptable to all groups. Clearly a new leader for the *umma* from the allied tribes was out of the question, as was a Madīnan candidate, because of the jealousies between the Aws and the Khazraj. Nor could the customary Arab practice of letting the most prominent member of the leading family, *bayt*, emerge as leader be applied since it would have been against the very nature of the notion of a supra-tribal leadership. Besides, who could name the leading family at the time? It was too early and it would have seemed far-fetched to apply the principle of *bayt* to the Prophet's own family. Furthermore 'Alī, only in his very early thirties, was too young for the responsibility, and the only other possible member, al-'Abbās, Muḥammad's uncle, was too recently converted to Islam. To apply the principle to the leading Qurayshite family would have meant the selection of Abū Sufyān, once an arch-enemy.

Finally, Abū Bakr emerged as the generally acceptable candidate. For many reasons he was the ideal choice. He was Qurayshite but his clan was unimportant. Above all he had been the closest friend of the Prophet and the man most familiar with his thinking. In addition he was an expert genealogist, *nassāba*, which was to prove a very useful skill politically in the *ridda*, apostasy, period when knowledge of the intricate tribal relationships was vital. He was a man who, while firm and decisive, was also easy and friendly in his manner, as the fact that he was always known by his nickname, *kunya*, indicates. The fact that he was chosen as leader shows the remarkable political good sense of the community, and the speed with which the choice was made is strong proof that they were determined to hold together and continue Muḥammad's work. He was chosen to maintain the *status quo*, to preserve the gains won by Muḥammad and to bring them to fruition.

One must be careful not to exaggerate the powers of Abū Bakr as *Khalīfat Rasūl Allāh*, Successor of the Prophet of God. The very title is so ambiguous that its definition even eludes lexicographers, and this is precisely why it was chosen.[1] Nobody could outline exactly the powers which the holder of this new office should be allowed so that he could fulfil his responsibilities; it was felt that only experiment could decide their extent. But it must be made clear that it was unthinkable that any ordinary man should wield the same powers as the Prophet. Thus Muḥammad could have no true successor, since no other man could ever have the same divine sanction behind his every act and decision. Therefore Abū Bakr had no religious authority and, in true Arab tradition, his secular authority as a leader was kept to a minimum. He only had the powers necessary to preserve the *umma* and his actions gained legitimacy only by following the precepts of the Qur'ān and the Sunna, i.e. the example given by the Prophet in his life. Seen in this light one can appreciate the limitations of Abū Bakr's authority as *Khalīfa*. He was in no sense a grand combination of Pope and Holy Roman Emperor. His emergence as leader was an *ad hoc* decision taken by the community in a moment of supreme crisis in the light of accepted Arab tradition. This decision should never be thought of as founding the Khalifate as a permanent institution. In fact for a period of six months Abū Bakr was only a part-time *Khalīfa* who also continued to be a merchant. He even had to milk his neighbours' sheep to supplement his income before the community realized that they needed a full-time leader. He was then allowed money from the communal purse but only enough for his and his family's subsistence.[2] There is no better proof of his limited secular authority.

In fact the community needed all the energies it could muster, let alone those of its leader, to face a major threat to the survival of the regime. At the time of Muḥammad's death all Arabia was by

[1] The clearest definition of *Khalīfa* is "one who takes the place of another after him in some matter". See W. Montgomery Watt, *Islamic Political Thought*, Edinburgh, 1968, p. 32.

[2] Al-Ṭabarī, Muḥammad b. Jarīr, *Tārīkh al-Rusul wa al-Mulūk*, ed. M. J. de Goeje *et al.*, Leiden, 1879–1901, I, pp. 2142–3; Ibn al-Athīr, 'Izz al-Dīn, *al-Kāmil fī al-Tārīkh*, ed. C. J. Tornberg, Leiden, 1866–71, vol. II, p. 325.

no means securely bound together within the *umma*. It was no secret that during the last years of Muḥammad's life rival prophets had arisen in South and Central Arabia, who were no doubt only checked by his vast prestige and success. To them the death of Muḥammad presaged the end of his regime. Whether their tribes were allied to Madīna or not, this was the time for them to rise against what they considered Madīnan hegemony or threat. The immediate effect of Muḥammad's activities had been to disrupt completely their trade and to deprive them of a considerable source of income. For those tribes allied to Madīna this situation was additionally burdensome because they were also obliged to pay a tax, *zakāt/ṣadaqa*, for which they got nothing in return.

The great majority of the tribesmen in Arabia, therefore, joined the various rival prophets against Islam and broke away from the Madīnan alliance. Ḥanīfa, a big tribal group in Central Arabia, which had never been a party to the Madīnan alliances, led the surrounding clans. It had its own so-called false prophet, Musaylima, whose aim apparently was to establish a commonwealth in Yamāma.[1] The agricultural productivity of this area was high and its main market had been Makka until the latter was brought under Muḥammad's control. Furthermore it was centrally located between east and west and therefore suffered a significant loss from the disruption of trade. Musaylima's main strength and probably also his main weakness was that he tried to lead the settled communities in Central Arabia in an attempt to control the nomads around them, in order to set up his commonwealth.[2] But this vast sea of nomads was too extensive and too involved in eastern and western Arabian tribal politics for him to control. Many of them were hesitant or did not see the advantage in openly declaring their support for Musaylima against the potentially greater power of Abū Bakr.[3] Some of these nomadic tribes had their own prophets like Ṭulayḥa of Asad and apparently they saw no common interest between themselves and Ḥanīfa, as is evident from the lack of any co-ordination between them against Madīna, in spite of the proximity of their respective territories.

[1] Ṭabarī, I, pp. 1930–2; Watt, *Muḥammad at Medina*, p. 136; Dale F. Eickelman, "Musaylima", *Journal of Economic and Social History of the Orient*, 1967, pp. 17–52, where the author treats this movement from the social anthropologist's point of view in addition to that of the historian.

[2] Ṭabarī, I, pp. 1930–4; Eickelman, "Musaylima", p. 42.

[3] Ṭabarī, I, pp. 1871, 1889, 1911, 1963, 1970; Athīr, *Kāmil*, vol. II, pp. 259, 264.

In Yaman and South Arabia the situation, though grave, was significantly hopeful for Madīna. There was what amounted to almost a national revival in the ancient civilized Yaman. It was led by yet another false prophet, al-Aswad al-ʿAnsī, who actually started his movement during the last years of Muḥammad's life. He probably thought that as long as Yaman had been extricated from the Persian sphere of influence, there was no reason why it should not wholly regain its independence. His supporters must have come from the agricultural communities of Yaman, but there was a definite split in the country. A considerable number of clans openly opposed his movement and actively sided with the Madīnan regime. These can only have been Yamanite clans whose main interest was trade. They were ready to fight their own countrymen for the reopening of the trade route to the north. They must have realized that without Madīnan support their life-line could not be restored and the cost was not really of great consequence. It is not insignificant that al-Ashʿath b. Qays al-Kindī, one of the leaders of the rebels, owned extensive agricultural land in Ḥaḍramawt, while Abū Mūsā al-Ashʿarī, an early convert who remained most faithful to Islam, was almost certainly a Yamanite resident agent in Makka before Islam. Furthermore he even continued to be engaged in trade later, during the conquests, while he was active as general and governor of Baṣra.[1]

In Madīna itself Abū Bakr was determined to carry out Muḥammad's plan for the ultimate success of the Madīnan commonwealth. Behind him stood the Madīnans solidly united. Surprisingly he also had the unwavering support of Makka and Ṭā'if.[2] The fiercest enemies of Muḥammad did not attempt to take advantage of the situation following his death and instead became the staunchest supporters of the Madīnan regime. Of course they were all new converts to Islam and one cannot rule out individual cases where the zeal of a new convert was the primary motive for the defence of his adopted religion. But it is more likely that they gave their unanimous whole-hearted support in deference to their own interests. They realized that having lost their own trade network they were now indissolubly bound to the Madīnan scheme. If they wanted to restore their prosperity they had no

[1] Ṭabarī, I, pp. 1994, 1996, 2004, see also Ibn Taghry Bardy, *al-Nujūm al-Zāhira*, ed. T. G. Juynboll and B. F. Matthes, Leiden, 1851, vol I, p. 142; for details of a different interpretation see Watt, *Muḥammad at Medina*, pp. 117–30.

[2] Athīr, *Kāmil*, vol. II, p. 259.

choice but to fight for its ultimate success which was almost in sight.

At this stage Abū Bakr had at his disposal the populations of Madīna, Makka and Ṭā'if and a few of the semi-nomadic tribesmen in their vicinity. The rest of the tribesmen of Ḥijāz were divided into those whose attitude was one of wait and see and those who were openly hostile.[1] To some extent this reaction represents the breaking point of the tension between the settled and nomadic elements in Arabia. The nomads saw the Madīnan regime simply as a renewed attempt by the settled communities to control them and at the first opportunity tried to rid themselves of it. They were not content merely to break away but aimed at its total destruction. The nomads surrounding Madīna attempted to attack the Madīnans themselves who were barely able to repel them.[2] The Madīnans were in fact in a very precarious situation because the bulk of their forces were already on an expedition to the north. Abū Bakr, in his determination to follow through all Muḥammad's plans, had lost no time in sending out an expedition along the northern route planned and prepared by Muḥammad before his death in accordance with his policy of impressing the Arab tribes on the Byzantine borders and their masters. This was done very much against the better judgement of his advisers, but Abū Bakr bravely ignored all the imminent dangers and insisted that the expedition must go through in 633/11. It was an enormous risk but it was also a move of immeasurable political value. It was a forcible declaration that the Madīnan regime was more than strong enough to meet all its enemies. Furthermore it reassured all those interested that the pursuit of restoring trade was one of the urgent priorities of Abū Bakr's policy. Under the circumstances this measure was a calculated risk but one of great political wisdom. Militarily it was of no significance and the expedition was back in Madīna in little over a month.

It was this unparalleled determination on the part of Abū Bakr which transformed the precarious situation of Madīna into a swift victory. It was also to his advantage that the rebels did not attempt a concerted action against Madīna. After his successful defence of Madīna he lost no time in taking the initiative against his enemies. He mobilized all his forces and sent them on expeditions in all directions. They came mainly from Makka, Madīna and

[1] Ṭabarī, I, pp. 1871, 1887, 1905.
[2] *Ibid.*, pp. 1872–4.

Ṭā'if, and they also included some tribesmen from the surrounding tribes.[1] It is not fortuitous that we find references, in our earliest sources, to these forces as *ahl al-qurā*, the people of the villages, i.e. the settled communities, and that some of their opponents from Ḥanīfa are also referred to in the same way in the same traditions.[2] Later traditions refer to these *ahl al-qurā* as *qurrā'* which is simply another derivation from the root *qry*.[3] This simple morphological difference has given rise to many misunderstandings of the nature of the groups involved because the word *qurrā'* has been wrongly taken to mean Qur'ān readers.[4] In this case the emphasis on *ahl al-qurā* in our sources is meant to draw our attention to the fact that the Madīnan attack on Ḥanīfa was different, in as much as it was a fight between two settled groups. In other words this fight was really between the commonwealth of Madīna and its projected rival in Yamāma. The predominant tension between settled and nomadic elements was of secondary importance in this particular case.

These famous *ridda*, apostasy, campaigns suffered some minor defeats but were soon impressively successful. Their success tipped the balance in favour of the Madīnan regime and those hesitant tribesmen who did not openly declare for the apostates were welcomed back into the fold and quickly recruited to fight the rebels.[5] On the other hand those who had been subdued were not trusted enough to be used to fight against the remaining rebels.[6] Most of the apostate tribes were defeated within a year of Muḥammad's death. The previously unconverted tribes were brought under Madīnan control equally quickly, the most important of them being the great Central Arabian tribe of Ḥanīfa which was defeated at the Battle of 'Aqrabā 633/11. This was certainly going beyond maintaining the *status quo* but Abū Bakr could not easily ignore the threat Ḥanīfa represented to the trade plans of the Madīnan commonwealth. Besides Khālid b. al-Walīd was involved.

Khālid, the victor of 'Aqrabā, was the chief general in the *ridda* wars in Central Arabia. His military genius was responsible for the only victory Quraysh achieved against Muḥammad at the Battle of Uḥud 625/3. He was a man of considerable standing in Makka

[1] *Ibid.*, pp. 1887, 1923, 1930.
[2] *Ibid.*, pp. 1946, 1947.
[3] Balādhurī, *Futūḥ*, p. 88.
[4] See below p. 51.
[5] Ṭabarī, I, pp. 1962–80.
[6] *Ibid.*, p. 2225.

and a leading member of Makhzūm, one of the most powerful clans of Quraysh. All his actions clearly point to his strong independence of mind and indicate a certain impulsiveness. In his campaign against the apostates he did not adhere strictly to Abū Bakr's instructions; he simply defeated whoever was there to be defeated.[1] Mention is made in our sources of many clans of Asad, Ghaṭafān, Fazāra, Ṭayy and Tamīm, most of whom were nomads. He then turned against Ḥanīfa and conquered its settlements. The Battle of 'Aqrabā left him a great general in command of a victorious army in close proximity to the rich Sāsānian empire. He knew that the tribesmen of Shaybān, who were Muslims and who did not take part in the apostasy wars, were busy raiding the border territories of Sāsānian Iraq. This they were doing of their own accord and without any direction from Madīna.[2] The temptation to join them was too great for Khālid. It is not clear whether he obtained Abū Bakr's permission; being Khālid he would either not have bothered to ask or would have ignored any objection on Abū Bakr's part.[3] After all, under the circumstances the great general Khālid of Makhzūm would not have viewed Abū Bakr of Taym with any great reverence. The latter was only a *Khalīfa* in Madīna and, in addition, a man of a lesser clan. Khālid invited his men to join him on this excursion but allowed those who did not want to follow him to go back to their homes. Those who followed him were undoubtedly driven by their desire for any booty lying within the Sāsānian domains. Such Arab forays in Sāsānian territories had been a pre-Islamic practice which continued in spite of the advent of Islam. In fact they were now an economic necessity, not because of over-population in Arabia, but because trade, especially after the *ridda* wars, was in ruins.

As a leader Abū Bakr must have been aware of this fact and of the general economic recession and, hoping for the best, he had no choice but to acquiesce in Khālid's impulsive though intuitive solution.[4] Soon Abū Bakr began to realize that this was the ideal if not the only solution. After over a decade of war trade in Arabia was at a standstill and there was no sign of its early resumption. If the new Madīnan regime wanted to survive and strengthen its hold over its followers a new source of income had to be found to compensate for the loss of trade, particularly when it was itself

[1] *Ibid.*, p. 1922.
[2] Balādhurī, *Futūḥ*, p. 241.
[3] *Ibid.*, p. 242; Ṭabarī, I, p. 2016.
[4] Ṭabarī, I, pp. 2036, 2041–2.

responsible for this loss. Almost as a reward, a new expedition was prepared in 634/13 from the men who had firmly stood by the regime in its direst hour, those of Makka, Madīna and Ṭā'if. Also included were the tribesmen who had fought with them in the *ridda* wars, especially the Yamanite clans who fought for the regime against their own countrymen.[1] Enemies of Madīna in these wars were completely excluded and deprived of these possible gains. This expedition was led by Qurayshites like 'Amr b. al-'Āṣ and Yazīd b. Abī Sufyān who, because of their former trade activities, were familiar with the expected field of action. In contrast to the previous expedition in this direction, it was now intended to reach into Byzantine territory in southern Palestine. The fact that it was composed of four separate contingents operating in various directions indicates that it was not meant to engage in a major military confrontation with Byzantine troops, but rather its purpose was to gain the greatest possible booty.[2]

The Arabs must have misjudged the state of affairs in the Byzantine empire, or at least have thought of it as being no different from that of the disintegrating Sāsānian empire. The Byzantines, however, were better informed about events in Arabia, and their loss of trade must have increased their awareness of the threat posed by the rising power of Madīna. The successive Islamic campaigns on their borders were a clear and growing threat to the security of their empire. A well-organized government, such as theirs, which had just fought a ferocious war against the Sāsānians (A.D. 614–28), would scarcely ignore such matters as frontier security. The news of Muḥammad's death and the subsequent widespread warfare in Arabia certainly increased their apprehensions. This situation must also have encouraged them to hope for advantage should they intervene. Therefore when the Arab army arrived in Palestine they were met by an alert enemy, ready for battle.

Although they achieved a minor victory against a small Byzantine contingent, the Arabs soon found that they would have to fight a pitched battle against an organized regular army. They immediately requested reinforcements from Abū Bakr, but as he was still adamant in his policy of excluding the *ridda* tribesmen, he had no forces at his disposal to send to Palestine. The only alternative was to use Khālid and his men who were still conducting a

[1] *Ibid.*, pp. 2004–5, 2082–4; Balādhurī, *Futūḥ*, p. 107.

[2] Ṭabarī, I, pp. 2085–7, 2107–18; Balādhurī, *Futūḥ*, p. 108.

campaign of lightning raids in Iraq. These raids met no resistance and were of no military significance, but their material advantages were of importance to both the participants and Abū Bakr to whom one-fifth of the booty was duly sent. However, the emergency in Palestine obliged Abū Bakr to direct Khālid to join his beleaguered fellow Muslims in Palestine with as many of his men as possible. Khālid did so in a celebrated forced march across the Syrian desert lasting five days.[1] Meanwhile the Arab forces gathered together and when Khālid joined them he assumed the generalship of a united army. This appointment was, interestingly enough, not authorized by Abū Bakr; it was dictated by Khālid's military ability.[2] His united forces numbered about 24,000 men, representing virtually the whole strength of the Madīnan regime at this stage. It seems likely that the Byzantine forces in Palestine, mostly Arab and Armenian mercenaries, did not greatly outnumber their opponents, and under the circumstances it is not surprising that when battle was joined the Arabs won a decisive victory at Ajnādayn (634/13).

Abū Bakr died before hearing the news of this great battle. He must have died a satisfied man because in his short reign of two years he had accomplished the main task facing him: he had re-established the threatened Madīnan regime. Not only had he brought the breakaway tribes back into the fold but he had also succeeded in converting those tribes who had previously resisted Islam. Through the *ridda* wars some semblance of unity had been imposed on all Arabia. Although this unity was qualified by the fact that the *ridda* tribesmen could not be active members of the *umma*, the door had been thrown wide open for the proper unification of the Arabs. For the first time tribesmen, who hitherto had had no common interest or activity, were now participating in such activities. Thus we see Makkans fighting alongside tribesmen from eastern Arabia in Iraq. We also see Yamanites from the south side by side with Makkans and Madīnans in Palestine in the north.

Abū Bakr's only failure was his inability to put an end to the disruption of trade. But ironically this brought Islam to the threshold of a career of conquest. The Arabs met no resistance in their raids in Iraq and were successful in their full-scale battle against the Byzantines. Probably they were surprised at their success but

[1] Ṭabarī, I, p. 2109; Balādhurī, *Futūḥ*, p. 110. [2] Balādhurī, *Futūḥ*, p. 113.

undoubtedly they were encouraged to push forward with their conquests. These wars had given Abū Bakr the opportunity to assume, in limited measure, the direction of affairs, but he was far from being an absolute ruler. As explained before, in his first six months in office he had been a part-time *Khalīfa* and this, together with his relationship with Khālid, illustrates very clearly the limitations of his powers. Nonetheless he would not have considered this a failure. The history of his reign and the fact that the community continued the experiment of the Khalifate with 'Umar show his government to have been a great success.

To be sure, Abū Bakr had differences with the other leaders of the community in Madīna, and of these much the most important concerned policy towards the rebels of the *ridda*. All were agreed that they had to be subdued; opinion varied about the treatment to be meted out to them. Khālid represented one extreme of contemporary opinion. He took brutal reprisals against the apostates on more than one occasion and his behaviour aroused considerable criticism in Madīna, particularly and significantly from such figures as 'Umar b. al-Khaṭṭāb.[1] With perhaps one exception, Abū Bakr himself took little brutal action against the rebels. For example, he not only spared the life of al-Ash'ath b. Qays al-Kindī, one of the leading rebels in Yaman, but set him free and married him to his own sister. But he agreed with the substance of Khālid's policy, namely that the apostates returned to the fold should not be trusted or treated as equals with those who had stood fast by the Madīnan regime in its hour of crisis. Therefore Abū Bakr kept al-Ash'ath under strict surveillance in Madīna and turned a deaf ear to the pleas of the tribesmen of Shaybān to enlist ex-rebels in their raids in Iraq.[2] The attitude of Abū Bakr and Khālid is understandable, considering how deeply involved both had been in the *ridda* wars. Nevertheless, in depriving the *ridda* tribesmen of the gains accruing from participation in raids they were also depriving themselves of a considerable source of manpower. However, Abū Bakr cannot have considered this important, feeling that the loyal troops who had fought the *ridda* wars would suffice to hold down Arabia. This was true as long as the Madīnan regime abstained from long campaigns outside Arabia. Abū Bakr can only have regarded the campaigns in Byzantine and Sāsānian territories as temporary and incidental.

[1] Ṭabarī, I, p. 1928.
[2] *Ibid.*, p. 2120.

3

'UMAR AND THE CONQUESTS

Before his death in 634/13 Abū Bakr designated 'Umar b. al-Khaṭṭāb as his successor. In spite of the fact that this was an unprecedented act, it seemed the most natural thing for him to do, and its general acceptance by the community only shows that they had decided to continue the experiment begun with Abū Bakr. They probably felt that two years were not long enough for them to draw any mature conclusions about this system of government, even though the experiment, so far, had been a success. Abū Bakr's designation of 'Umar was indeed an innovation, but it must be noted that it was made in the form of a recommendation, subject to the approval of the community. Indeed, there was nothing at all binding about it and the community could have rejected it had they wanted to do so. But 'Umar was a man with great qualities of leadership and during Abū Bakr's reign his stature had grown fast. He was certainly influential in rallying the Madīnans to accept Abū Bakr as *Khalīfa* at a moment of supreme crisis and one must conclude that he was trusted by them. The Qurayshites had accepted Abū Bakr and there was no reason why they should oppose 'Umar. According to Arab tradition he had already emerged as a man of proven ability and it was almost inevitable that he would be chosen as leader. In effect, therefore, Abū Bakr was not so much recommending an individual as he was recommending the continuation of the office of *Khalīfa*.

'Umar's first act was to reverse Abū Bakr's policy towards the ex-rebels of the *ridda*. He not only allowed but even encouraged their participation in the raids on Sāsānian territories. Appointing Abū 'Ubayd of Thaqīf to take charge of this front, he directed him to recruit, *en route*, as many tribesmen as possible regardless of their activities during the *ridda*.[1] This was a momentous decision entailing profound changes in Arabia. It was the most meaningful step towards the unification of the Arabs. Now none would be

[1] Balādhurī, *Futūḥ*, p. 250; Ṭabarī, I, pp. 2165, 2183, 2225.

excluded from the general activities of the community of all Muslims. Whether they were *ahl al-qurā* or *ahl al-wabar*, settled or nomads, they would all have a common interest and an equitable share in the gains of the Madīnan regime. With one simple decision the sinners were forgiven and their frustrated energies unleashed and directed to the advantage of all. Islamic Co-operation, which had been momentarily confined to a minority, was re-established among the whole body of Muslims. The basis of the Madīnan regime was widely expanded to include all Arabs. Without this decision there would have been no Arab empire.

The absence, in our sources, of any reference to the slightest objection to this new policy, indicates that it had the approval if not the whole-hearted support of all concerned. It must have been realized that a Madīnan commonwealth based on international trade was increasingly difficult to achieve, especially after the open hostilities with Byzantium. The passivity of the Sāsānians so far, and the defeat of the Byzantines at Ajnādayn, convinced the Arabs of the vast gains possible from raiding, compared with the futility of pursuing an elusive trade. Thus encouraged, they decided to utilize all their forces in pursuit of maximum possible gains. These gains went far beyond their expectations.

Sāsānian territories were the more promising in this respect not only because they probably offered more booty but also because they offered no resistance. However, as an imperial power they could not be expected to tolerate such raids for long. Confident of their own strength they had ignored the impetuous forays of Khālid as an inevitable hazard of having such raid-happy neighbours. But the arrival of Abū 'Ubayd accompanied by a menacingly increased number of tribesmen pointed to a new onslaught on their borders. Now they took the situation more seriously, began to mobilize their forces and sent an army to intercept the Arab raiders. The sight of the elephants of the Sāsānian force bewildered the Arabs and even Abū 'Ubayd's own valour against them was of no use. He, his brother and son were killed and his forces shattered at the Battle of the Bridge, in 634/13.[1]

On the Byzantine front the Arab situation was also getting serious. Alarmed by the defeat at Ajnādayn, the Byzantines mobilized new forces to meet the Arab threat. The simultaneous mobilization of the full forces of the two great world empires

[1] Balādhurī, *Futūḥ*, pp. 251–2.

forced 'Umar to bring forth all his strength. It is not difficult to imagine the enormous problems he encountered in mobilizing all the Arabs, let alone in organizing them to fight two imperial armies on two fronts. For these tasks the organizational abilities of the enterprising Qurayshites were his greatest asset. Their pre-Islamic trade connections, inter-tribal relations and their prestige in Arabia, which was conserved if not enhanced by Islam, were of the utmost value in meeting the new situation. Sa'd b. Abī Waqqāṣ, a Qurayshite of no particular military distinction, was appointed to take charge of the Sāsānian front. Although he was a choleric man and a mediocre general-administrator, as his career would later indicate, he was appointed because of his wide connections in Central Arabia and his readiness to co-operate in full measure with the *ridda* ex-rebels.[1]

He set out from Madīna at the head of a small army of about 2,000 tribesmen, half of them Yamanites who had quickly responded to 'Umar's call. On his way he recruited at least 7,000 men and eventually his army included such notorious former rebels as al-Ash'ath and Ṭulayḥa, the ex-prophet of Asad.[2] Arriving at the Sāsānian frontier this rapidly growing army was joined by the tribesmen of eastern Arabia who had already been involved in fights against the Sāsānians. In the ensuing battles the Arabs overcame their fear of the elephants and apparently learnt some of the tactics of their enemies. The Sāsānians, though alarmed, never really considered the Arabs a major threat to their empire and consequently they did not attempt to deploy all their military forces, especially in the first encounters. By the time they began to realize the possible outcome of the situation it was too late. The Arabs had already made considerable inroads into Sāsānian territories and had inflicted some significant defeats upon their adversaries. Furthermore they were able to hold their gains for more than two years living off the abundant booty from the rich countryside of Iraq. Arab morale was rising while that of the Sāsānians was badly affected. When the latter finally put a major force in the field, the result was an outstanding victory for the Arabs at the Battle of Qādisiyya, 637/16. It was the first clear portent of the collapse of the Sāsānian empire.

A similar situation prevailed on the Byzantine front. After the

[1] Ṭabarī, I, pp. 2202, 2215–16, 2221.

[2] Balādhurī, *Futūḥ*, pp. 257–60; Ṭabarī, I, p. 2222.

victory of Ajnādayn (634/13) the Arabs continued to hold their ground in Palestine and were duly reinforced by new arrivals mainly from Yaman. They did not have so many *ridda* tribesmen among them although they included such a prominent *ridda* leader as Qays b. al-Makshūḥ al-Murādī.[1] Nevertheless, 'Umar, in order to ensure harmony within this army in enemy territory, felt it wiser to replace the strongly anti-rebel Khālid b. al-Walīd by Abū 'Ubayda al-Jarrāḥ as general in charge of the whole Byzantine front. Undoubtedly Khālid was by far the more able militarily, but the situation now called for the milder Abū 'Ubayda who could easily co-operate with such men as Qays b. al-Makshūḥ. It was not personal animosity between Khālid and 'Umar that was responsible for this change in command. It was an act of statesmanship understood and complied with by Khālid, who continued to serve under Abū 'Ubayda. The latter's task seems to have been that of a co-ordinator rather than that of a commander-in-chief. Through co-ordinating the activities of his generals he was able to direct frequent strikes deep into Syria, yet still have all his troops united. When the Byzantines decided to mount a major counter-attack against the invaders, Abū 'Ubayda was able to meet them in full force at the Battle of the Yarmūk (637/16). The Arabs won a decisive victory which induced the Byzantines to relinquish Syria altogether. Subsequently the complete conquest of Syria was achieved without much difficulty.

It was inevitable that the conquest of Egypt should follow the fall of Syria, yet this new conquest is a classic example of the spontaneous and haphazard manner of the Arab conquests. 'Amr b. al-'Āṣ, the conqueror of Egypt, had been one of the Qurayshite generals in the early expedition in Abū Bakr's time, and later 'Umar put him under the command of Abū 'Ubayda. 'Amr knew Egypt well, for he had visited it several times before Islam. After the final conquest of Syria he was stationed with a small army in Palestine. Our sources leave no doubt that he simply set off for Egypt on his own initiative at the head of the 3,500 tribesmen under his command.[2] Now, 'Amr was not in the least an impulsive man; on the contrary he was well known for

[1] Balādhurī, *Futūḥ*, p. 256.

[2] *Ibid.*, p. 212; Ṭabarī, I, p. 2584; Ibn 'Abdilḥakam, *Futūḥ Miṣr*, ed. C. C. Torrey, New Haven, 1922, p. 57; Al-Kindī, *Governors and Judges of Egypt*, ed. R. Guest, Gibb Memorial Series, vol. XIX, London, 1912, p. 8.

BYZANTINE
EMPIRE
Taurus Mountains
DIYĀR BAKR
Āmid
Edessa
Tarsus
Antioch
Dābiq
Aleppo
Qinnasrīn
DIYĀR MUḌAR
Raqqa
Ṣiffīn
Qarqīsiyyā
CYPRUS
Mediterranean
Sea
SYRIA
Ḥimṣ
Palmyra
Syrian
Desert
Beirut
Damascus
JORDAN
Jābiya
Buṣrā
Qaysāriyya
Fiḥl
ʿAmwās
Jerusalem
Ajnādayn
Ghazza
PALESTINE
Mu'ta
36°
38°
40°
32°
34°

2 Syria, Ja

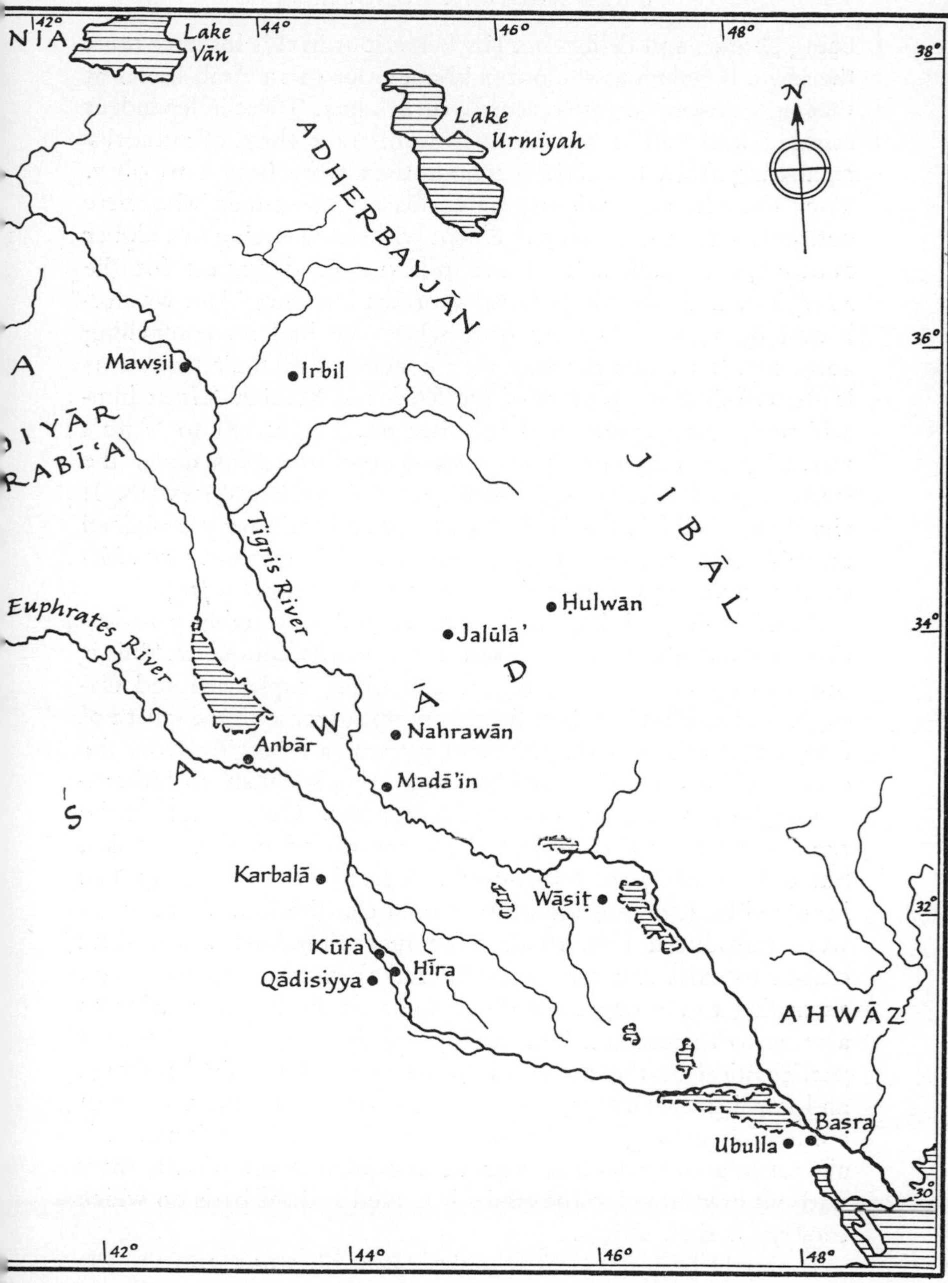
NIA
Lake Vān
ADHERBAYJĀN
Lake Urmiyah
N
A
Mawṣil
Irbil
DIYĀR RABĪ'A
JIBĀL
Tigris River
Ḥulwān
Jalūlā'
Euphrates River
SAWĀD
Nahrawān
Anbār
Madā'in
Karbalā
Wāsiṭ
Kūfa
Ḥīra
Qādisiyya
AHWĀZ
Baṣra
Ubulla
42°
44°
46°
48°
38°
36°
34°
32°
30°

l Sawād

being shrewd and deliberate. His behaviour in this instance must therefore be taken as the normal behaviour of an Arab leader at that time towards the government of Madīna. These independent minded leaders did not think in terms of a chain of authority emanating from the *Khalīfa* whom they were bound to obey. They thought rather of themselves as no lesser men who were entitled to use their own judgement without deferring to a higher authority in Madīna. This was not out of disrespect for the *Khalīfa* or a desire for personal glorification since 'Amr was followed by 3,500 tribesmen over whom he had no compelling authority. This was the way they conceived of their powers as leaders *vis-à-vis* the powers of the *Khalīfa* at Madīna. 'Umar himself must have appreciated this because he reacted to 'Amr's move by sending him at least 8,000 reinforcements under the leadership of another Qurayshite, al-Zubayr b. al-'Awwām. It should be noted that neither 'Amr's nor Zubayr's army contained any *ridda* leaders which would almost certainly mean that no *ridda* tribesmen were present at the conquest of Egypt (640/19).[1]

At this point, it is important to pause and consider the constitution of the Arab armies involved in these early conquests. This is not an easy task because of the essentially haphazard and disorganized fashion in which they were put together. One must not forget that this was seventh-century Arabia emerging from the chaos of the *ridda* wars and reacting spontaneously to hitherto unimagined situations outside its borders. Our sources make remarkable efforts to explain the composition of these armies, but unfortunately the terms used to describe the various groups involved lead to confusion rather than clarification. These terms were introduced then to describe new situations which soon ceased to exist and they also differed from place to place and according to the degree of glory some of these groups tried to ascribe to themselves. This was primarily due to the fact that participation in the early conquests entailed certain privileges and considerable status, which were soon to become a bone of contention among the Arabs in the conquered provinces. It is almost impossible to understand subsequent developments there without first knowing the Arabs involved and the basis on which they made their claims.

It should be made clear that the Arab tribesmen who actually

[1] See below p. 36.

achieved these first conquests considered the conquered territories as belonging to them and them alone. They did not think in terms of these conquests being made in the name of a king or a *Khalīfa*. These were their own conquests and all the accruing gains were theirs. According to their ancient tradition their leaders were entitled to one-fourth of these gains which was normally booty. Now the Islamic leader, to their advantage, was only entitled to one-fifth of this booty and this they were willing to yield. The tremendous amount of booty won at this stage was enough to satisfy everybody and helped to overcome any possible differences. But a conflict was in the making, mainly because the early conquerors were extremely reluctant to allow tribesmen who joined them later to share in what they considered their own by right of conquest.

In discussing the particular question of the composition of the Arab armies, it will be necessary to discuss also the wider question of the conditions and organization of the conquered provinces of Iraq, Syria and Egypt. The conditions of these provinces before the conquests and the circumstances of the conquests themselves were very different. As a result each province had its problems and no one solution was applicable to all three. These differences have created difficult problems for historians, and the very few scholars who have attempted detailed studies of the conquests have confused the conditions and solutions in the three provinces in their accounts.[1] But, pending much-needed new work on this subject, we must hazard an account of the situation, for without one, most subsequent developments in the Arab empire become inexplicable.

We shall deal first with Egypt because its historical problems are the least difficult to solve and our sources are unusually clear about some aspects of its conquest. We have detailed information about the composition of the conquering army. As previously noted, 3,500 men followed 'Amr b. al-'Āṣ from Palestine to Egypt and 8,000 men were sent from Madīna under Zubayr.[2] The striking feature of both groups is that they included no *ridda* tribesmen. Also, there were few Makkans and Madīnans, although Sa'd b. Abī Waqqāṣ, the leader at Qādisiyya, was

[1] See the "provisional" discussion of Cl. Cahen, "Djizya", *Enc. of Islam*, II, New Edition, Leiden, 1954– .

[2] Ibn 'Abdilḥakam, *Futūḥ Miṣr*, p. 61.

among Zubayr's men.[1] A number of tribesmen from the various clans of the Ḥijāz also joined Zubayr but they represented so many clans that they were all put in one unit and referred to as *ahl al-rāya*, those under one flag, as opposed to the usual practice of forming each clan into a unit, when there were enough men in a particular clan to make this viable.[2] The majority of Zubayr's reinforcements were clans from Yaman as far east as Mahra. These were tribesmen who may have accepted Islam at a later stage but who did not actually take part in the *ridda* wars. These *madadiyyūn*, reinforcements, were of slightly inferior status but soon achieved full status equal to that of their fellow conquerors.[3]

'Amr's group was of a similarly interesting composition. These were tribesmen who had been in action on the Byzantine front as early as Abū Bakr's time. Therefore their early and faithful services to Islam were easily recognized. Nevertheless they represented the minor clans who participated in this early campaign, clans from the extreme north of Ḥijāz who were living in areas adjacent to the Syrian desert; Balī of Quḍā'a was the most representative of them. In contrast, the tribesmen of Kalb, also from Quḍā'a, who were the original inhabitants of the Syrian desert and joined Islam only after the initial conquest of Palestine, were not represented at all in Egypt.[4] In 'Amr's group there were also tribesmen from the first wave of immigrants from Yaman who had been on the right side in the *ridda* wars. Most representative of these was the clan of Tujīb led by Mu'āwiya b. Ḥudayj whose power and prestige in Egypt testify to his early good standing.[5] It is significant that sister clans of Tujīb who all belonged to the tribe of Sakūn remained in Syria where they formed a considerable unit in the Arab army there. The fact that they were absent from the first campaign indicates that their arrival was a later one. Thus in Palestine, where 'Amr's men had been settled for at least four years, the situation arose where the tribesmen from minor clans, who had actually achieved the first victory, were being crowded out by more powerful clans of lesser standing in Islam. Of course, this may have created some tension between the two sides. The weaker group decided that it was to their advantage to attempt the conquest of Egypt where they would have a whole province for themselves. Although

[1] *Ibid.*, pp. 93, 114–15.
[2] *Ibid.*, pp. 98, 116–17.
[3] *Ibid.*, pp. 118–19, 122–8.
[4] *Ibid.*, pp. 116–19.
[5] *Ibid.*, pp. 123, 143.

'Umar had to accept their move, he realized that the loss of these men or the failure of their venture would have an adverse effect on the whole regime. He had no choice but to support them, and under the circumstances *ridda* tribesmen were deliberately excluded from the reinforcements under Zubayr.

Once the conquest was achieved, all the tribesmen were stationed in the newly built garrison town of Fusṭāṭ, now old Cairo. The Arabs were given small lots of non-agricultural land where they built their homes. From a strategic point of view, the location of Fusṭāṭ, between the crowded delta of the Nile and the long narrow valley to the south, made it possible for the Arabs to control the whole country. There were only two other centres of military activity in Egypt, of which the most important was Alexandria. Because of the considerable danger of Byzantine naval attack, the Arabs established a base there, manned by contingents sent on six months' rotation from Fusṭāṭ.[1] The other was at Khirbetā, a village on the western desert borders of the delta, where a similar base was created to ward off any Byzantine attacks from the western desert.[2] Except in the spring, when the tribesmen were allowed to graze their animals, they were kept out of the countryside.[3] The Egyptian population retained complete control of their lands. There was virtually no change in the structure of landownership. Of course there was a Byzantine community in Egypt before the conquest but it seems that they were more involved in trade with Byzantium itself than in agriculture. Although many of them fled from Egypt with the withdrawing Byzantine army and navy, the problem of lands being deserted which they had owned did not arise, in marked contrast to Syria, and for that matter Iraq. Apparently the only economic problem created by their departure was the shortage of gold coins, most of which they carried away with them.[4]

Except for minor modifications and the substitution of Arab for Greek rulers, the government and social system of Egypt continued exactly as before the conquest. The Coptic Church was sufficiently strong and the native officials were co-operative enough to be relied upon to see to the day-to-day business of local government. As for taxation, the general intention of the Arabs was to preserve the Byzantine system but the sudden

[1] *Ibid.*, pp. 130, 192.
[2] *Ibid.*, p. 142; Kindī, *Governors*, p. 21.
[3] Ibn 'Abdilḥakam, *Futūḥ Miṣr*, pp. 139–42, 162.
[4] *Ibid.*, pp. 82, 87.

shortage of coinage severely undermined this policy. 'Amr, now the governor of Egypt, was acutely aware that the prosperity of Egyptian agriculture was completely dependent on the efficient and expensive maintenance of an intricate irrigation network and the annual protective measures against the Nile flood.[1] On the other hand he was also aware that the peasants were understandably unable to meet any demands for tax payment in cash. The Byzantine system had to be modified to overcome this serious, if temporary, crisis.

In the agricultural economy of Egypt the Byzantine taxation system was based on a fixed tax on the land to be paid in cash. The system allowed for annual adjustment of the amount of this tax according to local conditions and subject to assessment by tax officials and the local community leaders. Each year such leaders of all the villages in every district met to discuss and decide on the allocation of taxes. For purposes of allocation and collection of taxes each village constituted a separate unit. It was the responsibility of the village leaders to divide the tax burden according to the actual number of cultivated acres in their respective villages, each farmer paying the amount of cash due on the land he held. They were also responsible for the assessment of taxes to be paid by tradesmen and labourers according to their financial abilities. The leaders also had to consider the assessment and collection of taxes of the absent residents, *jāliya*, who were registered as members of a village. In most cases these were men who were temporarily engaged in some public works or who permanently worked in another part of the country but left their families in the security of their own villages.[2] Having collected these taxes the leaders made allowances for the maintenance of their churches, public baths, ferries across the Nile and presumably for local administrative expenses. The remainder was then duly sent to the district centre concerned which in turn sent it to the capital Alexandria.[3]

1 *Ibid.*, p. 161.

2 The usual rendering of *jāliya* as fugitives is not correct in this case, because it implies peasants' flight from the land. See Cahen, "Djizya". It was more of a tax evasion practice applied by those who left their villages, where they were registered for poll-tax purposes, for more lucrative occupations elsewhere. Either their taxes would be assessed at a low rate if they had strong attachments to their villages, or better, they could evade the tax altogether. Ibn 'Abdilḥakam, *Futūḥ Miṣr*, p. 153; Al-Maqrīzī, Aḥmad b. 'Ali, *al-Khiṭaṭ*, ed. G. Wiet, Cairo, 1911–22, vol. II, p. 94.

3 The best source in this respect is the passage in Ibn 'Abdilḥakam, *Futūḥ Miṣr*, pp. 152–3, which was clearly understood by Maqrīzī, *Khiṭaṭ*, vol. I, part I, pp. 323–4.

'Amr left the allocation and collection of taxes in the hands of the native officials and with their co-operation he introduced some changes in the system which secured the money he needed for his administration. He allowed the tax-collectors to accept payment in kind, in any form of produce, from the peasants. Any land where clover was cultivated was exempted from tax and in return the Arabs were allowed to graze their cattle for a short time in the spring.[1] The most important innovation, which in fact brought in the badly needed money, was the modification of the poll-tax. This was essentially the tax that had been imposed on tradesmen, only now increased and strictly enforced. It was clear that at this time virtually no Egyptians had been converted to Islam; 'Amr took advantage of this situation and, with calculated exceptions, required all non-converts to pay a poll-tax of two dinārs a year. These included all the tradesmen in the villages as well as the majority of the urban population, particularly that of Alexandria and the other towns on the Mediterranean coast. Admittedly two dinārs was a considerable amount of money at the time, but exemption was easily obtained. Only capable adult males were required to pay the poll-tax; the clergy, the old, all females and the poor were automatically exempted. Of course the peasants who were already paying a land tax were also exempted.[2]

These tax adjustments were probably made in more than one stage and in accordance with the advice of the Egyptian leaders. The general population must have been satisfied with the arrangements because we hear of no objections of any sort on their part. The Arab tribesmen were also satisfied although they received little cash. Their leaders received a stipend of 200 dinārs a year,[3] but they themselves were paid in adequate amounts of foodstuffs and clothing.[4] We have no reports of them receiving regular stipends at this stage. Such reports refer to later developments in the Umayyad period. 'Umar demanded and eventually had grain sent to Madīna,[5] and, as it had been for Byzantium, Egypt became, for some time to come, the granary for the whole of Ḥijāz.

1 Ibn 'Abdilḥakam, *Futūḥ Miṣr*, pp. 141, 153.

2 *Ibid.*, p. 70; Maqrīzī, *Khiṭaṭ*, vol. I, part I, pp. 324, 331, vol. II, part I, p. 61; Balādhurī, *Futūḥ*, p. 218.

3 Ibn 'Abdilḥakam, *Futūḥ Miṣr*, p. 145.

4 *Ibid.*, pp. 152, 192. The food supplies distributed were of such quantities as to exclude the need for cash payments. Also they are referred to as *arzāq*, usually food supplies distributed monthly.

5 *Ibid.*, pp. 158–65; Balādhurī, *Futūḥ*, p. 216.

Although Syria had also been part of the Byzantine empire its situation was quite different. The composition of the Arab army that conquered Syria is again of some complexity. We recall that the first army sent to Palestine by Abū Bakr in 634/13 was recruited from tribesmen who stood fast by the Madīnan regime against the *ridda* rebels. It was more in the nature of a reward that these faithful tribesmen were chosen for this particular campaign. The core of this army was some 7,000 men from Makka, Madīna, Ṭā'if and the surrounding Qaysite clans of Ḥijāz such as 'Abs and Sulaym.[1] There were also men from north-western Arabia from clans of ancient Yamanite origin such as Balī who were related and attached to 'Amr b. al-'Āṣ. The bulk of the army was about 20,000 men from Yaman who had also been faithful to Madīna in its hour of need.[2] These were the heroes of Ajnādayn (634/13). In the following three years they penetrated deep into Syria and by 637/16 they dealt the Byzantines another decisive blow at the Battle of the Yarmūk. This battle was the major turning-point in the Arab conquest and settlement of Syria. Deciding to give up the whole province, the Byzantines withdrew accompanied by a large proportion of the population which included many of the original Arabs of Syria.[3] The majority of the remaining Arabs decided to accept Islam and accordingly joined the Arab forces.[4] These were tribesmen who, though late Muslims, had not taken any part in the *ridda* wars. The most prominent of these tribesmen were from the clans of Kalb.

Although 'Umar allowed the *ridda* tribesmen to join the army on the Syrian front, we hear of only 700 of them under the leadership of Qays b. al-Makshūḥ al-Murādī as part of the Arab army in Syria. This group was transferred to Iraq soon after the Battle of the Yarmūk, scarcely arriving in time to take part in the Battle of Qādisiyya.[5] Their removal from Syria left the province with no *ridda* tribesmen and no more were brought into Syria afterwards. This can only have been a planned move to rid Syria of a possible source of trouble. In fact there must have been some very serious problems emerging among the Arabs there, although our sources present us with a picture of complete harmony. Aware of these

[1] Ṭabarī, I, pp. 2079, 2083–4; Balādhurī, *Futūḥ*, p. 172.
[2] Ṭabarī, I, pp. 2082–7.
[3] Balādhurī, *Futūḥ*, p. 136.
[4] *Ibid.*, pp. 145, 150; Ṭabarī, I, p. 2081.
[5] Balādhurī, *Futūḥ*, p. 256; Ṭabarī, I, p. 2350.

problems 'Umar himself had to travel to Syria, after the Battle of Yarmūk, almost certainly at the end of 638/17, to help settle these problems.[1]

The original plan for the Arab settlement of Syria was to establish a garrison town at Jābiya on the Golan heights and to control the province from there.[2] The situation in Syria forced a radical change in this plan soon after the Yarmūk battle. Inhabited Syria covered a much larger area than the Nile valley. Moreover this province was much more vulnerable to Byzantine attacks by land from the north and along the whole of the Syrian Mediterranean coast. From a military point of view it was necessary to establish major defences on both frontiers. Another very important factor in the situation was that the Greeks and Arabs who fled from Syria left some of the towns and much of the cultivable lands there deserted, inviting quick appropriation by any covetous observer. The first to take advantage of this situation were the native Arabs of Syria.[3] Having accepted Islam and seeing that the conquering tribesmen were confined to Jābiya, they understandably saw no reason to miss such an opportunity. Nevertheless, this amounted in fact to depriving the conquerors of the fruits of their conquest. Since the native Arab Syrians outnumbered their fellow Muslim conquerors the situation was indeed very delicate and required all possible tact in dealing with it. It was precisely for this reason that 'Umar went to Syria to adjudicate, persuade and help find a solution. The threat of a Byzantine counter-attack meant that the Arabs in Syria must be in as strong and stable a position as possible and any disharmony could only bring disaster to all concerned. On the other hand the extent of the flight from Syria was so great that it was necessary to arrange for the re-occupation of practically abandoned towns and much deserted land if only to keep commercial life flourishing and the land in cultivation. The final arrangement endorsed by 'Umar was a redistribution of the available houses and lands among all Muslim Arabs, natives and conquerors alike.

The province was divided into four military districts, each called *jund*, army, corresponding to the Byzantine provinces before the conquest. These were Ḥimṣ, Damascus, Jordan and

[1] Balādhurī, *Futūḥ*, p. 136. [2] *Ibid.*, pp. 139, 151.
[3] *Ibid.*, pp. 113, 116, 122, 126, 138, 139, 142, 144, 150, 151, 152; Ṭabarī, I, pp. 2159, 2392.

Palestine. An appropriate number of tribesmen from related clans were settled in each of these districts. They were permitted to take a normal part in the economic life of their district but at the same time were charged with the responsibility of defending it as well as the whole province.[1]

Shortly after, some of the conquering tribesmen, feeling somewhat slighted, took the initiative and left to conquer Egypt. However, another group of the original conquerors, who probably also resented this settlement, opted for or were rewarded by a similar new conquest. These were the core of the conquering army, the 7,000 tribesmen from Makka, Madīna, Ṭā'if and the surrounding Qaysite clans of Ḥijāz. Their reward was the easy conquest of the vast and rich region of Jazīra, Mesopotamia, which they rapidly conquered and ruled as a separate province.[2] This conquest had the added advantage of securing the right flank of Syria against any possible Byzantine attacks down the Euphrates.

All these arrangements contributed to the security and harmony of the Arabs in Syria. The conquering tribesmen from Yaman, who numbered around 20,000 men, were given houses and properties partly in Damascus but mostly in Ḥimṣ. There they had a better chance to engage in trade and form a powerful defence line on the northern frontier. The acknowledged leader in Ḥimṣ was al-Ṣimṭ b. al-Aswad al-Kindī, and after him his son Shuraḥbīl, who had supported the Madīnan side in the *ridda* wars in Yaman.[3] The Syrian Arabs were given lands, especially along the fertile coast where they also were effective in its defence against Byzantine sea attacks.[4] These two most powerful groups in Syria began to forge a common interest based on maintaining these satisfactory arrangements. They became commonly known as the Yamaniyya, the first by virtue of being immigrants from Yaman and the other by an alleged descent from a Yamanite origin, but this tenuous genealogical relationship was the least important factor in their newly found harmony.

1 Balādhurī, *Futūḥ*, pp. 129, 151; Ṭabarī, I, pp. 2347–8, 2403, 2407, 2521, 2523; Ibn 'Asākir, *Tārīkh Dimashq*, ed. S. El-Munajjid, Damascus, 1951, vol. I, pp. 553, 556.

2 Balādhurī, *Futūḥ*, pp. 172–7; Ṭabarī, I, p. 2507.

3 Balādhurī, *Futūḥ*, pp. 122, 131; Ṭabarī, I, p. 2250; Ibn 'Asākir, *Tārīkh Dimashq*, vol. I, p. 591.

4 Balādhurī, *Futūḥ*, pp. 128, 133, 144, 150.

The preservation of this harmony became largely the responsibility of the family of Abū Sufyān, and in particular Mu'āwiya. As is well known, Abū Sufyān had had considerable trade with Syria before Islam, and had even owned a farm near Damascus. His son, Yazīd, was one of the first generals sent by Abū Bakr to campaign in Palestine, and after the death of Abū 'Ubayda in 639/18 he became the second governor of Syria. After his death in 641/20 his brother, Mu'āwiya, was appointed the new governor, a post which he held for the next twenty years. The cornerstone of his policy was the continued stability of the province by maintaining the arrangements of its settlement. This stability was absolutely necessary for its defence against any Byzantine threat, which could still not be ignored. Nothing was to be allowed to cloud the loyalty of the Arabs in Syria or distract them from their primary responsibility of defending the province. In order to be able to carry out this policy, Mu'āwiya gradually secured what amounted to complete control over immigration into Syria. After the initial stages of the settlement he shrewdly utilized his powers as governor to limit immigration to tribesmen related to clans already there.[1] Fortunately, this coincided to some extent with the Madīnan policy of excluding the *ridda* tribesmen from Syria. The net result was that this province was saved from the social upheaval and antagonisms caused by successive waves of tribesmen pouring into other provinces.

As for the fiscal organization of Syria, the system introduced by the Arabs was just as simple as the organization of their settlement there and corresponded to it. The Muslims paid their *'ushūr*, tithes, on the land they held.[2] The non-Muslims continued to pay their taxes according to the Byzantine system, and for this purpose many of the former tax officials were kept to serve the new masters. Although we are uncertain on many points of the Byzantine system in Syria, apparently a "duality of land tax and poll-tax existed at the taxpayer's level, under various conditions, for the greater part of the peasant population, while on the other hand a system of unitary contribution prevailed throughout Syrian towns".[3] From the peasants the Arabs required one dinār

[1] Al-Iṣfahānī, Abū al-Faraj, *al-Aghānī*, Cairo, A.H. 1285, vol. XVIII, pp. 69–70; Ṭabarī, I, pp. 2187–8, 2218.

[2] Balādhurī, *Futūḥ*, pp. 151, 152, 173, 177, 180; Ibn Sallām, Abū 'Ubayd al-Qāsim, *al-Amwāl*, Cairo, A.H. 1353, p. 500.

[3] Cahen, "Djizya".

and one *jarīb* (measure of wheat) on every head, probably in proportion to the lands they held. From the non-Muslim urban populations they continued to collect what was also called *jizya*, a poll-tax. Its rate was one, two or four dinārs according to the wealth of the taxpayer, and exemption was easily obtainable.[1]

At this early stage it does not seem that a system of distribution of stipends to the Arabs had yet been instituted,[2] although the leaders probably received an annual stipend of 200 dinārs. Apart from the usual administrative expenses, which could not have been very great, the balance of the taxes was used in building up fortifications on the coast, and above all to launch an Arab navy.[3] The grain collected was probably distributed only among the Arabs who settled in the towns and who had been given no cultivable land.[4] Those who settled in the countryside had to be satisfied with their own produce. One last interesting financial point is that Syria, with the exception of the customary one-fifth of the booty, sent absolutely nothing to Madīna from its revenues.

Iraq poses by far the most difficult and important historical problems among these three provinces. Just as it was the scene of unusually bitter conflict, so are the sources unusually partisan, exaggerating the confusion of a period already confused. Modern scholars have dutifully imitated their sources and made the obscurity almost complete. Failing to interpret the source material, they have applied irrelevant juristic formulae of centuries later to this early situation. Furthermore, as a result of their failure to study systematically the circumstances of the conquests of the areas concerned, they have applied these incomprehensible data to the wrong areas.[5] It is hoped that the following interpretation will at least help to clarify some of the confusion, and will provoke scholars to a further investigation of these problems.

The composition of the Arab army which conquered Iraq was the major factor in the troubles that plagued this province for a considerable time after its conquest. That our sources wished to emphasize this point is clearly indicated by the elaborate nomenclature they apply to the various groups who took part in the conquest and finally settled in Iraq. It will be recalled that raids in

[1] Balādhurī, *Futūḥ*, p. 124.

[2] Ibn 'Asākir, *Tārīkh Dimashq*, vol. 1, p. 556.

[3] Balādhurī, *Futūḥ*, p. 128.

[4] *Ibid.*, pp. 124, 125, 152.

[5] F. Løkkegaard, *Islamic Taxation in the Classic Period*, Copenhagen, 1950; D. C. Dennet, *Conversion and the Poll-tax in Early Islam*, Cambridge, Mass., 1950.

Sāsānian territories were initiated by tribesmen from eastern Arabia, mostly from clans of Shaybān, in the time of Abū Bakr. More to their credit is the fact that they did not take part in the *ridda* rebellions. Therefore they are accurately referred to in our sources as those of valour, *ahl al-balā'*, in recognition of their courage against the Sāsānians.[1]

When Khālid joined in the raids in Iraq, his men, except for those Makkans and Madīnans who remained with him, were mostly from clans of little importance.[2] Nevertheless they were the heroes of 'Aqrabā and other battles against the apostates and their faithfulness to Islam was beyond any doubt. Moreover, their penetration of Sāsānian territory gave their raids the distinction of military success. Minor as it was, this success was important in the sequence of the greater conquests. The battles these men fought and won were of the utmost service to Islam as well as being the major proof of their devotion. The Madīnans and Makkans amongst them had the distinction of being *anṣār* and *muhājirūn*, or at least of belonging to Quraysh. These otherwise undistinguished tribesmen came to be known as *ahl al-ayyām*, those who took part in the battles.[3]

The campaigns against the Sāsānian empire did not gather momentum until the apostates, *ahl al-ridda*, of 633/12 were allowed to join them, after 'Umar's succession. Their major role in the Battle of Qādisiyya 637/16 was duly recognized and the derogatory term *ahl al-ridda* was dropped in favour of the respectable *ahl al-Qādisiyya*. This last appellation was applied to all those who took part in this battle, *ridda* and non-*ridda* tribesmen alike.[4] Similarly, all the tribesmen who continued to pour into Iraq after Qādisiyya were called *rādifa*, i.e. those who follow or come after. Each group of these late-comers was also designated as first, second or third *rādifa* according to their time of arrival.[5]

These are not just empty terms invented for simple reasons of boasting. They are meaningful terms introduced at the time for the specific purpose of determining the credit of each group and its exact services to the cause according to which due reward was decided. Abū Bakr deliberately excluded the *ridda* tribesmen from

[1] Ṭabarī, I, pp. 2028, 2451; Athīr, *Kāmil*, vol. II, pp. 375–6.
[2] Ṭabarī, I, pp. 1887, 1905, 1911, 1930, 2021, 2028.
[3] *Ibid.*, pp. 2110, 2201, 2853, 2907.
[4] *Ibid.*, pp. 2165, 2183, 2217–22, 2633, 2852–3, 2907.
[5] *Ibid.*, pp. 2413, 2496, 2835.

the early raids and deprived them of such easy gains. When 'Umar allowed them to join in the Iraqi campaign, it was not his intention to treat them on an equal footing with the more trustworthy tribesmen already at that front. His policy was to make use of the former rebels without appointing their leaders to any responsible positions, either in the army itself or in the conquered territories.[1] In other words their influence on decision-making was kept to a minimum and in fact they were subjected to the decisions of none too sympathetic leaders. Of course the inequality of their treatment was shown most clearly in the division of the rewards of the conquests. As will be explained presently, they were given a lesser share than their non-*ridda* fellow tribesmen. In the case of the late-comers, most of whom were *ridda* tribesmen, this discrepancy was so great that it was bound to cause very serious problems. To understand the nature of these problems one needs to take into consideration the circumstances of the conquest, the treatment of the native population, the organization of the Arabs and their relations with Madīna.

The final collapse of the Sāsānian empire in Iraq towards the end of 637/16 left the Arab conquerors in complete control of the most fertile and thickly populated part of that empire. This area is known in our sources as the Sawād and it stretches from the head of the Persian Gulf to Mawṣil in the north and from the borders of the Syrian–Iraqi desert to Ḥulwān in the east. The Arabs in Syria were fortunate in the sense that so many of the native population fled to Byzantium leaving behind enough houses and lands to accommodate the conquerors. In Iraq this problem was not so easily solved. Certainly the Sāsānian king and many court and government officials fled eastwards in the hope of later regaining their positions, but the vast majority of the population and the local nobility remained on the land. The Arabs had, therefore, to determine the fate of their persons and their property. Arguably the rules applying to booty gained on the battlefield could offer guidance, but unfortunately, beyond the fact that a fifth should go to Madīna, the example of the Qu'rān and the Sunna, i.e. the Prophet's example, were very variable and did not offer consistent guidance on the question of spoils in these unexpected circumstances. The central difficulty was whether the booty gained on the battlefield should be interpreted so widely as

[1] *Ibid.*, pp. 2225, 2327.

to include the persons and properties of the territory conquered whatever the circumstances. The usual practice of the Arabs was to consider everything conquered the private property of the conquerors themselves. The later distinction between *ghanīma* and *fay'* had not yet been made; *ghanīma* being the booty won on the battlefield and *fay'* being all other gains.

In fact this question was decided empirically. Those Sāsānian subjects who went over to Islam posed no problem. Considerable numbers of the Sāsānian army did accept Islam, joined the Arab armies, were warmly welcomed and given the highest pay.[1] A few of the local nobility, *dihqāns*, also accepted Islam and were allowed to keep their property. The difficulty lay with the vast majority of the unconverted. At the very beginning some of them were enslaved and even sent to Madīna as part of the fifth of the booty.[2] Evidently the Bajīla group of tribesmen received slaves as part of the quarter of the booty they were promised to encourage them to go to the Sāsānian front. Soon they were given eighty or, according to other reports, 400 dinārs to relinquish this right. Some scholars have interpreted this right as referring to a quarter of the lands, and admittedly our sources sometimes say "a quarter of the Sawād",[3] but this is a complete misunderstanding since the traditions concerned clearly refer to people and not to land.[4] The term Sawād should here be understood to mean *ahl al-Sawād*, the inhabitants of that area. The idea of enslaving a whole nation was ludicrously impractical. First, the Arabs could have little use for so many slaves. Second, as in Egypt, the conquerors soon understood the significance of an agricultural economy as a source of revenue and decided it was to their advantage to maintain its structure.[5] Since the Arabs were comparatively few, economic necessity dictated that the conquered population should be free to cultivate the land.

More important, from a historical point of view, was the fact that the land was no more divided than the people. This is the

[1] Balādhurī, *Futūḥ*, pp. 280, 373–4; Ṭabarī, I, pp. 2499, 2563.
[2] Ṭabarī, I, pp. 2026, 2028, 2031, 2036, 2037, 2077, 2289.
[3] *Ibid.*, pp. 2197–8; Balādhurī, *Futūḥ*, pp. 267–8.
[4] Balādhurī, *Futūḥ*, pp. 266, 268; Ṭabarī, I, pp. 2369–75; Ibn Sallām, *Amwāl*, p. 59; Abū Yūsuf, *Kitāb al-Kharāj*, Cairo, A.H. 1302, pp. 16, 21.
[5] Some of the conquerors of Egypt initially thought that the native population should be enslaved and divided, but this opinion was soon revised and some of those enslaved were even set free; see Ibn 'Abdilḥakam, *Futūḥ Miṣr*, pp. 82–8.

essential point of the present interpretation. Sources, jurists, historians and modern scholars have widely disagreed on the distribution of land and its revenue in Iraq, producing the most confusing accounts of the situation. Some of the difficulty results from attempts to make fine distinctions between *kharāj* as a land tax and *jizya* as a poll-tax. At this stage the definitions of these words varied from place to place and from time to time, and they meant tax or revenue only in the most general way. The remaining difficulty results from the tendency to view the most rudimentary measures of the early conquerors as based on precisely formulated legal principles. Any effort to make the irregularities in this period appear well-planned according to theological–juristic formulas is decidedly mistaken. Measures were taken on an *ad hoc* basis in the most haphazard manner to meet unexpected situations. The essential point is that most of the land remained in native hands, provided that due taxes were paid, while the revenue from these taxes was distributed among the conquerors. No less a personality than Khālid in Iraq had set a precedent for this. In his initial campaigns, three or four localities surrendered without fighting and agreed to a treaty by which they kept their freedom and property in exchange for a small tribute. After one-fifth had been set aside to be sent to Madīna, the rest of this tribute was divided among Khālid's troops.[1] In fact, even after the final conquest of Iraq the population of these localities held fast to their treaties and continued to pay the same small tribute to their conquerors. This is but one of the many anomalies in the settlement of Iraq. Yet this minor incident in itself was important in that it set a pattern for the distribution of revenue. Following this unintentional precedent, most of the revenues from Iraq were treated as booty and were therefore, after one-fifth had been set aside to be sent to Madīna, divided among the conquering troops.

These revenues were the aggregate of the fixed tributes imposed upon certain localities, when they decided to surrender without a prolonged fight, and the taxes collected from other areas. It is not difficult to imagine that the fixed tribute was most probably less than the amount of tax required by the Sāsānians from the same districts. It is also clear that the allocation and collection of taxes needed to raise these tributes was left to the discretion of the local nobility and it is unlikely that there were any converts in such

[1] Ṭabarī, I, pp. 2026, 2028, 2031.

districts. Therefore the Sāsānian system of taxation was continued in what amounted to lightened taxation.[1] In the areas where there were no treaties, the Sāsānian system of taxation was continued under the same officials. This followed the usual Arab practice of making the least possible change, especially in such complicated matters as taxation. The Sāsānian system involved two kinds of tax, poll-tax and land tax. The poll-tax was imposed on every person, peasant or town-dweller, between the ages of twenty and fifty years, and was graded according to income. The nobility, the warriors, the priests and the civil servants were exempted from this tax.[2] Obviously this was a tax mainly intended for craftsmen and tradesmen. The land tax was of a fixed rate in kind or money assessed on area and kind of product. The Arabs continued the land tax on exactly the same scale and basis as the Sāsānians.[3] The poll-tax was also continued but the maximum was fixed at forty-eight dirhams which was probably less than that of the Sāsānians. The minimum was twelve dirhams, but again the range of those exempted was probably wider than under the Sāsānian system.[4]

By far the most complicated problem in the settlement of Iraq was that of the abandoned lands, the extensive properties belonging to the Sāsānian royal family, their close relatives, and the great notables who fled with them, and the huge holdings of the fire-temples.[5] We do not have enough information about the arrangements according to which peasants had kept these lands under cultivation, but it is reasonable to assume that such arrangements were to the great advantage of the prominent landlords. It may also be assumed that the peasants had been tied to these lands through some manipulation of the Sāsānian administrative regulations. These lands, therefore, now had the necessary manpower to work them but were without owners. The Arabs, who wanted these very fertile lands to remain under cultivation, left the peasants on the land to continue their work. It was, however, practically impossible to divide the lands between the Arab tribesmen, who considered themselves the owners by right of conquest, since, as the properties were scattered all over the Sawād, the whole

[1] *Ibid.*, pp. 2049–51.
[2] A. Christensen, *L'Iran sous les Sassanides*, Copenhagen, 1936, pp. 118–24, 315–16, 362.
[3] Ṭabarī, I, pp. 2467–8; Balādhurī, *Futūḥ*, pp. 269–70.
[4] Baladhurī, *Futūḥ*, p. 271.
[5] *Ibid.*, pp. 272–3; Ibn Sallām, *Amwāl*, p. 283; Ṭabarī, I, pp. 2371, 2467.

system would have collapsed.[1] In addition this would have had the result of scattering the Arab troops themselves all over the wide area. The only possible solution, therefore, was to hold the lands under collective ownership, such owners being described by the new term *ahl al-fay'*.[2] These new owners were probably more lenient towards the peasants than the Sāsānians because the Arabs do not seem to have demanded a special rate of rent for these particular lands. It is almost certain that the Sāsānian land tax rates were also applied which in this case was certainly a great improvement for the peasants involved.[3]

For the sake of administering these lands and collecting and distributing their revenues, a system of trusteeship was established.[4] Of course the trustees, *umanā'*, were to be chosen from *ahl al-fay'* who included both *ridda* and non-*ridda* tribesmen. Since such a responsible position could not be entrusted to the *ridda* tribesmen and the Makkans and the Madīnans generally returned to Ḥijāz,[5] the task fell automatically to those importuning tribesmen who had been loyal to Madīna during the *ridda*, had participated in all the stages of the conquest of Iraq and had remained there after Qādisiyya, i.e. *ahl al-ayyām*. Their early battles had been overshadowed by greater battles in which they had also taken part. To call these tribesmen simply *ahl al-Qādisiyya* would in fact mean equating them with *ahl al-ridda*.[6] Understandably this represented a threat to their hard-gained prestige and ultimately to their newly acquired gains. Determined to keep their distinction, and because of their trusteeship responsibilities, they eventually acquired a new nomenclature, the *qurrā'*.

This term has been understood to mean Qur'ān-readers even by some rather early historians. Although it is etymologically plausible, it is difficult to accept the idea of thousands of Qur'ān-readers, organized into separate contingents, all fighting at Ṣiffīn a few years later. If they were some latent form of clergy, as some historians see them, one is astonished to see them so numerous, especially at this early stage.[7] Their history shows without doubt that they were very bellicose, politically united, with many

[1] Ṭabarī, I, p. 2468.
[2] *Ibid.*, pp. 2371, 2468.
[3] Balādhurī, *Futūḥ*, pp. 269–71; Ṭabarī, I, pp. 2467–8.
[4] Ṭabarī, I, pp. 2469, 2496.
[5] *Ibid.*, pp. 2456, 2596.
[6] *Ibid.*, p. 2110.
[7] H. A. R. Gibb, "An Interpretation of Islamic History", *Studies on the Civilization of Islam*, London, 1962, pp. 7–8, where they are described as "the religious party".

common interests and all from those clans which had remained faithful to Madīna during the *ridda* wars. All these indications unequivocally point to the group previously known as *ahl al-ayyām*. The term *qurrā'* should be understood as no more than another derivation from the root *qry* and meaning the same as *ahl al-qurā*, those of the villages, which denotes their distinctive field of action as trustees.[1] The ambiguity about Qur'ān-readers may have been introduced by tenth-century Islamic chroniclers who were just as confused with the earlier *qurrā'* at 'Aqrabā. It is also possible that it was encouraged by the *qurrā'* themselves to enhance their ever waning prestige.

As for the organization of the Arabs in Iraq, there was a definite policy of keeping them together and separate from the native population. They first settled in the Sāsānian capital of Madā'in, living in the deserted houses of the city.[2] However, they soon moved to Kūfa in 639/18 because, if one is to believe the sources, the climate did not suit them. It is far more likely that the decision was taken because the town was more strategically placed to send help to Syria should it be needed.[3] Also from a military point of view Madā'in could be easily cut off by a thrust from the still unsubdued and powerful province of Fārs. Furthermore, in a large city like Madā'in it was probably not easy to control the tribesmen effectively, an easier task in the garrison town of Kūfa.

Another garrison town was soon established at Baṣra to relieve the pressures of ceaseless immigration into Iraq, and also as a result of the opening of a new front by the Arabs of Baḥrayn, on the Persian Gulf. These tribesmen took advantage of the collapse of Sāsānian power by crossing the Gulf and raiding the province of Fārs on their own initiative.[4] The Persian Gulf was no hindrance to these raids but rather a highway: the real hindrance was the

[1] In fact al-Farazdaq used *ahl al-qurā* in reference to the *qurrā'* who were killed in the revolt of Ibn al-Ash'ath (see below p. 110): *Dīwān al-Farazdaq*, ed. R. Boucher, Paris, 1870, vol. I, p. 151. This meaning of *qurrā'* is also confirmed by Aḥmad al-Manīnī in *Sharḥ al-Yamīnī 'alā Tārīkh al-'Utbī*, Cairo, A.H. 1286, vol. II, p. 207, where the author explains the usage of this term in Sīstān, and quotes lexicographers in support of his explanation. It is also significant to find Mas'ūdī using *ahl al-qar' wa al-ashrāf* instead of *qurrā'*: Al-Mas'ūdī, 'Alī b. al-Ḥusayn, *Murūj al-Dhahab*, ed. C. Barbier de Meynard and P. de Courteille, Paris, 1861–77, vol. V, p. 469. See also above p. 23 where the word had a slightly different emphasis.

[2] Ṭabarī, I, pp. 2443, 2444, 2451.

[3] *Ibid.*, pp. 2483–6, 2515; Balādhurī, *Futūḥ*, p. 275.

[4] Ṭabarī, I, p. 2546; Balādhurī, *Futūḥ*, p. 386.

unexpectedly fierce resistance of the province. Failing to establish a safe base in Fārs, the tribesmen withdrew to the safer area of Baṣra where they were joined mainly by their fellow-tribesmen of eastern Arabia.[1] In contrast to Kūfa, very few of the founders of Baṣra were from the tribesmen who took part in the early raids or the actual conquest of Iraq. The majority of the Arabs of Baṣra were tribesmen who did not take an active part in the *ridda* war, either for or against Madīna, and some of them may have accepted Islam only after the end of these wars. These were tribesmen from the clans of Tamīm, Bakr, 'Abdulqays and Azd.[2] The relative homogeneity of the Arabs in Baṣra was a major reason why it was spared much of the strife that prevailed in Kūfa.

The groupings into which the tribesmen were organized in Kūfa and Baṣra were of some complexity. The organization of the Arab armies during the conquests, as might be expected, was of the most rudimentary kind, but serious thought was given to the planning and organization of the new towns where they settled. The problem was particularly difficult because the clan, the usual unit of Arab society, was not wholly applicable in the new situation. Only in a few cases had a whole clan joined the Arab army; in most cases sections, and indeed very small sections, of clans had joined. This situation was aggravated by the fact that later immigrants into Iraq arrived in similar disorganized fashion. It is interesting to note that different terms were used in this situation to denote these groups. If a whole clan joined, they were called *barara*, i.e. those who proved true and obedient; if only a section, they were called *khiyara*, select or chosen. Thus the clans in Kūfa varied considerably in numbers.[3] For the purposes of housing and social organization in the new town, tribesmen of related clans were lumped together into seven major divisions. Each division bearing the name of the major clan or tribal group was granted a big lot of vacant land where members built their houses and their own mosque. Allowances were made for further immigrants to be absorbed by the clans to which they belonged or by other related clans.[4] For military and administrative purposes the tribesmen in Kūfa were divided into roughly equal small units, regardless of

[1] Ṭabarī, I, p. 2548.
[2] Balādhurī, *Futūḥ*, p. 386; for further details on Baṣra see Ṣāliḥ A. al-'Alī, *al-Tanẓīmāt al-Ijtimā'iyya wa al-Iqtiṣādiyya fī al-Baṣra*, Baghdad, 1953.
[3] Ṭabarī, I, p. 2495; Athīr, *Kāmil*, vol. II, p. 304.
[4] Balādhurī, *Futūḥ*, pp. 276–7; Ṭabarī, I, p. 2495.

which clan they belonged to. The number of men in each unit depended on its members' share in the revenue because each unit was allotted 100,000 dirhams. Each unit, *'arāfa*, was under an *'arīf* responsible for the distribution of its stipends and for its availability and readiness for military service. This same socio-military organization was followed in Baṣra. The only difference was that there was no need to create new divisions there,[1] since clear tribal groupings already existed, which served the same purpose as the divisions of Kūfa and which were duly recognized. Again Baṣra was more fortunate in that it was saved the agonies of artificial divisions. Twenty-five years later, when both towns were reorganized, drastic changes were introduced in Kūfa while the divisions in Baṣra remained basically the same.

While the Baṣrans had yet to establish their rule in newly conquered territories, the Kūfans had already established their rule over the Sawād. However, hardly any Kūfans lived permanently outside the garrison town. Some tribesmen were sent on so-called minor expeditions to establish Arab rule at the grass-roots, or alternatively to form minor garrisons, *masāliḥ*, in the countryside. At other times outright appointments were made by the Arab governors of Kūfa for the collection of revenue in a particular district. As we have seen, the task of tax-collection and local government remained in the hands of local notables and village heads, *dahāqīn*. Therefore these appointments represented the link between the Arab government in Kūfa and local governments. The duties of those appointed certainly included the receipt of the taxes collected by the *dahāqīn* and the transfer of the money to the public treasury. They probably also included the supervision of the assessment and collection of the poll-tax. This vital link and important responsibility could not be, and was not, entrusted to the *ridda* tribesmen. Again the *qurrā'*, who were already involved in the administration of the abandoned lands, were the obvious men to undertake such responsibility. This conclusion is clearly supported by our sources since practically all the names of tribesmen mentioned as being involved in any activities outside Kūfa at that time were from among the *qurrā'*.[2] While the *ridda* tribesmen were confined to Kūfa, the *qurrā'* were happily roaming the countryside where, during their tours of

[1] Ṭabarī, I, p. 2496.
[2] Ṭabarī, I, pp. 2455–6, 2463, 2474, 2478, 2497, 2596, 2597, 2628, 2637, 2645.

inspection, they lived off the fat of the land, the local populations being required to offer hospitality to any passing Arab for at least three days.[1]

It was only natural that the *ridda* tribesmen in Kūfa should resent the special position given to the *qurrā'* in the government of the Sawād. It must be remembered that the ex-rebels were generally from clans of high standing in pre-Islamic Arabia, in contrast to the *qurrā'* who belonged to relatively unimportant clans. Al-Ashʿath b. Qays al-Kindī, a notorious protagonist of the *ridda*, was no ordinary leader of an ordinary clan. His position before Islam had been that of a king in Ḥaḍramawt and his followers in Kūfa could not have easily forgotten his past position. Since many of the late-comers to Kūfa were *ridda* tribesmen, the rise to power and influence of their former leaders was inevitable. This was easier because the seven primary divisions of Kūfan society had still the right to choose their own leaders. In such a situation the *qurrā'* were gradually outnumbered and their newly acquired prestige was gravely threatened. No wonder they felt very jealous for their position in the new but rapidly changing society.

Although this tension was gradually building up to an explosion it was balanced, at the beginning, by the flush of the great conquest. The riches of the booty gained on the battlefield were so unimaginably great that all groups were, at least temporarily, satisfied. However the only point of agreement between them was that, after setting aside the fifth of this booty to be sent to Madīna, the rest was to be divided equally among the conquerors. This equal division, and the considerable size of the shares, helped to overcome such problems as the enslavement of the population of the Sawād and the management of the abandoned lands. Now that the great battles were over and there was practically no booty to be had from the battlefield, it was important to decide on the distribution of the revenues from the conquered Sawād. Since all the tribesmen involved in the conquest considered this territory their own by right of conquest, it was practically a matter of course that its revenues should be divided among themselves. There was some doubt as to whether Madīna was entitled to one-fifth of these revenues, as it was entitled to a share in the booty won on the battlefield,[2] but apparently the question was decided in favour of Madīna, though perhaps after

[1] *Ibid.*, p. 2470. [2] *Ibid.*, p. 2418.

some hesitation. The rest of the revenues from the land tax, the poll-tax, the abandoned lands and any tributes paid as a result of peace treaties were divided among the conquering tribesmen, as annual stipends. Meagre allowances were made to the newcomers. Therefore the stipends in Kūfa varied from 250 to 3,000 dirhams per annum. At the top of the scale the founders of Kūfa, that is the original conquerors of Iraq, received stipends varying between 2,000 and 3,000 dirhams. Obviously a good part of this was their share of the revenues from the abandoned lands. The highest figure was the stipend of *ahl al-ayyām*, i.e. the *qurrā'*, no doubt as an acknowledgement of their good standing and their special services in the government of the Sawād. The newcomers, who had no right to the abandoned land, did less well. Only a very few, the relatively early arrivals, received as much as 1,500 dirhams, while the majority were given only 250 to 300 dirhams.[1]

In Baṣra, only the recognized leaders received 2,500 dirhams, which came to be known as *sharaf al-'aṭā'*, the stipend of leadership. The remaining tribesmen received the usual 250–300 dirhams,[2] and, although this was not high, the situation was helped by the food supplies which were distributed each month from the accumulated land taxes paid in kind.[3] However, it must be noted that here high stipends were the exception, a fact which no doubt added to the homogeneity of Baṣra. In contrast, the disparity in the size of stipends in Kūfa was yet another cause of tension between the original conquerors, both *ridda* and non-*ridda* tribesmen, and the later arrivals. The unusual conditions of living in a garrison town, together with the anomalies of a socio-military organization, helped to accentuate these tensions in Kūfa and sooner or later an explosion was bound to occur.

Now we shall turn to examine the situation in Madīna, the centre of the rapidly expanding Arab empire. From the outset, it should be stated that, except for the broadest policy decisions for the regime as a whole, Madīna exercised virtually no control over the newly conquered provinces. Central government as such did not exist since such an institution demands a vast bureaucracy and Madīna had none. Only 'Umar, the *Khalīfa* of the *Khalīfa* of the Prophet, stood amid such a flux of events as would bewilder the

[1] *Ibid.*, pp. 2411–18; Balādhurī, *Futūḥ*, pp. 448–61.

[2] Ṭabarī, I, pp. 2413, 2496, 2538–9.

[3] Balādhurī, *Futūḥ*, p. 460.

most sophisticated modern government. He could rely only on the voluntary help and advice of other leaders in Madīna. Our sources describe 'Umar, while in office, counting under the burning sun the camels collected as *ṣadaqa* (alms or tax collected from Muslims at the time). For this task he had only the voluntary help of 'Alī and 'Uthmān to record the number, size, qualities and defects of these camels.[1] While it is true that he had the power to appoint commanders and governors, and at times gave them detailed directions about their responsibilities, he had no means of enforcing these directions. Once these leaders left Madīna they were on their own to meet new and unexpected circumstances and understandably felt free to act according to their own best judgement. They were probably restrained more by the wishes of their followers than by any directions from 'Umar. When 'Amr b. al-'Āṣ marched to conquer Egypt with 3,500 men who ought to have been garrisoning Palestine, he was acting on his own initiative without direction from 'Umar.

Despite the huge increase in the problems and responsibilities facing him and despite the imperious vigour of his character, 'Umar had in reality no more authority than his mild, part-time predecessor, Abū Bakr. The only difference is perhaps that 'Umar used his great vigour and force of character to bolster the limited powers in his office. However, all his recorded actions and utterances make it very clear that he was well aware of the limitations of his power. Like any other traditional Arab leader he was only to advise and persuade, never to command. 'Umar's original title was the *Khalīfa* to the *Khalīfa* of the Prophet, that is the successor to Abū Bakr, the successor of Muḥammad. What we have said of the term *Khalīfa* with reference to Abū Bakr holds equally true for 'Umar. However, it is clear that the title was getting cumbersome, so the shorter title of *Amīr al-Mu'minīn* was introduced and generally used instead.[2]

It is a grave misunderstanding to think that this change to a simpler title implied any change in the powers of the office. The usual translation of the new title as Commander of the Faithful is a gross misnomer. According to the fullest dictionaries the word *amīr* means prince, commander, leader of the blind, husband, adviser or counsellor. Of these alternatives the last translation, as counsellor, represents best the essential realities of 'Umar's

[1] Ṭabarī, I, pp. 2736–7.

[2] *Ibid.*, pp. 2735–76.

position. Significantly Theophanes, the ninth-century Byzantine historian, translated *Amīr al-Mu'minīn* as *protosymboulos*, or first counsellor, and even applied this translation to the far more authoritarian Umayyad *Amīr al-Mu'minīn*. Later Byzantine historians even apply it to the 'Abbāsids.[1] To the Arabs, the *Amīr al-Mu'minīn* was not a commander but rather a counsellor, very much in the tradition of Arab leadership. The only qualification that one must make is that the conquered peoples were far more accustomed to authoritarian rule than their conquerors. They looked up to him as the ultimate redresser of injustice and would almost certainly have thought of the *Amīr al-Mu'minīn* as a king.

The second part of this title, *mu'minīn*, also requires discussion. Many minds have laboured over the distinction between *muslimūn* and *mu'minūn*. The argument goes that *mu'minūn* signified the inner circle of the Islamic community, while *muslimūn* signified the whole body, but it is hard to see a conclusive solution in the Qur'ān or any of our other sources.[2] Fortunately one need not take refuge in theological niceties, for there is a very plausible explanation at hand. *Amīr al-Mu'minīn* was a political, not a religious title, and *mu'minūn*, that is believers, was clearly a more tactful and politic word than *muslimūn*, that is submitters. Nobody could object to being called a believer, but to be called a submitter would obviously have been repugnant to the pride of the rebels of the *ridda*, some of whose leaders, especially in the Yaman, were known as *malik* or king. Therefore no especial political significance should be attached to 'Umar's assumption of the title *Amīr al-Mu'minīn*, for it did not involve any new powers. It was merely a convenient way of avoiding the cumbersome term, *Khalīfa* of the *Khalīfa* of the Prophet.

The absence of any means of effective control of the vast empire and the limited power of the office of *Amīr al-Mu'minīn* were the main features of the relationship between Madīna and the provinces. 'Umar's institution, for example, of a registry, *dīwān*, in Iraq to organize the distribution of stipends, *'aṭā'*, should not be seen as an assertion of central power but as a formal acknowledgement of what had already been decided by the tribes-

[1] J. Wellhausen, *The Arab Kingdom and its Fall*, tr. M. G. Weir, Calcutta, 1927, p. 138.
[2] Gibb, "Interpretation", pp. 5–6; Watt, *Muḥammad at Medina*, p. 226; Serjeant, "The Constitution of Madina", *Islamic Quarterly*, vol. VIII, 1964, pp. 3–16.

men of Iraq themselves. It was perhaps a desperate attempt, on his part, to limit and contain the desires of the conquerors. At first, Madīna was satisfied with the fifth of the booty sent from the provinces because of its immense size. But once the flow of the riches from the booty of the conquests began to dry up, Madīna was compelled to seek new sources of revenue from the provinces.

In the meantime the fifth and the tithes of Arabia sufficed to keep Madīna rich, and indeed allowed the government to pay generous stipends from 2,000 up to 12,000 dirhams to the residents of Madīna and Makka. Makkans who accepted Islam only after the conquest of Makka received 2,000 dirhams each. Madīnans and early Makkan converts received from 3,000 to 5,000 dirhams, with special allowances being made for women and children. Thus 'Alī received 5,000 for himself and, as a special allowance, 5,000 each for his sons Ḥasan and Ḥusayn because of the Prophet's affection for them. The only stipends higher than 5,000 dirhams were for the widows of the Prophet who received up to 12,000 each.[1] But this happy state of affairs could not continue indefinitely, and Madīna was soon asking for more. The very rich abandoned lands in Iraq, for example, were soon to become a bone of contention between 'Uthmān and the tribesmen of Iraq. If 'Umar had difficulty in establishing control over the governors in the provinces, it was in fact equally difficult for the provincial governors to assert their power. 'Umar attempted to enforce both the governor's power and his own by initiating what can best be described as Islamic leadership. This involved appointing men whose distinction stemmed from their devotion to Islam, men of the calibre of 'Ammār b. Yāsir whom 'Umar appointed governor of Kūfa. However the attempt failed, for 'Ammār was clearly a novice in the art of government. 'Umar had to fall back upon seasoned politicians like al-Mughīra b. Shu'ba of Thaqīf, despite his shaky reputation as a good practising Muslim.[2]

By the time 'Umar was suddenly assassinated, he was painfully aware of the problems of the empire and his impotence to solve them. Events were moving too fast, the empire was growing too quickly, the tribesmen were too fiercely independent, too prone to

[1] Ṭabarī, I, pp. 2412–13; Balādhurī, *Futūḥ*, pp. 450–7.
[2] Ṭabarī, I, p. 2645; Balādhurī, *Futūḥ*, p. 279.

view the conquered provinces as their own private property, social tensions were too deep and governors too uncontrollable. The regime established in Madīna was of its nature neither suited nor meant to develop the strength to control the whirlwind of imperial politics. 'Umar's only weapon to combat and control this intractable whirl of events was his position as counsellor and it was becoming increasingly clear that it was far from adequate.

4
THE BREAKDOWN OF THE MADĪNAN REGIME

Undoubtedly there could have been no better judge of the regime that he headed for almost ten years than 'Umar himself, and the fact that he did not choose to appoint a successor is generally underrated in importance. There was no reason why he should not do so. It had seemed the most natural thing for Abū Bakr to nominate a successor, and 'Umar had equal if not greater moral authority to do exactly the same. That he did not do so, when there were so many leaders of good standing to choose from, is a clear indication that he himself was not convinced that the office of *Amīr al-Mu'minīn* could adequately meet the requirements of the empire and that he was not prepared to recommend its continuation.

Although the community had so far emerged intact from the birth pangs of the *ridda* wars and the growing pains of the conquests, there were already clear signs of an imminent explosion. The Makkans had been quick to seize the chance of making enormous fortunes throughout the empire, as also had been the provincial governors.[1] Not even 'Umar's decision forcing the governors to surrender to the public treasury at Madīna half their wealth at the end of their terms of office sufficed to check this tendency. The tribesmen were also unhappy at the self-enrichment of Makkans and governors, but they themselves were jealous for their own economic position and resented the efforts of the newcomers to share in the spoils of conquest. In Madīna itself 'Umar personally inspected the streets and market place to see that justice was done and seen to be done.[2] He attempted to make tours of inspection outside Madīna and visited Syria, but it was impossible for him to make any lasting impression in this respect. The *Amīr al-Mu'minīn* had neither the authority nor the means to

[1] The banking operations involved in the division of booty offered the best opportunities for fast profits. 'Amr b. Ḥurayth, a Qurayshite from the clan of Makhzūm, became the richest man in Kūfa as a result of such operations; see Ṭabarī, I, p. 2600.

[2] Ṭabarī, I, pp. 2742–5.

control what happened, so events in the provinces moved quickly towards chaos while he sat powerless in Madīna. The tribesmen were now beginning to realize their strength and to value their independence, and worst of all to identify themselves with their particular locality. A fiercly independent regional spirit had been born, and attempts by the governors to assert their leadership had little power against it.

'Umar's appointment of the *shūra*, or the committee of six, should be seen in this context. It was not set up as a council of state to advise the future *Amīr al-Mu'minīn* for it disbanded after the election of 'Uthmān. Nor was it an Islamic equivalent of the conclave, a body specifically appointed to elect 'Umar's successor from among its number. This is the usual interpretation, and it does have support in the sources. But the sources may well have been looking at these events through the eyes of a century later, by which time the Khalifate was a truly established institution and later generations could not imagine its utility ever being questioned.

Like Muḥammad before his death, 'Umar preferred to leave the question of leadership open, and let the community as represented by the committee of six eminent companions decide the issue for themselves. Even if the usual interpretation is correct it does not contradict this argument since the person of the successor and the type of leadership required were of their nature inextricable questions. It is clear that the six soon decided that the office of *Amīr al-Mu'minīn* was to the best advantage of the community. After a few days of hard bargaining and extensive sounding of leading members of the Madīnan community, the choice narrowed down to two candidates, 'Alī b. Abī Ṭālib and 'Uthmān b. 'Affān.[1] The former was the first cousin and son-in-law of the Prophet, and the second a member of the great Umayyad clan of Quraysh and the husband of two of the Prophet's daughters.

Evidently the six were split not only on personal grounds but in their conception of what the functions of *Amīr al-Mu'minīn* should be, for, in the event, 'Alī was offered the job on the condition that he continued the policies of Abū Bakr and 'Umar. This was probably a compromise between those opposed to 'Alī on grounds of policy and those who supported him on political and personal grounds. 'Alī flatly refused this condition, insisting

[1] *Ibid.*, pp. 2783–5.

that he should be allowed to use his own judgement as the occasion demanded. In other words ʿAlī refused the office unless its minimal secular authority was increased, probably by giving it for the first time some religious authority. ʿUthmān was then offered the office on the same terms; he accepted unconditionally and was promptly acclaimed as the new *Amīr al-Muʾminīn*.[1]

ʿAlī's refusal to follow obediently in the footsteps of Abū Bakr and ʿUmar and his insistence that he should be an *Amīr al-Muʾminīn* with enhanced power and responsibility shows him to have been strongly aware of the strains that constant change had inflicted on the community. This insistence on the necessity for new policy to meet new circumstances automatically made him the leader of the forces of change, and the hero and rallying point for the opposition. In time his remarkable foresight was acclaimed as a semi-divine "knowledge", the cornerstone of Shīʿite dogma and politics.

ʿUthmān was the choice because, as the conservative candidate, he was a safe man. It was in many ways an unfortunate choice, for ʿUthmān was too closely associated with Makkan interests. ʿAlī had the advantage in this respect, for although he was a Qurayshite and Makkan born, he was practically a Madīnan in spirit. His formative years were spent under Muḥammad's roof, during the most difficult period for the Prophet in Makka, which can hardly have given him a good opinion of his fellow clansmen, and from the *hijra* onwards he had lived continually in Madīna. He was certainly the favourite candidate of the Madīnans and he held their steadfast support until his death. This support must have been his strongest asset in the deliberations of the six. ʿUthmān, on the other hand, despite his very early conversion and lifelong devotion to Islam, was a Makkan to the core. He had lived most of his life in Makka and, as a man of considerable wealth, had many trading connections there and well understood the interests of Quraysh. His deep devotion to Islam made him less objectionable to his fellow Muslims than he might have been as a thorough Qurayshite and, at that, a member of Umayya, once the most notoriously anti-Muslim clan.

The major flaw in ʿUmar's appointment of the *shūra* is that it was an essentially Makkan body. No doubt by calling the six most

1 *Ibid.*, pp. 2786, 2788, 2793–4; Balādhurī, *Ansāb al-Ashrāf*, vol. v, ed. S. D. Goitein, Jerusalem, 1936, p. 22.

eminent companions from among the *muhājirūn*, to settle the problem in the name of the community, 'Umar hoped to initiate in Islamic form the Arab practice of the tribal council; but by definition these companions were ex-Makkans, which excluded direct reference to the interests of the Madīnans and the many other tribes of the community. The time factor arguably justified the exclusion of the tribal leaders, but the exclusion of the Madīnans, the *anṣār*, seems a curious mistake. Perhaps the latter was a deliberate decision, or alternatively it was taken for granted that the ex-Makkan *muhājirūn* were competent to settle the affairs of the community, but whatever the reason, it does not alter the fact that the six were essentially unrepresentative. A similar body might have been suitable, indeed was so, for pre-Islamic Makka, but for Madīna, let alone the rest of the Muslims throughout the empire, the *shūra* was quite inadequate. Six ex-Makkans could never have the breadth of vision to appreciate the conflicting interests of a great empire. It was surprising that they even thought of 'Alī in the first place, and it was natural that they finally made the safe conservative choice of 'Uthmān.

'Uthmān began his reign quietly and for some time seemed to give universal satisfaction. Our sources divide his Khalifate (644–56/23–35) into six good years and six bad.[1] This is a little too neat to be completely accurate but it does reflect a genuine truth. For the first half of his reign 'Uthmān stood by his election promise to follow the policies of his predecessors, but events were moving too fast for these policies to be tenable for much longer.[2] His reign coincided with a new wave of immigration to Iraq and Egypt, and 'Uthmān must have eventually decided that he could no longer leave the initiative in the hands of the tribesmen, merely giving formal acknowledgement to their decisions.[3] He had to assert himself and establish some measure of control over the provinces but these positive policies eventually brought him to his death. His celebrated weakness was not one of character – his only reported fault in reliable sources is that he was extremely polite, which scarcely seems very grave – but rather one of policies.[4] His new line of policy involved an assumption of more authority than he was supposed to possess, and might well have

[1] Balādhurī, *Ansāb*, vol. v, pp. 25, 26. [2] *Ibid.*, p. 42.

[3] Ibn 'Abdilḥakam, *Futūḥ Miṣr*, pp. 123, 128; Ṭabarī, I, p. 2814. Balādhurī, *Futūḥ*, p. 226.

[4] Balādhurī, *Ansāb*, vol. v, pp. 4, 5, 10.

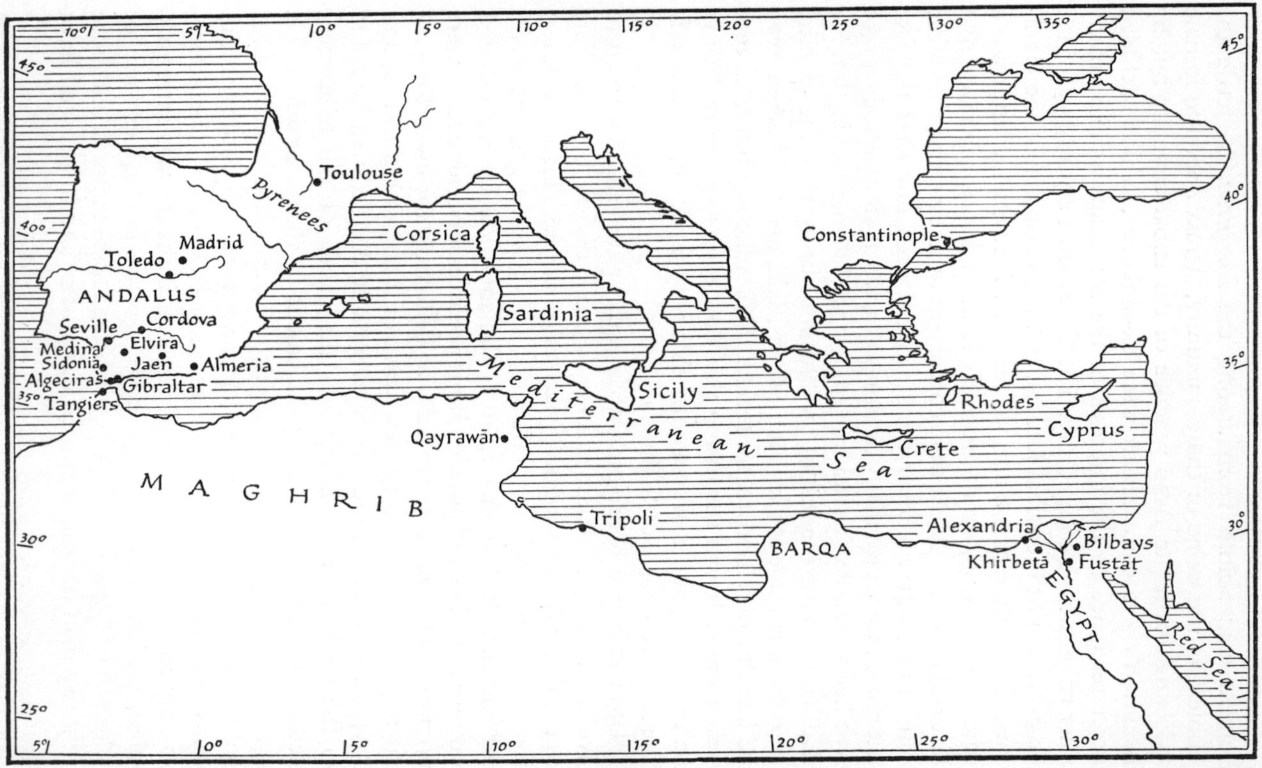

3 The western provinces

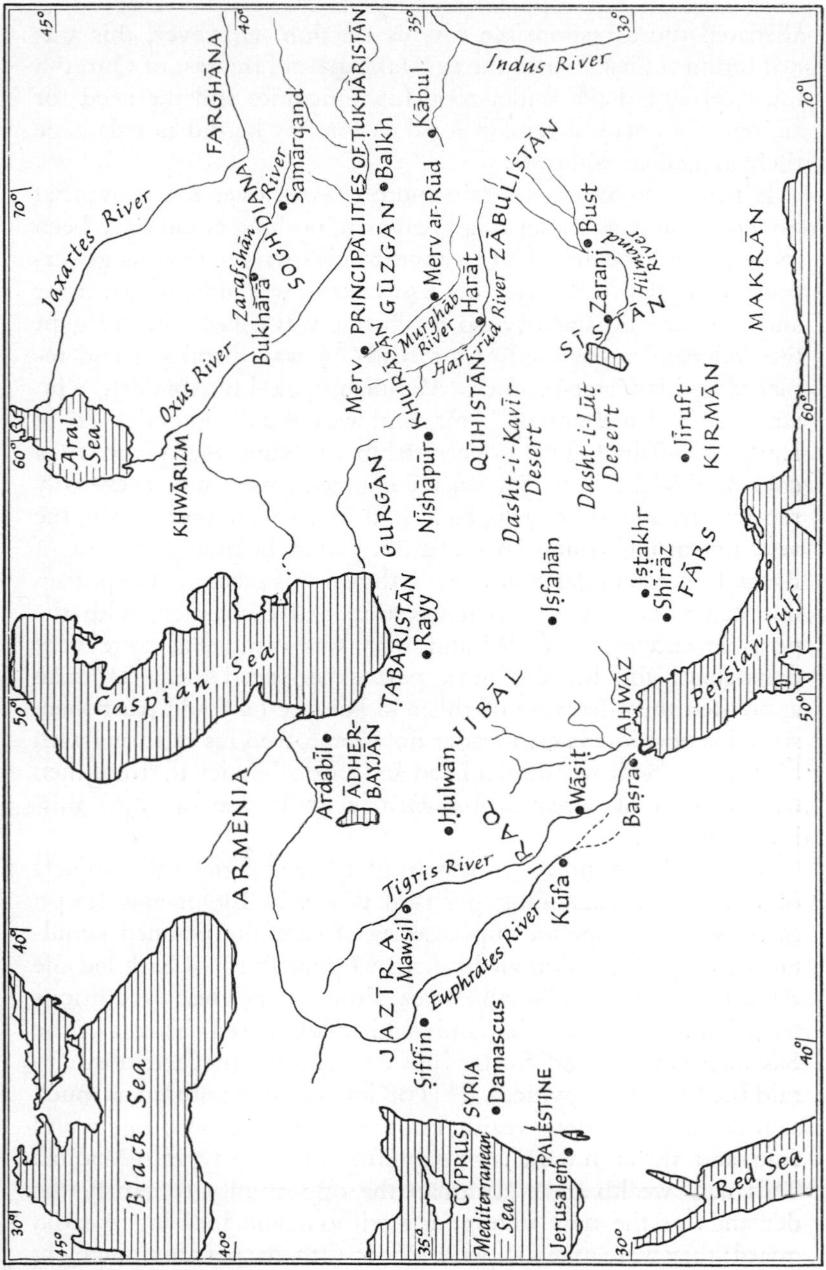

4 The eastern provinces

alienated those responsible for his election. However, this was not serious in itself since the ex-Makkans and the rest of Quraysh must certainly have understood his difficulties and the need for action. They would remain loyal as long as he did not damage their immediate interests.

His first move was to gain more control over the provincial governors and, as leader of a great clan, nothing could have been more natural for him than to appoint his own relatives as governors. In Syria, Mu'āwiya, his first cousin, was already governor and was very satisfactory, so no change was called for. In Egypt the independent-minded 'Amr b. al-'Āṣ was dismissed and replaced by his foster-brother, 'Abdullah b. Sa'd b. Abī Sarḥ, who was also a lieutenant of 'Amr, and was equally experienced in Egyptian affairs.[1] The governorship of Kūfa was given to a cousin, al-Walīd b. 'Uqba, an incompetent, who was eventually replaced by another cousin, Sa'īd b. al-'Āṣ. Yet another cousin, the very promising young 'Abdullah b. 'Āmir, became governor of Baṣra. One can understand why 'Uthmān was accused of nepotism but that is not the point in question. All these men, with the possible exception of al-Walīd who was dismissed, were very competent, and for the most part experienced men. 'Uthmān appointed them because of this and because he could trust them since his position as clan-leader now reinforced his relations with his governors. It was a calculated and shrewd policy to strengthen the position of *Amīr al-Mu'minīn*, even if one open to misinterpretation.

'Uthmān's second move was to give the energies and conflicts of the rapidly expanding garrison towns in Egypt and Iraq a safety-valve by opening up a series of carefully planned simultaneous expeditions on all fronts. In Egypt Ibn Abī Sarḥ led the Arab forces far into North Africa. From Baṣra great expeditions were led by 'Abdullah b. 'Āmir which conquered the rest of the Sāsānian empire, and from Kūfa expeditions marched north to raid the Caspian provinces. This policy was successful in as much as it brought vast new wealth, booty and revenues into Egypt and Iraq, and, through the customary fifth of the booty, into Madīna. This new wealth gave 'Uthmān the opportunity to satisfy the demands of the new immigrants without antagonizing the old guard; they were given stipends of 300 dirhams per annum which,

[1] Kindī, *Governors*, pp. 10–11.

together with their shares of the booty, proved satisfactory. This was especially so in Baṣra, because the riches of Khurāsān were far greater than those gained by Kūfa from the Caspian provinces, and because Baṣra was happily not bedevilled by the irregularities of distribution of booty existing in Kūfa.[1] Baṣra was satisfied and generally remained grateful and loyal to 'Uthmān and his memory.

The problem of Kūfa, however, was by no means solved and 'Uthmān's first great failure lay in his attempt to strengthen his power and regularize the situation in Kūfa and its domains. His policy brought the wrath of the *qurrā'* upon his head; they were particularly important for they were effectively in control of the administration of the countryside of Iraq, and what is more they administered, and from their point of view almost owned, the extensive abandoned Sāsānian lands of the Sawād.[2] Unless their power in Iraq was broken the *Amīr al-Mu'minīn* could never establish his power.

It was around the abandoned lands that the conflict centred. They were not divided, but were administered by the *qurrā'*, and their revenue was distributed among the veterans of the wars of conquest. As we have said, the *qurrā'* regarded themselves almost as the owners of these very rich properties. 'Uthmān did not dare openly to challenge this alleged right, but adopted a gradual approach. First, arguing that the veterans who had returned to Makka and Madīna had not therefore forfeited their rights to these lands, he claimed for them their just rewards. The *qurrā'*, in reply, claimed that without their own continued presence in Iraq these revenues would never be collected at all, thus proving that the Kūfan veterans did have a greater right to these lands. But it was not a very convincing argument, and so, wooed and lulled by the blandishments of Sa'īd b. al-'Āṣ, they fell in with 'Uthmān's plan and consented to the institution of an exchange of land rights system of a baffling complexity. For example Ṭalḥa, a leading ex-Makkan, gave Khaybar in Ḥijāz in exchange for the rights of residents of Madīna to some of the richest farms in the Sawād, and al-Ash'ath b. Qays exchanged his lands in Ḥaḍramawt for far richer property in the Sawād.[3] It has been claimed that 'Uthmān parcelled out much of the Sawād to many other

[1] For details see M. A. Shaban, *The 'Abbāsid Revolution*, Cambridge, 1970, pp. 31–2.

[2] Ṭabarī, I, p. 2908; Balādhurī, *Ansāb*, vol. v, p. 40.

[3] Ṭabarī, I, pp. 2854–6.

ex-Makkans, but that probably happened through some of the rather more dubious of these exchange deals. The net result of this operation was that the *qurrā'* belatedly discovered that their economic power base was being destroyed as their lands were distributed, regardless of their rights.

'Uthmān added insult to injury by finally breaking down the distinction between *ridda* and pre-*ridda* Muslims. 'Umar had used the *ridda* tribesmen, but had made a point of keeping their leaders out of responsible positions. Under 'Uthmān this policy was discarded and a man such as al-Ash'ath b. Qays was appointed, through Sa'īd b. al-'Āṣ, commander of the Adherbayjān front.[1]

The *qurrā'* decided to fight back, and in 655/34 encountered Sa'īd b. al-'Āṣ, on his way back from conferring with 'Uthmān at Madīna, at an obscure village near Kūfa called Jara'a. They prevented him from entering Kūfa, chose Abū-Mūsā al-Ash'arī as their governor and forced 'Uthmān to recognize this violent act.[2] This is significant for it was Abū Mūsā whom these very *qurrā'* chose as arbitrator after Ṣiffīn. Jara'a is also crucial for it was the first time that the growing authority of the *Amīr al-Mu'minīn* was openly challenged by the tribesmen. It was a minority indeed which delivered this challenge but it was an articulate minority whose clamorous self-righteousness was equalled by its dangerously articulate power.

In Egypt quarrels over money were also damaging to 'Uthmān's position, but here conflict arose not over land but over the distribution of booty. Ibn Abī Sarḥ, wishing to attract more recruits from new arrivals for his campaigns, promised the newcomers a larger share of the booty. The old guard, like old guards at any time, objected strongly to inequality when they were at the lower end of the scale. They pointed in indignant reproof to the previous custom of equal shares for all.[3] But one need not set much store by this righteous indignation for the governor could equally point to precedents justifying his actions in the Prophet's own life. Neither of the two parties was entirely right or wrong, for the Prophet's policy on the distribution of booty had been variable: the interpretation adopted was more a matter of political than theological taste.

[1] *Ibid.*, p. 2927.
[2] *Ibid.*, pp. 2929–36; Balādhurī, *Ansāb*, vol. v, pp. 44–7.
[3] Ṭabarī, I, pp. 2814–15.

A further dispute arose when Ibn Abī Sarḥ became very strict in his financial methods, showing the greatest rigour in the collection of revenues and the greatest stringency in their distribution. Again there were perfectly sensible reasons of policy for this – the money was needed for the campaigns and for the building of an Arab navy to check Byzantine domination of the Mediterranean. But all that the old guard could appreciate was the alarming threat to their own position. Also, and more creditably, it is possible they feared that Ibn Abī Sarḥ was squeezing the Egyptian population too hard and driving them into rebellion.[1]

When complaints reached ʿUthmān, he decided to send ʿAmmār b. Yāsir to investigate the situation. It soon became clear that ʿAmmār was the wrong man for such a mission. He did not possess the objectivity of the ideal ombudsman, for to him all virtue lay in the earliness of a man's devotion to the cause. He had been governor of Kūfa under ʿUmar, but his origins were obscure. He had started, though an Arab, as a slave, so in fact his only claim to fame was his conversion in the very earliest years of Islam. This being the case it was almost inevitable that he would side with the old guard. His report was worse than useless and he returned a bitter and vehement opponent to ʿUthmān's regime.[2] Indeed after the murder of ʿUthmān the Umayyads and their party looked upon him as one of the prime movers of the conspiracy.

ʿUthman's drive to assert his authority as *Amīr al-Mu'minīn* resulted in yet another unforgivable error. Again it was concerned with money, this time the distribution of the fifth of the booty sent to Madīna. As we have already indicated the guidance of the Qur'ān and the Sunna on this most delicate of matters was subject to the different interpretations of the interested parties. Even Muḥammad had been openly criticized for his handling of the question,[3] and it is therefore not surprising that Abū Bakr and ʿUmar were tactfully discreet, perhaps claiming some freedom with a fifth of this fifth. ʿUthman was less discreet and boldly assumed freedom in dealing with the whole sum,[4] paying the stipends and then using the rest as he saw fit for the public good.

[1] Ṭabarī, I, pp. 2819, 2867, 2993; Balādhurī, *Ansāb*, vol. v, 26; Ibn ʿAbdilḥakam, *Futūḥ Miṣr*, p. 190.
[2] Ṭabarī, I, pp. 2943–4; Balādhurī, *Ansāb*, vol. v, p. 51.
[3] Ṭabarī, I, pp. 1682–3.
[4] *Ibid.*, p. 2953; Balādhurī, *Ansāb*, vol. v, p. 25.

Since he was a very rich and generous man he could not be accused personally of corruption, but he gave large sums to his relatives as well as to others, and by this indiscretion laid himself wide open to charges of nepotism.[1] What we have here is in fact probably some form of political patronage. Marwān b. al-Ḥakam, a cousin of 'Uthmān and one of his closest advisers, was the favourite target for accusations of corruption, but he does not seem to have lived in any great style. He was most probably a type of secretary of patronage, buying the political support of leading figures for 'Uthmān's policies.[2]

'Uthmān also laid himself open to attack on the religious as well as the secular front. Hitherto there had been slight and unimportant variants in the reading of the Qur'ān. 'Uthmān, to prevent any possible dispute, decided to impose uniformity by issuing an authorized version and suppressing all variant readings. This was sensible enough but it aroused strong opposition, stronger than he may have anticipated. His opponents could argue quite plausibly that since the *Amīr al-Mu'minīn* was not meant to have any greater religious authority or insight than any other Muslim, he had not the authority to issue a standard edition. In other words, they argued, 'Uthmān was usurping a religious power which he did not hold.[3]

The circumstances of the day had forced 'Uthmān to assume more power than he originally intended. His well-meant and often reasonable efforts to keep the empire in order had provoked the opposition of various groups. By the end of his reign this opposition had become so powerful that even those who owed him a debt of gratitude were forced to dissociate themselves from his policies. Finally a deputation of a few hundred tribesmen from Iraq and a similar number from Egypt arrived in Madīna to demand redress for their grievances. The people of Madīna abandoned 'Uthmān and left him unprotected, face to face with his most bitter critics, virtually besieged in his own house. Sheer inability to conceive of the lengths to which the opposition was prepared to go, allowed the situation to get out of control. After nearly fifty days of angry arguments, discussions and fruitless deputations,

1 Balādhurī, *Ansāb*, vol. v, pp. 7, 8, 38, 39, 58; Ibn A'tham al-Kūfī, Abū Muḥammad Aḥmad, *Kitāb al-Futūḥ*, Istanbul manuscript, Library of Ahmet III, No. 2956, vol. I, p. 2A.

2 Balādhurī, *Ansāb*, vol. v, p. 28.

3 *Ibid.*, p. 62; Ṭabarī, I, p. 2952.

the Egyptians broke in and butchered the helpless old man, abandoned by his fellow Madīnans.[1]

The shock of the murder of the *Amīr al-Mu'minīn* left the Madīnans stunned for five days. Eventually 'Alī emerged as 'Uthmān's successor. He was without doubt the most obvious candidate and, even if others were suggested, no one else made an open bid for the succession. In fact the problem lay rather in persuading 'Alī to accept, for he was naturally hesitant to take power in such intimidating circumstances. He eventually let himself be persuaded in order to prevent the situation from falling into complete chaos.[2]

'Alī's position could have been worse had he not had the unwavering support of the *anṣār*. His strength is shown by the ease with which he suppressed the revolt of Ṭalḥa and Zubayr shortly afterwards. These two Qurayshites were leaders of the *muhājirūn* and had been members of the *shūrā* which elected 'Uthmān. Their political stand centred around the continuance of a purely Qurayshite leadership of the community. They were looking back to the severely limited powers of the *Amīr al-Mu'minīn* under Abū Bakr and 'Umar. Although they had backed 'Uthmān in the *shūrā*, he had disappointed them and had therefore lost their support. They must have been aware that 'Alī would be even more likely to make radical changes in the organization of the empire and the position of the *Amīr al-Mu'minīn*.[3]

This being the case, it is not surprising that they were able to obtain some financial support in Makka and the collaboration of 'Ā'isha, the widow of the Prophet and the daughter of Abū Bakr, in their revolt.[4] 'Ā'isha no doubt felt that what had seemed good to her father and to his hand-picked successor should hold good for all time thereafter, and therefore decided to oppose 'Alī. The three conspirators departed for Baṣra, hoping to whip up opposition to 'Alī among the tribesmen, thereby reminding them of the gratitude they owed to the murdered *Amīr al-Mu'minīn*. The Baṣrans, to their credit, mostly refused to become involved. The Kūfans, most bitterly opposed to 'Uthmān's policies, even marched to join 'Alī. The latter, supported by the *anṣār*, was in hot pursuit of the rebels. The two forces met at the Battle of the Camel

[1] Ṭabarī, I, pp. 2941–3050; Balādhurī, *Ansāb*, vol. v, pp. 59–105.

[2] Ṭabarī, I, pp. 3073–5.

[3] *Ibid.*, p. 3081; Athīr, *Kāmil*, vol. III, p. 169.

[4] *Ibid.*, pp. 3100–3.

and the vastly superior forces of 'Alī rapidly won the day. Ṭalḥa and Zubayr were killed, and 'Ā'isha was reprimanded and sent back to Madīna.[1]

'Alī entered Baṣra and was publicly acclaimed. It was now that he gave an important indication of his policy, for he divided all the money he found in the public treasury equally among his supporters.[2] This did not mean that he rejected the special prestige and position of the early Muslims, but that he gave equal value to the great role played by the later Muslims, *ridda* or non-*ridda*, in the conquest and settlement of the empire. Virtually every group which had felt itself slighted or underprivileged rallied around 'Alī. Thus the *anṣār* were solidly behind him, as were the *qurrā'* who saw him as the only hope of regaining ground lost under 'Uthmān. These two groups were compact and well organized, but they were far outnumbered by the late immigrants into Iraq. 'Alī's policy on booty division would be particularly appealing to the latter. Some of them had indeed benefited from 'Uthmān's policies, but they must have put greater trust in 'Alī, considering his famous stand in the *shūrā* for positively welcoming change. It is no coincidence that notorious former *ridda* leaders, like al-Ash'ath b. Qays, were prominent among 'Alī's supporters, along with men like 'Ammār b. Yāsir.

'Alī then had an impressively wide coalition of interests behind him. The only trouble was that it was too wide. None of the three main constituents of this coalition had any common interests; the *anṣār* had nothing in common with the Iraqis, and satisfying the demands of the *qurrā'* involved damaging the interests of the later immigrants and vice versa. Such a broadly based coalition, comprising so many conflicting interests, could not be expected to hold together for long. In fact it is surprising that it was launched at all. The main reason for its existence is the remarkable character of 'Alī. His political stand was clear, relevant and decisive. His unusual insight into the rapidly changing nature of the empire had led him to the firm conviction that the guide-lines laid down by

[1] The traditions related by al-Ṭabarī, mostly on the authority of Sayf and Madā'inī among others, agree on most of the details. They tend to exaggerate these details and hence the importance of the incident itself (Ṭabarī, I, pp. 3091–233). Perhaps Ibn al-Athīr presents a more reasonable narrative (Athīr, *Kāmil*, vol. III, pp. 165–217). On the other hand Ibn Khayyāṭ offers the most concise and accurate account: *Tārīkh Khalīfa b. Khayyāṭ*, ed. A. D. al-'Umarī, Najaf, 1967, vol. I, pp. 160–73.

[2] Ṭabarī, I, p. 3227; Al-Ya'qūbī, Aḥmad b. abī-Ya'qūb, *Tārīkh*, Beirut, 1960, vol. II, p. 130.

the Qur'ān and by the lives of Muḥammad and his first three successors were inadequate unless reinterpreted to meet the needs of the time. Failing divine inspiration Muslims had to use their own judgement in the light of their knowledge of Islam. If this were true of ordinary Muslims, how much more true was it of the *Amīr al-Mu'minīn*, the responsible leader of all Muslims.

'Alī was laying claim to some religious authority in order to solve political problems. This is the origin of the view of 'Alī held by his partisans, *shī'a*, as the *Imām* who would apply his knowledge to the achievement of justice for every Muslim. This notion of *Imām–Amīr al-Mu'minīn* became the basic objective of all later Shī'ite sects. Such a leader was particularly needed in Iraq, to defeat the attempts of the *qurrā'* to find Qur'ānic support for their privileges, and to reinterpret the Qur'ān to the equal benefit of all Muslims. Whatever one thinks of the abilities of such a controversial figure as 'Alī, the devotion he inspired can only be explained by his remarkable foresight and force of character.

Meanwhile, although Baṣra had acclaimed him, 'Alī only had active support there from the few hundred *qurrā'* who had moved there in order to join their clansmen, some of whom they had also converted to 'Alī's cause. These Baṣrans, mostly of Tamīm, moved with 'Alī to his new camp outside Kūfa.[1] It would, however, be a mistake to consider this a definite transfer of the capital from Madīna to Kūfa. At this time 'Alī did not intend to settle permanently in Kūfa; he had only gone there to establish his power, as the pitching of his camp outside the town indicates.[2]

At the same time he made moves to establish his position in other provinces of the empire. Although the situation in Egypt was still unsettled – for example the grain shipments to Madīna had been stopped – 'Alī's nominee as governor of Egypt was accepted without much demur.[3] 'Alī's initial gestures towards Syria were unsuccessful. Whether he sent emissaries requesting allegiance, whether he dismissed or confirmed Mu'āwiya in office, the Syrians refused their allegiance. On the other hand they did not proceed with the selection of an *Amīr al-Mu'minīn* of their own. Their excuse was that Mu'āwiya as first cousin of 'Uthmān was justified in refusing allegiance until such time as 'Uthmān's death was properly investigated and avenged.

[1] Naṣr b. Muzāḥim, *Waq'at Ṣiffīn*, ed. A. M. Hārūn, Cairo, 1946, pp. 28–31.
[2] *Ibid.*, pp. 5, 8, 136, 147.
[3] Ṭabarī, I, pp. 2577, 3238.

Mu'āwiya, indeed, had some justification in his demand for revenge and, what is more, he had the military power in Syria to make his protest effective. But all the same, the idea that the loyalty of the Syrians to him was so great that it could bring a whole province to the point of revolt to avenge a single murder is incredible. It is more likely that vengeance for 'Uthmān made an excellently pious cloak for more realistic differences. All the circumstances lead us to believe that the difference between 'Alī and Mu'āwiya centred around the special position of Syria. In the past 'Umar and 'Uthmān had been convinced of the necessity of keeping Syria free from the uncontrolled immigration which plagued Iraq, in order to guarantee its stability and security in the face of the Byzantine threat. Mu'āwiya and his Syrians were equally convinced of this. 'Alī saw it differently. He saw no reason why the Syrians should have a privileged position just because they performed their duty by defending their own frontiers; and this all the more so with the Byzantines despairing of Syria and the Arabs coveting Byzantium itself. Every province had its frontiers and its wars, and if they all behaved like Syria there would be nowhere to put new immigrants. It was ridiculous for Iraq to be overwhelmed with uncontrolled immigration, while Syria remained inviolable. Syria had to share in the solution of the whole community's problems even if it meant the loss of treasured privileges and the destruction of Mu'āwiya's life's work.[1]

Lengthy and ultimately fruitless negotiations followed between 'Alī and Mu'āwiya, their length being no doubt increased by the difficulty Mu'āwiya experienced in persuading the Syrian leaders of the necessity of going to war at all.[2] However, Mu'āwiya won his argument and events moved swiftly towards war. The Syrians concluded a truce with the Byzantines even though it was at the humiliating price of a tribute, and the Iraqi tribesmen responded enthusiastically to 'Alī's call to arms.[3] All this speed and enthusiasm unfortunately evaporated on the battlefield. The two armies met each other at Ṣiffīn in the spring of 657/38, and then followed one of the most curious battles in history.

[1] It must be noted that 'Uthmān included Jazīra in the governorship of Mu'āwiya. However there was some distinction between Syria and Jazīra as far as immigration is concerned. Nevertheless the majority of the tribesmen of Jazīra supported Mu'āwiya because they were afraid that they would fare less well if 'Alī's policy should prevail. See below p. 83.

[2] Muzāḥim, *Waq'at Ṣiffīn*, pp. 49–58.

[3] *Ibid.*, pp. 42, 49.

The confrontation at Ṣiffīn lasted three months, as compared with the few hours of the Battle of the Camel. No one had the will to fight, and so hostilities flared up between negotiators rather than soldiers. Apart from a few skirmishes, most of these three months were spent on negotiations which led nowhere. When battle was finally joined, it was just as abruptly stopped when the Syrians raised the Qur'ān on their spears to symbolize yet another appeal for peace and talks. After some discussion both parties enthusiastically agreed that arbitration was the universal panacea. Most of the *qurrā'* accepted arbitration, but the decisive factor in 'Alī's acceptance was the action of al-Ash'ath b. Qays.[1] As the leader of the biggest bloc in 'Alī's army he held the balance of power. His followers included all the *ridda* tribesmen of Kūfa in addition to all newcomers from their clans. These men, who had actually benefited from 'Uthmān's policies, were the least enthusiastic group in 'Alī's coalition. After three months of almost peaceful encounter with the Syrians, they began to realize that the fight would not particularly serve any of their purposes. Once Ash'ath saw that his followers' hearts were not in the fight, the decision to accept arbitration was irresistible.[2]

'Amr b. al-'Āṣ, the conqueror of Egypt, was chosen as the Syrian representative at the arbitration and Abū Mūsā al-Ash'arī, despite 'Alī's vehement objection, was chosen as the Iraqi. It is at first hard to see why the latter was chosen, particularly since 'Alī was so opposed to him. It appears that it was the *qurrā'* who insisted on this choice of Iraqi representative.[3] Abū Mūsā had been involved in the early stages of the conquest of Iraq both as general and as governor of Kūfa and Baṣra. He had also been opposed to the policy of 'Uthmān and had been the choice of the *qurrā'* as governor of Kūfa when they expelled 'Uthmān's governor, Sa'īd b. al-'Āṣ.[4] Abū Mūsā's only special qualifications were a long-standing political connection with the *qurrā'* and an intimate knowledge of the conquest of Iraq and its government, and this is no doubt why he was chosen. 'Amr b. al-'Āṣ also, as one of the conquerors of Syria, as the conqueror and governor of Egypt and as a resident of Palestine, could lay claim to similar knowledge.

Our sources are very vague about the issues discussed at the

[1] *Ibid.*, pp. 549–50, 553, 560, 571, 576; Ṭabarī, I, pp. 3330, 3332–3.
[2] Muzāḥim, *Waq'at Ṣiffīn*, pp. 231, 255.
[3] *Ibid.*, p. 572; Ṭabarī, I, p. 3333.
[4] See above p. 68.

arbitration, and there are few clues to give us any idea of what happened. The most significant point is that both arbitrators had almost unrivalled knowledge of their two provinces. This would indicate that the basic issues at stake were the terms of the relationship between Syria and Iraq, and the solutions to the problems caused by the conquest. The fact that Abū Mūsā was so closely connected with the *qurrā'* shows that the *qurrā'* were determined to turn the negotiations between Iraq and Syria to their own advantage. In fact the *qurrā'* wished to become almost a third party in the dispute.

However when the agenda for the arbitration were drawn up, it became painfully clear to most of the *qurrā'* that neither Syrians nor Iraqis were at all interested in restoring their privileges. It is at this point that the final collapse of 'Alī's coalition began. The *qurrā'*, who were among those who had forced 'Alī to accept arbitration and who imposed on him the choice of Abū Mūsā, now changed their minds and rejected the idea out of hand, deciding to strike out on their own.[1] They split away from 'Alī's army and started towards districts they had come to consider their own, in the hope of re-establishing their former power and position.[2] These ex-*qurrā'* came to be known as the *khawārij*, those who seceded.[3] They must be sharply distinguished from all later *khawārij*, and above all they must not be considered heretics. 'Alī partially saved the situation. He overtook them at Nahrawān, before they dispersed to their various destinations, and was able to persuade some of them of the futility of their plan. Those whom he persuaded returned to Kūfa. The others were forced to fight and many were massacred. The rest scattered and fled into "their" countryside. For this generation and the next these *khawārij* carried on their hopeless fight. Small groups of tribesmen from various clans, sometimes numbering even as few as thirty, established themselves at various places in the countryside, collecting and distributing their revenues among themselves. Some of these groups even had an *Amīr al-Mu'minīn* of their own, though significantly with no power whatsoever. These fierce little republics almost invariably lacked the support of the local population, yet such was their belief in their own inviolable

[1] Muzāḥim, *Waq'at Ṣiffīn*, pp. 587–90; Ṭabarī, I, pp. 3338–9.

[2] Ṭabarī, I, pp. 3364–5, 3380.

[3] *Ibid.*, p. 3330; Muzāḥim, *Waq'at Ṣiffīn*, pp. 560, 572, Athīr, *Kāmil*, vol. III, p. 264.

rights, a belief at once fanatical and pathetic, that they fought for two generations before they collapsed in exhaustion and defeat.[1]

Meanwhile ʿAlī returned to Kūfa to wait for the results of the arbitration but his position was disintegrating with alarming speed. The arbitrators evidently did not consider the situation urgent for they did not meet till more than a year later. In fact by the time the arbitrators had met with their grand retinues of 400 men each, it really did not make any difference what was decided, for events had already decided the issue. The arbitrators came to no decision, but it no longer mattered, for the events of Ṣiffīn had already fatally injured ʿAlī's position.[2] For ʿAlī, the recognized *Amīr al-Muʾminīn*, to accept arbitration made rather a joke of his claims to special insight and religious authority in all matters affecting the community. This was one of the worst blows to his position, and following it his ramshackle coalition fell apart. The *qurrāʾ* were the first to go, and those of them who neither surrendered nor were killed became bitter enemies. Now that the *qurrāʾ* had been broken at Nahrawān, the majority of the newcomers had little reason to fight for Alī, especially since the Syrians would in due course be amenable to a peaceful solution.

ʿAlī tried to strengthen his hold over the tribesmen by re-organizing the tribal groups in Kūfa so as to supplant men like al-Ashʿath by men of early standing in Islam, personally devoted to ʿAlī. Thus Ḥujr b. ʿAdī, a leader from the *qurrāʾ* who did not desert ʿAlī, replaced al-Ashʿath as leader of Kinda and related clans.[3] This was hopelessly ineffective, and indeed positively helped to hasten the disenchantment of the tribesmen with ʿAlī. Thus, however hard ʿAlī tried to organize a new army, he failed, because the grand coalition of the beginning of his reign was irrevocably torn apart by its own contradictions. Only the *anṣār*, the remnants of the *qurrāʾ* and a few of their clansmen remained faithful to ʿAlī, and their fights with the Syrians were of little importance.

This uneasy and unofficial truce moved further into peaceful co-existence when ʿAlī was assassinated in Kūfa (661/40). His eldest son, al-Ḥasan, succeeded but very soon abdicated. ʿAlī's coalition had evaporated, Egypt had fallen into Muʿāwiya's hands

[1] Ṭabarī, I, pp. 3418–29; Ṭabarī, II, pp. 17, 20, 127; Athīr, *Kāmil*, vol. III, pp. 290, 308, 313, 314.

[2] Ibn Khayyāṭ, *Tārīkh*, vol. I, p. 174.

[3] Ṭabarī, I, pp. 3371, 3385, 3447.

through the good offices of ʿAmr b. al-ʿĀṣ, and Muʿāwiya's power was by now irresistible. The latter sensibly helped al-Ḥasan come to a decision by offering him a large sum which would keep him in comfort in Madīna for the rest of his life. With ʿAlī dead and al-Ḥasan having abdicated, the office of *Amīr al-Muʾminīn* fell naturally to Muʿāwiya, and he was acclaimed the new ruler by all except the *khawārij*. The Madīnan regime was bankrupt; Quraysh's bid for the leadership had been brushed aside with contemptuous ease; and ʿAlī's new-style Khalifate had proved a pathetic failure. It now fell to Muʿāwiya to devise a new regime for the empire.

5
MU'ĀWIYA AND THE SECOND CIVIL WAR

Mu'āwiya was a man of *ḥilm*. This word is both complex and comprehensive and is not easily translated, but it is the best if not the only way of describing Mu'āwiya's special ability as a leader. However extreme and intimidating the pressures were, as a man of *ḥilm* he kept absolute self-control and made decisive judgements. He took decisions after long and judicious thought, and whenever possible rejected a show of power as a solution to his problems. He looked squarely at a problem to see what forces were at work so that through the subtle readjustment of these forces, he could reach an ingenious compromise. Thus Mu'āwiya was always quick to offer reconciliation and treated his fallen enemies with an unassuming generosity and magnanimity which saved their dignity and self-respect and gained him their loyalty. His mind was eminently pragmatic and political, characterized by restraint and self-control. Such a leader was exactly what was needed at this time. Mu'āwiya's attempt to establish a stable regime was successful, at least until he died, but its failure after his death clearly indicates how intractable were the problems of this period. One cannot over-emphasize how precarious the situation was at the death of 'Alī. The empire had just emerged from a civil war which had created more problems than it had solved. A comprehensive and permanent solution was not possible since the aims of the various political groups were so different and frequently irreconcilable.

The special quality of *ḥilm* which Mu'āwiya possessed was very much to the point. Appreciating that no group could have its claims completely satisfied, he capitalized on the widespread desire for peace to gain a general reconciliation based on compromise, avoiding any imperious show of authority. He was indeed *Amīr al-Mu'minīn*, but he acted as, at most, *primus inter pares* towards the other Arab leaders. Having witnessed the humiliating failure of 'Alī's reign he scrupulously avoided any claim to religious authority. But although his rule had the appearance of being like that of Abū Bakr or of ʿUmar, Muʿāwiya had the advantage of an ultimate sanction to his ingenious political manœuvring in the form of the Syrian army. He was able, therefore, to carry out with some success his policy of reconciling society and unobtrusively strengthening the central government.

At first Muʿāwiya did not particularly want to change anything. He respected the existing powers, confining himself to a judicious balancing of one power against the other. He relied on Quraysh for his appointments to responsible office, preferring that their undoubted prestige and abilities be used for, rather than against him. At the same time he was sufficiently deft as a politician to dissociate himself from the extremist Quraysh who had rebelled with Ṭalḥa and Zubayr. He was also very careful to respect the power of the various tribal groups. Those who had supported ʿAlī he treated with the unassuming and unhumiliating magnanimity of a man of *ḥilm*, and in return received their needed support.[1]

To keep the support of the fiercely independent tribesmen in the provinces, whether they had been for or against him in the civil war, Muʿāwiya knew that he had to allow them some measure of autonomy. His policy was to assert the central government's power only when feasible. When the tribesmen objected, Muʿāwiya gracefully surrendered. This respect for both the tribesmen's autonomy and for the power of the central government required all the *finesse politique* of Muʿāwiya and his extremely well-chosen governors in the provinces. It was also helped by a new wave of wars of expansion on all fronts. Again new booty and new wealth diverted the attention of the tribesmen to foreign soils. At the same time these expansionist wars helped to replenish the central treasury depleted after the civil war and gave the government badly needed time to shape its policies.

Egypt was again entrusted to the able and loyal hands of ʿAmr b. al-ʿĀṣ. He directed the Arabs from Egypt in North Africa with great success, for the battles were easily won and the booty very satisfactory to all involved. Apparently the tribesmen were so satisfied that ʿAmr was now able to send some of the surplus from the revenues of Egypt to the central treasury at Damascus.

[1] Ṭabarī, II, pp. 7–8; Ibn Aʿtham, *Futūḥ*, vol. I, pp. 99B–100A.

It should be stated here that, so far, apart from stipends of 200 dinārs paid to the leaders only, there are no reports in our sources of stipends being distributed to the bulk of the tribesmen in Egypt. Furthermore, 'Amr does not seem to have been as interested in naval operations as Ibn Abī Sarḥ, 'Uthmān's governor, and naturally this would save considerable expense. The financial crisis of the time of the conquest had by now been overcome and 'Amr, after meeting public expenses, could afford to send the surplus of 600,000 dinārs to Mu'āwiya.[1] After 'Amr's death in 663/43 his successors continued on the same pattern and with further success in North Africa.

In Syria itself the tribesmen were happy with their victory and the maintenance of their privileged position under Mu'āwiya. Before Ṣiffīn some of them demanded and probably acquired certain lands for themselves.[2] However, after the civil war they all returned to their districts in Syria to resume their normal lives. Although they formed Mu'āwiya's power base they were discreetly kept in Syria and were never used in other provinces during his reign. Nevertheless, and probably to their advantage, they were sent out on summer expeditions every year to raid deep into Byzantine territory and these expeditions, no doubt, rewarded them with a good deal of booty. At first these expeditions were small, but the apparent weakness of Byzantine resistance encouraged the Arabs to extend their military activities. Some of these summer campaigns continued into the winter and were even supported by Arab naval forces. The occupation of Rhodes (672/52) and Crete (674/54) was followed by the securing of a naval base in the Sea of Marmora which served as winter headquarters. From these headquarters attacks were mounted in the spring against Constantinople itself for a period of seven years 674–80/54–60 until the death of Mu'āwiya.[3]

It is only in connection with the naval operations of long duration, like the occupation of Rhodes,[4] that we hear of regular stipends being paid to the Arabs. We know that the native Egyp-

[1] Kindī, *Governors*, pp. 32–3; Ibn 'Abdilḥakam, *Futūḥ Miṣr*, pp. 193–4; Maqrīzī, *Khiṭaṭ*, vol I, part I, p. 331.

[2] Ibn A'tham, *Futūḥ*, vol. I, pp. 112A–B; this is a fuller version of the tradition related in Muzāḥim, *Waq'at Ṣiffīn*, pp. 492–5.

[3] Ṭabarī, II, pp. 16, 27, 67, 81, 82, 84, 85, 86, 87, 111, 157, 163; Balādhurī, *Futūḥ*, p. 236.

[4] Ṭabarī, II, p. 157.

tians and Syrians, who were engaged to work as oarsmen, helmsmen and sailors for this Arab navy, were paid wages for the duration of the campaigns,[1] and it is only logical that the Arabs, who were the actual fighting forces, should be compensated for relinquishing their regular means of livelihood. The other Arabs in Syria who took part only in the summer expeditions, had to be satisfied with their share of the booty. The institution of regular stipends for all the Arabs in Syria does not seem to have been established at this stage.

Jazīra, i.e. Mesopotamia, presented a problem to Mu'āwiya. It was not originally part of the governorship of Syria, but 'Uthmān had placed it under his jurisdiction.[2] This was an unfortunate decision as the tribal composition of the Arabs there was very different from that of the rest of Syria. To understand the reason for this difference one must go back to the beginning of the conquest. The first troops sent out to Syria by Abū Bakr were some 7,000 men from Makka, Madīna and the surrounding areas. These were mostly tribesmen from the Qaysite clans of Ḥijāz and western Arabia. They were the heroes of Ajnādayn and they also formed the most privileged group in Abū 'Ubayda's army at the Yarmūk.[3] Thus when he split up his troops to complete the conquest of Syria, he assigned, almost as a reward, the conquest of the rich Jazīra to these Qaysite veterans. Although this area was the front line of the Byzantine eastern defences, and as such very well fortified, it was now completely cut off and its conquest was rapidly and easily achieved.[4]

As a result of the Sāsānian–Byzantine wars and the Arab conquest, the vast and rich countryside of Jazīra was somewhat depopulated leaving an abundance of deserted cultivable lands. The Qaysite conquerors were quick to establish their claims to much of these lands, paying only the Islamic tithes.[5] In other words these few thousand men treated a whole province as their private property and as such established their rule there. During 'Umar's Khalifate these tribesmen continued to control Jazīra and to rule it as a separate province. While it is true that on the one hand they performed a service to Syria by protecting its right flank

1 *Greek Papyri in the British Museum*, vol. IV, *The Aphrodito Papyri*, ed. H. I. Bell, London, 1910, Introduction, pp. xviii, xxxii, xxxv, and nos. 1349, 1353, 1374, 1434.

2 Balādhurī, *Futūḥ*, p. 178.

3 See above p. 40.

4 Balādhurī, *Futūḥ*, p. 172.

5 *Ibid.*, pp. 173, 177.

from any possible Byzantine attacks down the Euphrates, they also benefited a great deal from their raids into Armenia. They expected to have the same treatment as the Arabs of Syria, especially in so far as immigration into Jazīra should be prohibited or at least controlled. But because of the small number of inhabitants and the vast size of the province, this was not only unfair but also impractical. The pressures of immigration in 'Uthmān's time forced him to seek a solution in Jazīra. When he decided to add it to Mu'āwiya's governorship, he was in fact trying to break the hegemony of these original conquerors.

Mu'āwiya proceeded to reduce the status of this privileged group and forced these Qaysites to accept immigrants from the unrelated clans of Muḍar and Rabī'a. However, he did compromise slightly by arranging for these newcomers to be given lands and to be settled in the many depopulated areas of the region.[1] Apparently these new immigrants were also excluded from the profitable raids into Armenia. Some of them were made to settle at strategically situated points at the intersections of military roads or at entrances to narrow mountain passes, to protect Jazīra from Byzantine surprise attacks. Malaṭya, by the upper Euphrates, was such a place where a *maslaḥa* or *rābiṭa*, a garrison or a frontier post, was established.[2] Again, it is only with regard to those tribesmen who were on permanent military duty that we hear of regular stipends, *'aṭā'*, being issued.[3] It is characteristic of Mu'āwiya that these new arrangements in Jazīra were effected gradually and over a long period of time. His compromises seem to have satisfied all groups concerned, as is evident from the fact that they supported him against 'Alī. Perhaps the Qaysites considered Mu'āwiya the lesser of two evils. It is significant, in the light of later developments, that we do not hear of any Qays against Kalb, or Muḍar against Yaman conflicts at Ṣiffīn. It is only after Mu'āwiya's death that we hear of such divisions in Syria and Jazīra. It seems that after the reorganization of Kūfa and Baṣra, which we shall presently discuss, Mu'āwiya forced the Arabs of Jazīra to accept more immigrants.[4] They tolerated this during his lifetime but after his death they seized the opportunity to give vent to their indignation. The Qaysites resented that they,

[1] *Ibid.*, p. 178. [2] *Ibid.*, p. 185. [3] *Ibid.*, p. 178.
[4] Ṭabarī, I, pp. 2673–4, II, pp. 127, 142; Ibn Ḥazm, 'Ali b. Muḥammad, *Jambarat Ansāb al-'Arab*, ed. A. Hārūn, Cairo, 1962, p. 426.

rather than the Yamani tribesmen of Syria proper, should be singled out for this unjust treatment, and they considered it an unforgivable blow to their pride, prestige and prosperity. The explosion between Qays and Yaman after Mu'āwiya's death shows how precarious was the situation in Jazīra and how difficult Mu'āwiya's task in devising compromises and solutions for such intricate problems.

Of course, Iraq was the most difficult province of all, and here Mu'āwiya had to use all his tact to bring the tribesmen into line with his policies. At first he did not propose any changes and tried only to restore the situation as it had existed before the civil war. To Kūfa he appointed Mughīra b. Shu'ba, a man long acquainted with its problems and well known for his political acumen. As governor (661–70/41–50) he tried hard to assuage the Kūfans while Mu'āwiya attempted to win over their leaders by giving them considerable sums of money. In Baṣra, the energetic general 'Abdullah b. 'Āmir was restored as governor in 661/41 and he immediately proceeded to reactivate the campaigns in the East.

Ibn 'Āmir's initial campaigns, during 'Uthmān's reign, had virtually achieved the conquest of the eastern Sāsānian domains. The various towns and districts of the East surrendered to the Arabs and agreed to peace treaties concluded with the local leaders. These peace treaties stipulated the payment of a fixed tribute by each locality. Most significant was the fact that the Arabs explicitly agreed not to interfere in the assessment and collection of taxes. These were to remain the responsibility of the local nobility, *dahāqīn*, who were also responsible for delivering the fixed tribute to the Arabs. These treaties formed the basis of the relationship between Arab rulers and the subject people, and continued to be so throughout the Umayyad period. The surrender of Merv in 651/31 brought the Arabs to the old Sāsānian frontier, where they realized that any further advance to the east would involve them in hostilities with the strong forces of the Hephthalite principalities. They decided the wiser course was to recoup their strength and consolidate their position in Khurāsān before embarking on new adventures. So far there was no plan for any tribesmen to settle permanently in Khurāsān. Arab policy, at this time, was to send an expedition every year from Baṣra to raid those areas which had not yet made peace treaties with the

Arabs. At the end of the campaign, in the autumn, they would return to Baṣra, leaving in Khurāsān a garrison of 4,000 men to secure the area for their return. This garrison would stay in the villages of the Merv oasis where, according to the treaty of Merv, provision had been made for them to be quartered in the houses of the local population.[1]

It was in the campaign of 652/32 that western Sīstān of the Sāsānians was conquered and a small Arab garrison stationed in its main town, Zaranj. Meanwhile, a significant development had taken place in the province of Kirmān. On his way to Khurāsān in 650/30 Ibn ʿĀmir had conquered parts of Kirmān and had left some of his troops there to continue the conquest. They were able to achieve this task but many of the conquered fled, leaving their lands and houses. These properties were divided among the Arab conquerors, who settled there, cultivated the land and paid the tithes due on it.[2]

During the civil war no expeditions were sent to Khurāsān and Arab authority there was threatened by several uprisings. However, the Arab garrison at Merv was able to subdue these minor revolts and to hold the province. In Sīstān the small garrison was driven out of Zaranj. Again it was Ibn ʿĀmir's responsibility to re-establish Arab control in the East. In 661/41 he prepared a big expedition directed to Sīstān. First of all, Zaranj was recaptured. Then a new front was opened against Zunbīl, king of Zābulistān. The Arabs besieged Kābul for a few months and finally entered it, defeating Zunbīl in their first encounter. However, this effort was in vain because Zābulistān continued to offer fierce resistance to the Arabs for more than two centuries. This mountainous region was more suited to the tactics of the indigenous population than to those of the Arabs. Indeed mountains proved always to be a decisive barrier in the path of the Arab armies. The interesting thing in this case is that Ibn ʿĀmir seems to have held high hopes for the Sīstān front in preference to the Khurāsān front. This is the only explanation for his apparent inaction with regard to the latter. He satisfied himself by simply rotating the garrison of Merv and made no particular effort to reopen the Khurāsān front. He seems also to have had some difficulties in his dealings with the tribesmen in Baṣra itself. This was because large numbers of new

[1] Shaban, *The ʿAbbāsid Revolution*, pp. 20–4.
[2] Balādhurī, *Futūḥ*, p. 392.

immigrants coming into Baṣra had caused some tension between the different tribal groups.[1] Muʿāwiya, who was alarmed by this situation, removed Ibn ʿĀmir in 664/44 in favour of the redoubtable Ziyād b. Abīhi, his father's son.

This man, as his name rather euphemistically implies, was illegitimate and of no tribal standing. But at an early age his exceptional abilities found him a post and soon important offices in the administration of Iraq. He served ʿAlī to the end, but Muʿāwiya with his instinct for talent lured him into his own service. Part of the bait was recognition, on trumped-up evidence, of Ziyād as the son of Muʿāwiya's own father. Thenceforward he was to be known as Ziyād b. Abī Sufyān and his new brother entrusted him with the governorship of Baṣra which included Khurāsān and Sīstān.

Ziyād, like Ibn ʿĀmir, supported an expansionist policy, but whereas his predecessor had chosen the more difficult front, Ziyād preferred Khurāsān. The Baṣrans, however, were not altogether willing to go to such far away fronts and were still less willing to campaign on the less rewarding Sīstān front. Under the circumstances Ziyād's choice was more in accordance with their general wishes. As his lieutenant in Khurāsān Ziyād appointed al-Ḥakam b. ʿAmr al-Ghifārī, who had been a companion of the Prophet and who would, Ziyād hoped, give campaigning in Khurāsān a special appeal. Nevertheless, Ḥakam had some difficulty recruiting for his expedition, taking more than two years to muster enough men. When he appeared in Khurāsān in 667/47, he advanced eastwards against the Hephthalite principalities of Gūzgān and Gharchistān. Although he met with some strong resistance he was able to establish Arab authority in these areas. It is not clear from our sources whether Ḥakam undertook more expeditions or whether he died in 667/47 or 670/50. He was, however, succeeded by another man of the same calibre, who had also been one of the companions of the Prophet. This was Ghālib b. Fuḍāla (or ʿAbdillah) al-Laythī who continued to carry out Ziyād's expansionist policy in the East. The expedition which arrived in Khurāsān in 667/47 does not seem to have returned to Baṣra as usual in the following autumn but instead seems to have remained in Khurāsān. Therefore it is possible to conjecture that its members did not have particularly strong ties in Baṣra. In

[1] Shaban, *The ʿAbbāsid Revolution*, p. 29.

other words they may have been recruited from the latest immigrants coming into the garrison town.[1]

Meanwhile, Ziyād was busy in Baṣra carrying out a new administrative reorganization of far-reaching effects. It was also possible, practically at the same time, for him to apply the same reorganization to Kūfa. After the death of its governor, Mughīra b. Shu'ba, in 670/50 it was added to Ziyād's governorship. Thus, for the first time one governor was responsible for almost half the empire and also had the unqualified support of the *Amīr al-Mu'minīn*. These circumstances gave Ziyād the opportunity to proceed with a radical plan to overhaul the entire organization of his extensive and troublesome governorship.

The system set up in Kūfa and Baṣra, in the time of 'Umar, had clearly lost its meaning under the strain of the disorganized influx of tribesmen. The basic unit of this system was the *'arāfa*, a small group of tribesmen lumped together for the purpose of the distribution of revenue. Since these stipends varied according to the date of the recipients' arrival, these *'arāfas* did not at that time necessarily coincide with the clan divisions. This was an unnatural situation. The clan was still very much the basic unit in Arab society, as the housing arrangements of the tribesmen very clearly showed. If at the beginning of the settlements there were not enough men from one clan to form an *'arāfa*, the increasing immigration of tribesmen who joined their clansmen had by now remedied this imbalance. In fact 'Alī had become aware of this new situation and had made ineffective gestures towards reform, but Ziyād had the ability and the time to carry out a more comprehensive plan. First of all, he rooted out corruption and abuses by purging the records of the *dīwān* of the names of the dead and the *khawārij*. He then reorganized the distribution of stipends to meet social needs and realities. Each clan was made an independent unit and for administrative purposes was divided into *'arāfas*. The *'arīf*, head of the *'arāfa*, was appointed by the government and was made responsible not only for receiving and distributing the stipends, but also for the discipline of his men. For wider purposes Ziyād grouped ethnically related clans into larger tribal divisions of roughly equal size, five in Baṣra and four in Kūfa. The government appointed a leader for each division and saw to it that his authority was recognized and enforced. Since

[1] *Ibid.*, pp. 29–32.

the tribesmen within each division often had conflicting interests, there was a satisfactory amount of disunity within the division itself. The various divisions could be played off against each other, and their leaders' powers were checked by the governor's. Thus Ziyād's reorganization ultimately worked to the benefit of the central government and towards the stability of Kūfa and Baṣra.[1]

However, as a result of this organization, large numbers of tribesmen were found who did not fit into the newly created units and were not included in the registers of Baṣra and Kūfa. Ziyād's solution to this problem was as simple as it was drastic; he arranged for 50,000 men and their families to be transferred from Kūfa and Baṣra to Khurāsān to settle permanently there. He was probably encouraged by the fact that the men who had gone to Khurāsān on the campaign of 667/47 were still there and he hoped that with a little persuasion these tribesmen would agree to make their homes there. Their families must have been included with the rest of the 50,000 families who were sent to Khurāsān in 671/51. The purpose of this move was to secure those conquests already made and to provide the forces needed for further expansion. The new governor of Khurāsān, al-Rabīʿ b. Ziyād al-Ḥārithī, was an old veteran of the early campaigns there. During his governorship (671–3/51–3) and that of his son, who succeeded him for a few months, Arab authority was extended to the banks of the Oxus. It should be added that these 50,000 families were settled in the villages of the Merv oasis, making the best possible use of the treaty of Merv which stipulated that the local population there should make room for the Arabs in their houses.[2]

Khurāsān, therefore, provided the solution for the overflow of newcomers in Iraq and was now an integral part of the empire. Muʿāwiya tried to establish the central government's right to more of the revenues from the new conquests there. His subtle, yet perhaps too obvious device was to revive and extend the Prophet's practice of appropriating certain items of the booty, *ṣawāfī*. He instructed Ḥakam to set aside for the central treasury all the cash collected in Khurāsān, but neither Ḥakam nor his men were ready to accept such an intrusion by the central government and they bluntly refused to contribute anything other than the ordinary fifth. Muʿāwiya, in his usual fashion, gracefully surrendered, at least for the time being.[3]

[1] *Ibid.*, p. 29. [2] *Ibid.*, pp. 32–4. [3] *Ibid.*, p. 31.

The application of the principle of *ṣawāfī* to Iraq had far more serious results. Here, the issue at stake was the vast abandoned Sāsānian lands which the *qurrā'* treated as their private property. Mu'āwiya declared most of these lands to be *ṣawāfī*, and required that their revenues be sent to the central treasury.[1] The *qurrā'* realized that this new dispensation denied completely all their claims to these lands or their revenues, and their agitation soon threatened the new precarious peace in Iraq. However, little could be done with an enemy as openly implacable as the *qurrā'-khawārij*. They had by no means given up their fight for their alleged rights, nor could they be easily stamped out. However often they were evicted it was all too easy for them to erect their minute republics in other quarters in what they considered their rightful domains; but the menace was kept under control.[2]

Where Mu'āwiya miscalculated was in his attitude to the ex-*qurrā'* peacefully living in Kūfa and Baṣra. Underestimating their desperate belief in the validity of their claims, he imagined that they would settle down quietly to being ordinary tribesmen under Ziyād's new organization. However, far from settling down, their open and persistent agitation in Kūfa increased to the extent that it threatened the authority of the government and the stability of the town. After a few unsuccessful warnings the government took drastic action. The leaders of the ex-*qurrā'* were arrested and sent to Damascus where seven of them were ordered to be executed. These included Ḥujr b. 'Adī al-Kindī, a leader who had fought against the *ridda*, had taken part in the first conquests of both Syria and Iraq, had contended the leadership of Kinda against the rising power of the *ridda* leader, al-Ash'ath b. Qays, and had remained one of 'Alī's most loyal supporters until his death. Ḥujr and the other six who were executed stand out, in our sources, as the exemplary leaders of the *qurrā'*.[3] Their execution was an unusual error on Mu'āwiya's part but indicates how powerful a threat Ḥujr and the *qurrā'* were to the stability of Kūfa. This was the first time that the *Amīr al-Mu'minīn* had assumed the power of life and death over his fellow Muslims and it was the first political execution in Islam. It was effective, but for Mu'āwiya

[1] Ya'qūbī, *Tārīkh*, vol. II, pp. 233–4.

[2] The clearest narrative on this point is that of Ibn al-Athīr, *Kāmil*, vol. III, pp. 344–7, 352–3.

[3] Ṭabarī, II, pp. 111–55; Ibn Sa'd Muḥammad, *al-Ṭabaqāt al-Kabīr*, vol. VI, ed. K. V. Zettersteen, Leiden, 1909, pp. 151–4.

it was unusually rash and high-handed. For the time being the tribesmen in Kūfa and Baṣra held their peace, but these executions brought the Khalifate that much nearer to monarchy and made these tribesmen understandably nervous for their cherished independence.

Muʿāwiya compounded this error by again appearing authoritarian in his arrangement for the succession. He contended, with good reason, that the stability of the regime depended upon a smooth process of succession. Therefore he determined to nominate a successor in the manner of Abū Bakr. Had there been one single and obvious candidate the slight element of high-handedness involved might have passed unnoticed. Unfortunately this was not the case. There were two obvious candidates, in terms of ability and standing in the Umayyad family, the Syrian army and the empire generally. One was Marwān b. al-Ḥakam, who had the great advantage of being the expected successor to Muʿāwiya as leader of the house of Umayya. On the other hand Marwān had spent too little time in Syria for Muʿāwiya to be sure that the former would receive the crucial support of the Syrian *jund*. It was here that Yazīd, the other candidate, was at a greater advantage. He was the son of Muʿāwiya, his mother was of the Syrian tribe of Kalb and he had lived all his life among the Syrians, and Muʿāwiya could therefore be almost completely sure of their allegiance to his son. This clinched the matter, despite the obvious dangers of accusations of dynasticism. Muʿāwiya was gambling on this innovation, and he must have realized this for he tried to make his gamble as safe as possible by arranging for allegiance to be paid publicly to Yazīd before his own death, even if it meant intimidating the dubious and the recalcitrant.[1]

It is hard not to sympathize with Mu'āwiya's motives. But that a cautious man like him, who always preferred indirect methods, should feel forced to act in such an authoritarian and innovating manner shows the precarious nature of his regime. Muʿāwiya had provided temporary peace and stability, but the essential problems had been evaded. The tribesmen were still too powerful and independent; indeed Ziyād's reforms in Iraq aggravated the problem by reasserting and consolidating the clan as the basic unit of society. Muʿāwiya did not give up the attempt to establish a regime which could exist without coercion, but the attempt re-

[1] Ṭabarī, II, pp. 173–7.

quired political and diplomatic skills of such a high standard and so much self-abnegation on the part of the government that not even he could always live up to the standard required.

The reign of his immediate successors made these facts all too clear. The moment the great Muʿāwiya was dead the regime that he had tended so painstakingly began to distintegrate. The first challenge came from Ḥusayn, the younger son of ʿAlī. He was so convinced that the time was ripe for a bid for power, and so confident of gathering enough support among the partisans, *shīʿa*, of his father there, that he marched, or rather rushed, on Kūfa accompanied only by his family and a few followers. But he was mistaken. The Umayyad forces found it an easy matter to massacre the entire party at Karbalā just outside Kūfa. A routine police operation sufficed to deal with this Shīʿite rebellion. Yet although this wild venture ended in humiliating failure, in the long term it did nothing but good for the Shīʿite cause, for it gave it its first authentic martyr. Soon the call to avenge Ḥusayn and his family was a standard part of Shīʿite propaganda, their banner and their rallying cry.

This venture also helped to establish the idea of *bayt*, the leadership of a certain privileged and hallowed family in Islam. The origins of this idea were old; in Arab tradition there was always a leading family or house, *bayt*, in each clan, which owed its prominence to some remarkable act of bravery, generosity or *ḥilm* in general. Muḥammad's family, Hāshim, had not been the leading family of Quraysh, but since it had produced the Prophet of God there, there were very plausible reasons for considering it the leading family of Quraysh and of the whole Islamic community. The Khalifate of ʿAlī and his son al-Ḥasan, however ineffective or brief, naturally helped this idea to gain a greater hold on the public imagination. Even the Umayyads inadvertently encouraged the growth of this idea when they claimed that their own house had gained the rights of *bayt* because of Muʿāwiya's outstanding success and *ḥilm*, and owing to the abdication of al-Ḥasan.[1] This was a very doubtful argument. It was dangerous to put forward the idea of *bayt* in support of the Umayyads, because once the idea of *bayt* was admitted, the claims of Hāshim were just so much stronger. There was even less justification for bringing in the abdication of al-Ḥasan, for by that token the *bayt* of the ʿAlīds was

[1] Ibn Aʿtham, *Futūḥ*, pp. 117B–118B; Ṭabarī, II, p. 380.

admitted as having once existed, and it did not then follow that al-Ḥasan's abdication invalidated the claims of other branches of Hāshim. And now ʿAlī's other son had laid claim to leadership, dying a martyr's death in the process. Thus a pathetic and abortive revolt had considerable political repercussions, for it put the last touch to a mythology which would inspire many malcontents in the future.

More immediately dangerous was the revolt of ʿAbdullah b. al-Zubayr. As we have already indicated, Muʿāwiya was not particularly associated with the extremist Qurayshites who had been behind the revolt of Ṭalḥa and al-Zubayr twenty years before. This group was by no means politically extinct, and it had always distrusted Muʿāwiya who had risen to power and remained there by the force of Syrian arms. Quraysh could claim no credit for Muʿāwiya's victory and they felt, correctly, that the new regime could never truly represent their interests. Therefore, these Qurayshites made one last bid to restore their position, and significantly the man they chose as their *Amīr al-Muʾminīn* was ʿAbdullah the son of al-Zubayr, who had rebelled against ʿAlī for exactly similar reasons. This revolt was serious and the sudden death of Yazīd added to its threat. The Syrian blockade of Makka, which would certainly have succeeded otherwise, had to be withdrawn. The Umayyad succession was thrust upon Yazīd's unwilling and protesting nineteen-year-old son, Muʿāwiya II. So unwilling was he indeed that within a few weeks he was dead. As a result ʿAbdullah b. al-Zubayr found himself in a remarkably strong position and he received the allegiance of every province except Syria.

At first the Syrians were not at all sure where to turn. The Qaysites of Jazīra, now part of Syria, were the only group who took a clear stand. They had never forgiven Muʿāwiya for opening "their" region to further immigration and they had no reason to support the cause of his family. They were quick to acclaim ʿAbdullah b. al-Zubayr, probably hoping that he would restore their autonomy in the province. Furthermore, much of the support of Ibn al-Zubayr came from Ḥijāz, whence these tribesmen of Jazīra had originally come.[1]

The rest of the Syrians were divided. Many were for accepting

[1] Balādhurī, *Ansāb*, vol. v, pp. 132, 133, 136; Ṭabarī, II, pp. 468, 471, 472, 473, 474, 482, 483.

Ibn al-Zubayr, who certainly did not propose any changes in their status. On the other hand they were not willing to support him to the extent of fighting for his cause. Some of the tribesmen of Kalb wanted to continue the office of *Amīr al-Mu'minīn* in the house of Mu'āwiya, but none of his descendants were old enough to assume this office. Moreover the Kalbites did not have the strength to force their choice upon their fellow Syrians.[1] At first the Kindite tribesmen of Sakūn from the district of Jordan favoured accepting Ibn al-Zubayr, but they soon realized that only an Umayyad could unite the Syrians and assure them of their privileges.[2]

Marwān b. al-Ḥakam emerged as a compromise candidate. Although Mu'āwiya had passed him over in favour of his son Yazīd, Marwān was still the most senior member of the house of Umayya. It also seems that he promised to grant the tribesmen of Sakūn more lands at Balqā' in the Jordan district.[3] Soon Marwān was acclaimed as the new *Amīr al-Mu'minīn* and most of the Syrians were united behind him. His first task was to secure his base and bring back the tribesmen of Jazīra into the fold. The Battle of Marj Rāhiṭ decided the issue in his favour and he now proceeded against the other provinces which had acclaimed Ibn al-Zubayr. Egypt was his first and easiest target. Without any difficulty Marwān persuaded the Egyptian tribesmen to renounce their allegiance to the Makkan contender and discontinue the grain shipments to Ḥijāz.[4] These were Marwān's achievements before his death after nine months in office. The task of continuing the fight against Ibn al-Zubayr fell to his son and successor 'Abdulmalik who now had the means for a massive counter attack.

Deprived, like 'Alī before him, of Egypt and Syria, and not possessing the advantage of a united and militarily strong province, Ibn al-Zubayr had to turn to Iraq for his main support. Admittedly Baṣra was quick to recognize him, and many of the clan leaders of Kūfa were inclined to do the same if only in the interests of social stability.[5] Still the only point the Kūfans were agreed

[1] Balādhurī, *Ansāb*, vol. v, pp. 128, 129, 133, 134; Ṭabarī, II, pp. 468, 470, 471.
[2] Baladhuri, *Ansab*, vol. IV, pp. 51–2, 55; vol. v, pp. 128, 134, 149; Ṭabarī, II, pp. 431–2.
[3] Balādhurī, *Ansāb*, vol. v, p. 149; Ṭabarī, II, p. 487.
[4] *Ibid.*, pp. 148–9, 189; Kindī, *Governors*, pp. 42–8; Ibn A'tham, *Futūḥ*, vol. II, pp. 52A–B.
[5] Balādhurī, *Ansāb*, vol. v, pp. 188, 207, 212, 218.

s a unanimous dislike of the Umayyads. Among the rank of the Kūfans the Shīʿite mythology was beginning to ot, as they came to realize how much ʿAlī's egalitarianism have been to their advantage.[1] Certainly very few of them saw any reason to support actively yet another outside domination. Taking advantage of this Shīʿite sentiment the remnants of the ex-*qurrā'* in Kūfa even went so far as to declare their fault in failing to support Ḥusayn, thus gaining the nomenclature the Penitents. Opposing both ʿAbdulmalik and Ibn al-Zubayr, they decided that the former was the more immediate enemy and accordingly marched upon Syria to destroy his power, grossly overestimating their own strength and underestimating that of their opponent. The Syrian army defeated them with the utmost ease and only a few escaped to return to Kūfa and to agitate.[2]

In such troubled circumstances the field was wide open to any man with sufficient skill and daring. The next man to try his luck in Kūfa was al-Mukhtār b. Abī ʿUbayd of Thaqīf. He came from a distinguished family with strong connections in Iraq. His father had led the first campaign in Iraq and had died at the Battle of the Bridge. His uncle had governed Madā'in under ʿAlī and al-Ḥasan, and Mukhtār himself had frequently deputized for him. Although he had a profound knowledge of the factions of Kūfa and owned property in the Sawād, he had preferred to withdraw to his family's home town of Ṭā'if. He had offered his help to Ibn al-Zubayr at a price, but the latter felt strong enough to do without it. Therefore al-Mukhtār decided to strike out on his own. Our sources are very hostile to him, but it appears that he was a very able and astute, if an ambitious, opportunist. Politicians less acute than al-Mukhtār might have imagined the vitality of the Shīʿite movement exhausted with the failure of the Penitents' expedition. He rapidly grasped its essential strength as a rallying point for the discontented. He therefore took over the Shīʿite cause and established what was then known under the name *shurṭat al-khamīs*, i.e. those distinguished and devoted in the army. These were the hard-core partisans of ʿAlī in Kūfa whose number was less than 12,000 tribesmen.[3] Mukhtār's revolt to avenge the blood of Ḥusayn was proclaimed in the name of Muḥammad b. al-Ḥanafiyya, the son of ʿAlī by a woman of the tribe of Ḥanīfa. We do not know how

[1] *Ibid.*, p. 221. [2] *Ibid.*, pp. 204–13; Ṭabarī, II, pp. 497–509, 538–76.
[3] Ṭabarī, II, pp. 1, 3, 7; Balādhurī, *Ansāb*, vol. V, pp. 249, 253, 260.

Muḥammad reacted to this honour so unexpectedly thrust upon him. In fact he was probably not consulted at all, and if he was he can only have agreed to this revolt in the most ambiguous terms. Whatever the truth of the matter, it was of no importance in Kūfa for Mukhtār proclaimed him the *Mahdī*, the divinely guided leader. This was a very shrewd move and the first example of the central Shī'ite idea of an *Imām–Amīr al-Mu'minīn* who would give justice to all. Mukhtār also declared that until such time as the revolt succeeded he would hold the secular authority as the helper, *wazīr*, of the *Imām*. This again set a very important precedent in Shī'ite revolts, which was followed by the leaders of the 'Abbāsid revolution.

Mukhtār's revolt was, for a time, sensationally successful. Its Shī'ite paraphernalia naturally won it the support of the remaining Penitents and the hard-core *shī'a*, led by Ibrāhim b. al-Ashtar, whose father had never deserted the cause of 'Alī. He was also able to win over the recent arrivals, whose allegiance to the established Umayyad-appointed clan leaders was easily shaken. This coalition was sufficiently strong for Mukhtār to expel al-Zubayr's governor of Kūfa and set himself up as the *wazīr* of the *Imām*. Mukhtār managed to keep it together by a most unusual propaganda campaign, proselytizing in a grand Qur'ānic style, prophesying events which sometimes happened, and presenting his followers with a Shī'ite Ark of the Covenant in the shape of an old chair once owned by 'Alī. One point to emphasize is that he did not, as is generally believed, make a great appeal for the support of the non-Arab converts, the *mawālī*. Admittedly we do hear of 2,300 *mawālī* among his followers. Although probably exaggerated, this is a small number compared to the number of his Arab supporters. Their unimportance becomes clearer when one notes that they were only recruited as an emergency measure to keep order in Kūfa when the bulk of his supporters had been sent out to evangelize the countryside, particularly to the north. This was an emergency measure, and these *mawālī* proved in battle to be very unreliable and ineffectual. The only real point of interest, in this respect, is that there must have been a number of unemployed native Iraqis who had gravitated towards Kūfa. This was to become a serious problem later.

In fact Mukhtār's regime was no more than that of a demagogue taking advantage of a troubled situation. It was far too flimsy to challenge the genuine power of the Umayyads or Ibn al-Zubayr. Even in Kūfan terms it was very precarious. It was a malcontents' regime, and the established clan leaders, *ashrāf*, of Kūfa soon threw their lot in with Ibn al-Zubayr as the only way of re-establishing their own position. They withdrew to Baṣra, joined up with the Makkan ruler's army, and marched back to Kūfa. Mukhtār's bluff had been called, and even Ibn al-Ashtar deserted him. His wazīrate collapsed and he met his death with some two hundred of his most fanatical followers.[1]

This was by no means the end of the disorders set in motion by the temporary collapse of Umayyad authority. The worst was to come in what was virtually a repeat performance of the *ridda* wars; although it is usually viewed as a Khārijite revolt. Our sources refer to these neo-*khawārij* as the Azāriqa or the Najdiyya after the names of two of their prominent leaders, who were both members of the tribe of Ḥanīfa. Although other leaders of this revolt were also Ḥanīfites, there were leaders as well as supporters from other tribes. Therefore it would have been wrong to call them all Ḥanīfites. It is characteristic of our sources to call them after their outstanding leaders: Najdiyya, i.e. the followers of Najda b. 'Āmir and Azāriqa, i.e. the followers of Nāfi' b. al-Azraq.

Ḥanīfa, in Central Arabia, was one of the greatest and most powerful tribes of the peninsula, and had never gladly submitted to any external domination. It was indeed one of the tribes of the wars of the apostasy which had never apostatized at all, since it had never in any way allied itself with Muḥammad.[2] Now, fifty years later, Ḥanīfa offered its help to Ibn al-Zubayr in the hope of throwing off the Syrian domination. The latter answered Ḥanīfa as he had answered Mukhtār – by refusing the offer – for their price would have been greater independence. Ibn al-Zubayr was both fearful of the example that these concessions would have set to his other followers, and sufficiently confident of his strength to run the risk of a refusal with all its consequences. Here he was unwise, for the great tribe of Ḥanīfa was not to be treated in the same way as a Mukhtār. The insulted Ḥanīfites, proud in their strength, decided to throw off the Makkan domination as well as the Syrian by breaking Ibn al-Zubayr's power in

[1] The best and most complete source for this episode is Balādhurī, *Ansāb*, vol. v, pp. 214–73.

[2] See above p. 20.

Iraq.[1] Eventually they sought an alliance with their fellow tribesmen among the *khawārij* and planned a concerted attack upon Baṣra. It was because of this alliance that our sources describe this as a Khārijite rebellion. Nothing could be further from the truth. The Ḥanīfite revolt had no connection with the social and economic disputes in Iraq which had caused the revolt of the *qurrā'–khawārij* against 'Alī. This so-called Khārijite movement was in fact a major revolt in Arabia itself, led by a tribe with a long tradition of independence, which happened to be in alliance with the *khawārij* for the purposes of an Iraqi campaign. It was not an ideological alliance, but one between two groups who had their independence and similar, if not identical, interests to protect. Indeed it was a very advantageous alliance to both sides for their strengths and weaknesses were complementary. The *khawārij* could raise more wealth from any areas they might control in Fārs and Khūzistān, and the Ḥanīfites could raise more men both from their own numbers and the tribesmen they were able to muster from the other clans of eastern Arabia.

The Ḥanīfites were ideally located to cut off Ibn al-Zubayr completely from Iraq. Moreover, they were in control of Yamāma, the alternative supplier of grain to Ḥijāz. This became very important after the stopping of grain shipments from Egypt.[2] First of all, the Ḥanīfites began to extend their control eastwards to the Persian Gulf and, after little resistance, were able to establish themselves in Baḥrayn. There, many tribesmen of the clans of Tamīm and 'Abdulqays joined the Ḥanīfite revolt.[3] But when the Ḥanīfites tried to dominate 'Umān, they met with fierce resistance from the tribesmen of the clans of Azd.[4] It was these very Azdites who were finally able to end this revolt, though not before it had extended itself across the Gulf.

Large numbers of tribesmen from Ḥanīfa, Tamīm and 'Abdulqays crossed the Persian Gulf to join their fellow tribesmen from among the *khawārij* in their depredations on Baṣran territory.[5] Soon they controlled huge agricultural areas in Fārs and Ahwāz,

[1] Ṭabarī, II, pp. 401–2, 513–17; Balādhurī, *Ansāb*, vol. IV, p. 47.
[2] Balādhurī, *Ansāb al-Ashrāf*, vol. XI, ed. W. Ahlwardt, Greifswald, 1883, p. 139.
[3] *Ibid.*, pp. 81, 128, 131–3.
[4] *Ibid.*, p. 135; Ibn Hazm, *Jamhara*, p. 382.
[5] Balādhurī, *Ansāb*, vol. XI, pp. 86, 93, 135, 148; Ṭabarī, II, pp. 517, 520, 588; Ibn Khayyāṭ, *Tārīkh*, vol. I, p. 252; al-Dhahabī, Muḥammad b. Aḥmad, *Tārīkh al-Islām*, Cairo, 1367–9, vol. II, p. 360.

depriving the Baṣrans of their revenues and providing themselves with a secure base for raids upon Baṣra itself. These neo-*khawārij* roused tribesmen of other clans in eastern and central Arabia to imitate them, and thus their numbers, wealth and power grew uncontrolled and unchecked. This new wave of uncontrolled and hostile immigration gained such momentum that the authorities in Baṣra trembled for their safety. Luckily for them and for Ibn al-Zubayr other tribesmen still in Arabia were encouraged to emulate the success of the new emigrants. These came mostly from the Azd clans of 'Umān, who made natural allies for the Azdite clans of Baṣra. The two groups soon came to terms: the new immigrants agreed to accept the leadership of al-Muhallab b. Abī Ṣufra in campaigns against the neo-*khawārij* in return for, at least, three years' revenues of every district they recovered for Baṣra.[1] It was an excellent investment. Al-Muhallab and the new immigrants won victory after victory against the neo-*khawārij*, and eventually forced the survivors into the arid regions of Kirmān and Sīstān, where they were sufficiently far away from the central government for neither to be a major annoyance to the other.[2]

But it was an investment that benefited the Umayyads rather than Ibn al-Zubayr, for al-Muhallab and his armies had no difficulty in reconciling themselves to the Umayyads, and continued their campaigns on to final success under the aegis of Damascus.[3] Meanwhile the Syrians for the first time turned the full force of their strength upon Ibn al-Zubayr. His Iraqi army was routed, and he lost Iraq to the Umayyads. Naval expeditions were sent from Egypt to the various ports of Arabia.[4] Makka itself was attacked and Ibn al-Zubayr killed. 'Abdulmalik, the son of Marwān, who was acclaimed the new *Amīr al-Mu'minīn*, was recognized by the whole empire after he had efficiently foiled the attempt of his cousin 'Amr b. Sa'īd to claim the throne. 'Amr based his claim on his rights as head of the Umayyad family, but it was all in vain for it ended in his capture and death at the orders of 'Abdulmalik.[5]

[1] Balādhurī, *Ansāb*, vol. XI, p. 103; Ṭabarī, II, p. 584, 587, 590, 591; Al-Mubarrad, Abū al-'Abbās Muḥammad, *al-Kāmil*, ed. W. Wright, Leipzig, 1874–82, vol. II, pp. 627–8.

[2] For the construction of al-Muhallab's army, see Shaban, *The 'Abbāsid Revolution*, p. 55.

[3] Ṭabarī, II, pp. 821–2.

[4] Kindī, *Governors*, p. 51.

[5] Balādhurī, *Ansāb*, vol. IV, pp. 138–46.

One important result of this second civil war was the gradual extension of the institution of *'aṭā'*, stipends, to the Syrians. When Yazīd I was threatened by the unrest in Iraq and the revolt of Ibn al-Zubayr in Ḥijāz, he felt obliged to recall the garrison of Cyprus to Syria,[1] practically the only full-time troops who were paid regular stipends. The troops who were sent to blockade Ibn al-Zubayr in Makka were paid the sum of one hundred dinārs each to undertake this particular expedition.[2] Marwān promised to grant land to some of the tribesmen of Syria when he needed their support to establish his rule.[3] We have a few reports of stipends of 200 dinārs, or 2,000 dirhams, being paid in Jazīra to leaders who were probably serving in an official capacity,[4] but until Marwan's death there are no references to stipends being paid on a large scale, like that of Iraq, in Syria, Jazīra or Egypt.

'Abdulmalik needed the support of the Syrians against Ibn al-Zubayr in Iraq and Ḥijāz. Many of these tribesmen demanded and were granted the highest stipends in exchange for their services outside Syria. During 'Abdulmalik's reign this practice was extended either as a reward or as encouragement to join in a particular action.[5] As we shall see, there were many such occasions at that time so that by the end of his reign most of the Syrians were paid regular stipends, and their services were required all over the empire.

1 Balādhurī, *Futūḥ*, p. 153.

2 Ṭabarī, II, p. 407. Balādhurī, *Ansāb*, vol. IV, p. 33. Although stipends are mentioned in these reports, these were most probably the stipends of the men brought from Cyprus.

3 Balādhurī, *Ansāb*, vol. V, p. 149; Ṭabarī, II, p. 487.

4 Balādhurī, *Ansāb*, vol. V, p. 136; Ṭabarī, II, pp. 477–8.

5 Ṭabarī, II, p. 893; Balādhurī, *Ansāb*, vol. V, 368; vol. XI, p. 58; Mas'ūdī, *Murūj*, vol. V, p. 200.

6

THE AGE OF ḤAJJĀJ

When ʿAbdulmalik came to power in 685/65, he probably had no clear political purpose other than the restoration of the stability of Muʿāwiya's reign through the implementation of the same cautious policies. Of course this was to the Syrians' advantage and obviously that was the reason for their support of Marwān and ʿAbdulmalik. While this approach assured the stability of Syria, the power base of the central government, it offered no solution to the chronic problems of the rest of the empire. ʿAbdulmalik must have realized that the second civil war had shown the inadequacy of such an approach, but he was also aware of the inherent risks involved in introducing any fundamental changes, particularly when such unstable conditions existed in the empire. Consequently, he proceeded to rule very carefully, proposed no basic changes and tried to cope with new situations in the empire with effective pragmatism. His approach to government was that of a practical ruler who saw no reason to depart from inherited policies until events absolutely demanded that he should. Undoubtedly he was an able ruler, but he seems to have lacked the imagination and foresight necessary to devise long-range policies on a systematic basis. He acted forcefully mainly in response to events in the empire rather than on his own initiative, and such actions provoked strong opposition which in turn called for still stronger measures. As a result measures which were meant to be of a temporary nature solidified into hard policies and became characteristic of the authoritarian rule of the last half of ʿAbdulmalik's twenty-year reign. What was worse, his policies became the political orthodoxy of all but five of the fifty years of power remaining to the Marwānids.

One of the main reasons why the policy which we always associate with ʿAbdulmalik and his trusty lieutenant Ḥajjāj was so long in emerging, is that a major change in policy also involved Iraq which, from the time of the conquests, had been the most turbulent and ungovernable of all the provinces. In the first half of his reign ʿAbdulmalik had far too many pressing concerns elsewhere to involve himself in the maelstrom of its politics. In the first place, the rival *Amīr al-Mu'minīn* in Makka was by no means completely defeated. In fact it took eight years to eliminate Ibn al-Zubayr and subdue the remaining centres of opposition, Makka and Madīna. When the problem was settled 'Abdulmalik had to turn his attention to North Africa where the Berber tribes had taken advantage of the civil war to throw off Arab domination. In 694/74 Syrian troops poured into North Africa, subdued the Berbers and eventually advanced the Arab front to Tangier. So successful were they that many Berbers were converted to Islam and 12,000 of them were recruited into the Arab army. Indeed, the subsequent conquest of Spain was their achievement rather than that of the Arabs.[1]

Even if 'Abdulmalik had given thought to the problems of Iraq, at no point in the first ten years of his reign was he in a position to put his thoughts into action; nonetheless, something had to be done there. Although Syria was the main pillar of the Marwānid regime, Iraq effectively dominated internal politics in the sense that its problems occupied most of the time of every ruler, rather than that her interests dominated all political decisions. For it was not only by far the most turbulent and unstable of the provinces, it was also the province with the most Arabs. At a very rough estimate it had three times as many tribesmen as Syria. While Syrian expeditions never exceeded about 30,000 men, Ziyād and Ḥajjāj at different times organized emigrations of a similar number to the East to get rid of Iraq's excess Arab population.[2]

At first 'Abdulmalik entrusted the governorship of Iraq to his own brother, Bishr b. Marwān. Bishr seems to have done little and to have been rather ineffectual. This was, no doubt, the reason for his appointment, since 'Abdulmalik would not at that time have risked an energetic governor in Iraq. As one might expect, affairs in Iraq were far from satisfactory during Bishr's governorship. The main problem was the lukewarmness of the Kūfans' support of the Marwānid regime and of the Baṣrans towards the campaign against the neo-*khawārij* in their own dependent territories. The lack of Kūfan interest in a fight for Baṣran terri-

[1] Ibn Khaldūn, *Kitāb al-'Ibar*, Cairo, A.H. 1284, vol. VI, p. 109; Ibn 'Abdilḥakam, *Futūḥ Miṣr*, p. 201; Athīr, *Kāmil*, vol. IV, p. 302.

[2] Balādhurī, *Ansāb*, vol. V, 167.

tories was perhaps not surprising. But the Baṣrans themselves gave virtually no help to Muhallab and his men in the reconquest of Baṣran lands from the neo-*khawārij*. To make matters worse they even grudged Muhallab's army the promised share of the revenues from the reconquered territories.[1] The tribesmen were convinced that they deserved their stipends not for serving in the army but merely for being Arabs.

It had always been a danger that these tribesmen might fail to join the annual expeditions, and as the problem became more serious the penalties became more severe. Under 'Umar and 'Uthmān the penalty was public humiliation by the formal throwing off of the offender's turban. Under Ibn al-Zubayr such an offender was made to shave his head and beard. Bishr allegedly took even more severe measures: the offender was virtually crucified on a wall.[2] But savage though this penalty was, stopping just short of death, it did not solve the problem, and the neo-*khawārij* were still not defeated by the end of Bishr's governorship.

The turning-point of 'Abdulmalik's reign was the year 695/75. By then he had defeated Ibn al-Zubayr and the Berbers, so at last he had the time and the power to attend to the problems of Iraq. After the death of the ineffectual Bishr he appointed al-Ḥajjāj of Thaqīf as the new governor. Ḥajjāj, still a young man in his thirties, had given proof of his remarkable abilities in the civil war. It was he who finally defeated Ibn al-Zubayr, and as governor brought Ḥijāz back under Marwānid control. 'Abdulmalik wished to avoid the threat to his family's reputation which the failure of another Marwānid in Iraq would cause, and Ḥajjāj was therefore the natural choice as the new governor. At first, neither 'Abdulmalik nor Ḥajjāj had any clear idea what should be done in Iraq, but they were resolved to replace the passive rule of Bishr by something altogether more energetic and efficient. This simple yet vague aim was to involve a major change in policy.

The first three years of Ḥajjāj's governorship were spent in getting control of the situation. As so often in Iraq, this first stage meant suppressing a large number of rebellions. Ḥajjāj's first duty was to break the tribesmen's habit of neglecting to go on campaign. As in all his activities Ḥajjāj's solution was ruthlessly simple; if a man did not join his expedition he was beheaded, and

[1] Balādhurī, *Ansāb*, vol. XI, p. 103; Ṭabarī, II, pp. 584, 857.
[2] Athīr, *Kāmil*, vol. IV, p. 308; Balādhurī, *Ansāb*, vol. XI, p. 270.

no excuse was acceptable. The results were encouraging, if rather surprising for Muhallab. Kūfans and Baṣrans, and even some of the ex-*qurrā'*, joined his army to fight the neo-*khawārij*.[1] It was a rather uncomfortable campaign for it was hard to get Iraqi tribesmen and Muhallab's mainly 'Umāni forces to co-operate, but it did fulfil its aim and the neo-*khawārij* were again chased out of Ahwāz and Fārs into Kirmān farther to the east. At this point the uncomfortable coalition was dissolved and Muhallab, perhaps to his relief, was left to follow up this success with his own forces.[2]

Some, though not many, prominent Iranian converts, for example Fairūz Ḥuṣayn, a very rich landowner in Iraq, had fought against the neo-*khawārij*,[3] for it was in the interests of this class that the established government should be stable. The same did not apply to the native population in Kirmān, the last refuge of the neo-*khawārij*. The history of Kirmān had been rather unusual. As mentioned before, it was finally subdued during 'Abdullah b. 'Āmir's first campaign to Khurāsān in 651/31. Our sources are exceptionally clear about the details of the subsequent Arab colonization. Many of the local inhabitants fled, abandoning their lands, and the small number of Arab tribesmen who decided to settle in Kirmān duly divided this land amongst themselves, cultivated it and paid their tithes.[4] Thereafter our sources do not indicate any disturbance in Kirmān, so we must conclude that these Arabs were assimilated unusually quickly into the indigenous population. It is also very probable that many of the original inhabitants accepted Islam as a result of this close association with the Arabs. They all paid their taxes and tithes and since there were no Kirmāni Arabs registered in the *dīwān*, especially after Ziyād's reorganization, the revenues went to Baṣra.

At first, the arrival of the neo-*khawārij* did not disturb this happy state of affairs. They set up as usual an independent republic of Kirmān under their own *Amīr al-Mu'minīn* and proceeded to appropriate the revenue, dividing it among themselves. This arrangement had considerable advantages for the Kirmānis. To begin with they were very leniently treated by their new masters. In fact the *khawārij* in general had a reputation for mild-

[1] Athīr, *Kāmil*, vol. IV, p. 316; Mubarrad, *Kāmil*, vol. II, p. 670; Ṭabarī, II, p. 876.
[2] Ṭabarī, II, pp. 877–8.
[3] *Ibid.*, pp. 1019–20; Mubarrad, *Kāmil*, vol. II, p. 654.
[4] See above p. 85.

ness towards a conquered people whether converted, i.e. *mawālī*, or not. Equally it was to the advantage of the Kirmānis, Arabs and non-Arabs, to break the tie with Baṣra, which was after all merely one between tax-payer and tax-collector. Now that Kirmān was a *khawārij* republic the tax revenues stayed in Kirmān and what was more were spent there. It was an arrangement which suited everyone, but it was not to last for very long. Muhallab was moving uncomfortably close to Kirmān, and the local population had a shrewd idea of the perils involved in harbouring the rebels against him. Therefore under the leadership of a *mawlā*, one 'Abdurabbihi, the whole population, Arab, *mawālī* and non-Muslims, rose against the neo-*khawārij*, who were forced to flee to the Caspian mountains.[1] There they were annihilated by the Syrian troops recently sent to Iraq.[2] Kirmān returned to the Baṣran fold and Iraq was finally free of the neo-*khawārij*. This particular movement, stemming from the alliance of Ḥanīfa and other tribesmen of eastern Arabia with the remnants of the *qurrā'-khawārij*, was now definitely at an end. Ibn al-Athīr was certain of it, and it is unfortunate that modern historians are often not quite clear about which *khawārij* were under discussion.[3]

'Abdulmalik was less successful in dealing with the source of the trouble in central and eastern Arabia. He succeeded only in cutting off the rebels from the sea and thus from their fellow tribesmen across the Gulf.[4] However they merely retired inland, where indeed pockets of them are still to be found, notably in 'Umān.

This was by no means the end of Ḥajjāj's problems. Baṣra was faced with a large financial deficit because of the loss of so much of its revenue and the expense of recovering it. Ḥajjāj therefore felt himself justified in cancelling the 100 dirham increase of the stipends ordered by Ibn al-Zubayr in the hope of encouraging the Baṣrans' enthusiasm.[5] Although economically he was justified, it was an unwise risk to take before he had established himself in a position of real strength. This problem was further complicated by the fact that Ḥajjāj was trying to strengthen his position in Iraq. Realizing that even strong measures against the tribesmen

[1] Mubarrad, *Kāmil*, vol. II, pp. 657, 686; Ṭabarī, II, p. 1007.

[2] Ṭabarī, II, pp. 1018–21.

[3] Athīr, *Kāmil*, vol. IV, p. 359.

[4] Ṭabarī, II, pp. 852–3.

[5] *Ibid.*, p. 874; Balādhurī, *Ansāb*, vol. V, p. 271.

were not sufficient to make them a reliable force to carry out the government's plans, he began to recruit the nucleus of what can best be called a standing army. Of course the main problem was to find enough tribesmen to enrol anew in such a force, especially when Ḥajjāj fixed the rate of payment at 300 dirhams a year.[1] Nevertheless, after the suppression of the neo-*khawārij* uprisings there were enough men with no particular ties, and probably other young men in Kūfa and Baṣra, to start such a project, given enough encouragement. Ḥajjāj's genius for discovering and training young leaders and his need for forces to hold the countryside, by now free from the ravages of the neo-*khawārij*, provided the answer. He gathered around him young men of the calibre of Qutayba b. Muslim and appointed them sub-governors of the districts of Iraq and western Iran.[2] In the long run these new appointments, at what may be called Ḥajjāj's "school" of governors, proved an invaluable training in the art of government. In the short run they also proved their value by encouraging tribesmen to enlist in the new force and join these new appointees in their districts.[3] It must be emphasized that this project was then only at the formative stage and these sub-governors were not supposed to be accompanied by great armies. The biggest number of newly enlisted recruits was 3,000 men stationed at Rayy, presumably to secure the main route to Khurāsān.[4] It should also be noted that this force could be called upon, when needed, to help enforce Ḥajjāj's will in Iraq.

The Baṣrans were the first to be immediately affected by Ḥajjāj's decision to cancel the 100-dirham increase of the stipends. They regarded this measure as a means of enabling Ḥajjāj to recruit a new force which would eventually be used against their interest, and were quick to revolt. Ḥajjāj was only just able to ride out the storm and then only because of the unexpectedly devoted support of men like Qutayba b. Muslim.[5] 'Abdulmalik himself reprimanded Ḥajjāj for such unwise conduct, and the latter had to give way with as much grace and speed as he could muster.

Ḥajjāj was lucky to escape so lightly for immediately afterwards a rather obscure revolt broke out among the slaves working

[1] Balādhurī, *Ansāb*, vol. XI, p. 273.
[2] Ṭabarī, II, pp. 962, 979–80.
[3] *Ibid.*, pp. 890, 899, 948.
[4] Ṭabarī, II, p. 996.
[5] Athīr, *Kāmil*, vol. IV, p. 311; Ṭabarī, II, pp. 873–4.

in the farms around Baṣra. We have no information about the working conditions of these slaves or even about the circumstances under which they had been brought there and put to such work. Nevertheless, the fact that they were used at all indicates the extent of land reclamation in the marches around Baṣra at this early stage. Their living and working conditions must have been intolerable because they seized the first opportunity to revolt. Their leader was a certain Ribāḥ, who took the high-sounding title of Shīr-i Zanj, the Lion of the Negro slaves. The numbers involved in this revolt must have been small for the Baṣrans put it down with ease, but it is interesting as the precursor of the much more dangerous slave revolt of two centuries later.[1]

Much more serious in its immediate results was yet another "Khārijiṭe" revolt in the district of Mawṣil. Its causes, as with most such risings, were complex, but basically it was precipitated among some *qurrā'-khawārij*, who had fled from Kūfa and settled in the district of Mawṣil. Eventually 'Abdulmalik decided to reorganize the area, bringing it under greater control. There were several reasons for this decision. The district was part of Kūfan territory but it was relatively unimportant from the point of view of revenue. Its principal inhabitants were the Christian clans of Taghlib who held a privileged position, since they were hostile to the Byzantines. They were exempted from the normal land taxes and the poll-tax that Christians had to pay, being required to pay only twice the amount of Muslim tithes.[2] Their main occupation was raising cattle on the rich pasture lands of the region, which were also basically good arable lands. The Qaysite tribesmen of the adjacent districts of Jazīra took advantage of the civil war to try to appropriate these lands[3] and naturally this led to fighting, particularly dangerous in this frontier area. The Byzantines began to take action and the situation could have become very serious. Vigorous action was clearly called for and 'Abdulmalik provided it in full measure. He bought off the Byzantines at the humiliating price of 1,000 dinārs a week, and ended the struggle by threatening to interfere in the fight on the side of Taghlib against the Qaysites, a move which won him the vociferous gratitude of their famed poet al-Akhṭal.[4] He also decided to

[1] Athīr, *Kāmil*, vol. IV, pp. 314–15.
[2] Balādhurī, *Futūḥ*, pp. 181–3.
[3] Balādhurī, *Ansāb*, vol. V, pp. 313, 314, 317.
[4] *Ibid.*, p. 324; Ṭabarī, II, p. 796.

incorporate Mawṣil in the newly formed province of Jazīra so that the governor could prevent any further incidents of this kind. Nobody in Kūfa objected and there the matter might have rested had not some of the *qurrā'-khawārij* settled in Mawṣil.

These were some of the few remaining *khawārij* of Nahrawān who had fled as far north as Mawṣil. Although they had still kept contact with their colleagues in Kūfa, Mu'āwiya seems to have left them alone.[1] Presumably he regarded them as a group of no importance who were actually doing the state some service by settling in a vulnerable frontier area. But 'Abdulmalik underestimated their capacity for mischief. Now that they were losing their freedom of action through his reorganization they became desperate and rose in revolt. Some 120 men from various clans joined under the leadership of Ṣāliḥ b. Musarriḥ of Tamīm, and after his death, under the leadership of Shabīb b. Yazīd b. Nu'aym of Shaybān.[2] Shabīb was born at the end of 646/25, his mother being a Greek slave whom his father had acquired while on an expedition in Byzantine territory.[3] His father was one of the *qurrā'* along with Ṣāliḥ b. Musarriḥ and the latter expressly invited Shabīb, who was in Kūfa at the time, to join the revolt.[4] Shabīb was a virtuoso in guerrilla warfare and a man with an extraordinary flair for the dramatic. The same is true of his wife Ghazāla who was his constant companion in his exploits. Together they worked wonders with little material. At no stage did their following exceed 800 and most of the time it was much less. None the less it is reported that Shabīb with a force of only 181 men defeated a Kūfan force of 6,000 led by no less a person than Ibn al-Ash'ath himself. Shabīb's great advantage was his extreme mobility and immense tactical skill. No matter how many expeditions Ḥajjāj sent against him from Kūfa, Shabīb invariably baffled them. Shabīb's other great advantage was his tremendous popularity. Many Kūfans sympathized with him, for in a sense he was defending their interests. In addition Shabīb possessed a sense of humour which greatly enhanced his popularity, particularly in comparison with the dour Ḥajjāj. Twice he had the audacity to enter Kūfa when the mighty Ḥajjāj was in residence and play practical jokes on him. Ghazāla even made her prayers in the central mosque, reciting the two longest chapters in the Qur'ān,

[1] Ṭabarī, II, pp. 127, 142. [2] *Ibid.*, p. 887. [3] *Ibid.*, p. 977.
[4] Ibn Ḥazm, *Jambara*, p. 237; Ṭabarī, II, p. 885.

to the infinite humiliation of Ḥajjāj and the endless amusement of everyone else. But all this had a serious side to it. There was no better way than ridicule to undermine the already precarious authority of Ḥajjāj and ʿAbdulmalik. The Baṣran revolt over, the stipends policy had done considerable damage to Ḥajjāj's prestige, and now this small group of guerrillas was laughing to scorn what little was left of it. Indeed Shabīb had started secret talks with Kūfan notabilities like Ibn al-Ashʿath and even Muṭarrif, the sub-governor of Madā'in, a cousin of Ḥajjāj and the son of al-Mughīra b. Shuʿba, whose loyalty to the Umayyads was almost exemplary. The situation was rapidly becoming impossible, and ʿAbdulmalik and Ḥajjāj were forced to deploy 6,000 Syrian troops in Iraq. This put an end to the lackadaisical activities of the Kūfan expeditions and soon Shabīb was defeated and killed in battle.[1]

Almost immediately after this, another so-called Khārijite revolt took place. This was the most unusual of these risings as it was led by an important member of Ḥajjāj's "establishment", Muṭarrif b. al-Mughīra b. Shuʿba of Thaqīf, the sub-governor of Madā'in. The ex-*qurrā'* were in no way involved, and although Muṭarrif had indeed been flirting with the idea of allying himself with Shabīb, in reality the two had nothing in common.[2] Muṭarrif was quite explicit and specific in his aims; he opposed the ʿAbdulmalik–Ḥajjāj policy of using Syrian troops in Iraq and the inexorably increasing authority of the *Amīr al-Mu'minīn*; he wanted the revival of the Madīnan regime under Qurayshite leadership, conceding a large measure of autonomy to the provinces.[3] The dangerous aspect of this revolt was that Muṭarrif tried to arouse the new Iraqi recruits against Ḥajjāj and was almost successful, as is evident from the fact that Ḥajjāj had to call in the Syrian troops to quell the revolt.[4] These soon crushed the rebellion with all their usual efficiency. They were temporarily stationed in Kūfa and forcibly quartered in the houses of its inhabitants.[5] They were to all intents and purposes an army of occupation. Ḥajjāj had at last gained control of the situation and his triumph was

[1] Attempting to emphasize the importance of this episode, Ṭabarī (II, pp. 880–979) devotes no less than one hundred pages to its details.

[2] Ṭabarī, II, pp. 983–7.

[3] *Ibid.*, pp. 984, 988, 993.

[4] *Ibid.*, pp. 989, 993, 996.

[5] *Ibid.*, p. 1069; Athīr, *Kāmil*, vol. IV, pp. 376, 385.

rewarded by 'Abdulmalik's decision to entrust him with the East as well.

It was now 698/79 and the positive policy characteristic of Ḥajjāj began to emerge. The next three years formed a transitional period between the long series of revolts in his first years as governor and the emergence of a fully fledged policy with the defeat of Ibn al-Ash'ath's revolt in 701/82. It cannot be overemphasized that affairs and policies were still very much in flux. To take the most important question, it had not yet been decided to have a permanent Syrian garrison in Iraq. As we have already shown it had originally been neither intended nor possible to use Syrian troops in Iraq. Even the 6,000 men sent in to defeat Shabīb had been asked for and sent with great reluctance, and it was hoped to withdraw them at the earliest possible opportunity.

Now that the province was at peace, Ḥajjāj could turn his attention to the social and economic consequences of the civil war and the long succession of rebellions. The ravages of these wars had caused the peasants to leave their land, either for safety or to avoid the taxes which were becoming all too difficult to pay because of the damage done to the delicate but vital irrigation system, or through a combination of both. This influx of peasants into the towns was creating a major social problem, since there was not adequate employment for them, and also a major economic problem, since the fall in agricultural production meant a corresponding fall in tax receipts. As always Ḥajjāj's solution was ruthlessly simple and logical: he ordered all the peasants back to their lands.[1] Many of them had become Muslims and were therefore in theory entitled to go where they pleased and be treated in all things like any Arab Muslim. Ḥajjāj was not the man to put theological niceties above the interests of the state, and such protests as were raised he simply ignored.

As for the Arabs, Ḥajjāj felt he had seen far more of their military abilities in Iraq than he liked, so following a long-standing tradition he determined to direct them outwards. He first got rid of al-Muhallab's army, which was still in Kirmān, by appointing al-Muhallab as his deputy in Khurāsān. The army, of course, followed its general.[2] Then, in 697/78, he dispatched an Iraqi

[1] Ṭabarī, II, pp. 1122–3; Balādhurī, *Ansāb*, vol. XI, pp. 336–7.
[2] Ṭabarī, II, p. 1033.

army, recruited from Kūfa and Baṣra, to Sīstān in the south-east to reopen the front against Zunbīl, the king of Zābulistān. As had happened before, Arab tactics were inappropriate in this mountainous region. The expedition was a disaster; the army was virtually wiped out and its general died of grief. Ḥajjāj was not to be deterred. The situation inspired him to repeat the mass emigration organized by Ziyād thirty years earlier. Deciding to kill two birds with one stone, he encouraged all the most troublesome elements in Kūfa and Baṣra to join the expedition of 40,000 men that he planned, carefully concealing the fact that this was no ordinary expedition but an enforced emigration. No expense was spared and the "Army of Peacocks" was truly royally equipped. But it was not for that that it was so called: "Peacocks" referred to the men rather than their accoutrements. It included many of the proudest and most distinguished leaders in Iraq, led by the proudest and most distinguished of them all, ʿAbdulraḥman b. Muḥammad b. al-Ashʿath, grandson of the great leader of the *ridda* and the conquest of Iraq, al-Ashʿath b. Qays. It also included many of the highly distinguished old men who had fought in the first armies of conquest, such as ʿĀmir b. Wāthila, an acknowledged companion of the Prophet. Even some of the ex-*qurrā*ʾ, who had been at Ṣiffīn, and who were still alive, were persuaded to join.[1]

The army arrived in Sīstān in the spring of 699/79 and then advanced eastwards into Zābulistān winning several victories. None the less, no one was very happy about fighting in such inhospitable territory, and the army began to get restive. At this point Ḥajjāj showed his hand, and instructed them to continue advancing into the heart of Zābulistān regardless of the time of year or of how long it took. The army felt it had been tricked. Ḥajjāj had given no sign that this was not an ordinary expedition; that they should not return home in the autumn as usual after a spring and summer campaign. If it had merely been a question of *tajmīr al-buʿūth*, keeping the army on campaign for too long, that would have been bad enough, but enforced emigration was more than they could stand. Therefore the army mutinied and turned back vengefully upon Iraq. They gained considerable support on

[1] *Ibid.*, pp. 1065, 1076–7, 1086; Ibn Aʿtham, *Futūḥ*, vol. II, pp. 107B, 108A; Ibn Khayyāṭ, *Tārīkh*, vol. I, pp. 282–8; Dhahabī, *Tārīkh*, vol. II, p. 276, vol. III, pp. 82, 232.

their return. The Kūfans drove out their unwelcome guests, the Syrian army of occupation; they captured the treasury and divided the money equally, each receiving 200 dirhams, thus compensating themselves for not being members of the *dīwān*. At first the Kūfans tried to keep their rebellion and that of the Army of Peacocks separate, but they were soon compelled to join forces. The Baṣrans also joined the revolt and forced Ḥajjāj out of the city.

Ḥajjāj was now encamped outside Baṣra, sending desperate calls for reinforcements to ʿAbdulmalik and only just able to hold his ground against the rebels.

ʿAbdulmalik wasted no time and sent every Syrian he could spare or find, not waiting to assemble them into sizeable contingents, but sending them as they came to him, often in groups as small as fifty or one hundred. Eventually ʿAbdulmalik was able to send two large Syrian contingents under his son ʿAbdullah and his brother Muḥammad. The assembled forces inflicted a crushing defeat on the rebels at the very beginning of 701/82. The leader of the revolt, Ibn al-Ashʿath, fled to Sīstān where he met his death in 704/85, while some of his followers scattered to the East. After such a rebellion ʿAbdulmalik and Ḥajjāj had no choice but to impose a permanent Syrian occupation on Iraq. Kūfa and Baṣra were completely demilitarized and a new garrison town was built at Wāsiṭ, half-way between Kūfa and Baṣra, to house the permanent Syrian garrison in Iraq, and in addition those Iraqi tribesmen who preferred to join the Iraqi army, *muqātila*.[1]

After this Ḥajjāj never had to face a serious rebellion for the remaining fourteen years of his governorship. Nothing of major importance happened in the remaining five years of ʿAbdulmalik's reign, so we can now sum up the fully developed policy which we must always associate with him. The easiest way of describing it is as the centralization of government around an authoritarian *Amīr al-Muʾminīn*. It is at this stage, when there was some semblance of administrative machinery to control the empire, that one can properly speak about a central government. It would be an exaggeration to talk about such things as existing under the Madīnan regime, though, perhaps, ʿUthmān had made some tentative moves in this direction. But, beginning with Muʿāwiya, there had been clear signs of the development of such institutions. Undeniably there was a central government in

[1] For details see Shaban, *The ʿAbbāsid Revolution*, pp. 67–9.

Damascus which had some control over the provinces, at least, through the full co-operation of Mu'āwiya's carefully chosen governors. But it was a very tenuous control completely dependent on the maintenance of a delicate balance of power. No doubt Mu'āwiya's power was strengthened by the solid support of the Syrians, but he was also helped by inheriting a viable administration in Syria from the Byzantines. While the Madīnan regime had no such asset, Mu'āwiya could try to expand this machinery to the level of an imperial administration.[1] This was not an easy task and there were not enough Arabs properly trained to take over all the functions of such a complex machine. However, it was possible to correlate the policies of the provincial governments in Iraq and Egypt with the general policies of the central government. Certainly, the appointment of Ziyād b. Abī Sufyān, who was well versed in the administration of Iraq, as governor of this province, was a significant step in this direction. During Mu'āwiya's reign the central government could only be concerned and effective at the highest level of general policies; it could not exercise direct control over the provinces and refrained from doing so.

Although Mu'āwiya's government proved inadequate, 'Abdulmalik had no choice at first but to follow along the same lines. He probably hoped that in due course the existing administration would mature into a more comprehensive imperial government, first by strengthening provincial administrations and then by integrating them all into a central government. The Syrian administration was being methodically developed and was well under control.[2] Iraq had problems which had to be solved before any attempt could be made to introduce innovations. Egypt, where peace prevailed, was the ideal province to put such a plan into effect. Its governor was 'Abdulmalik's own brother, 'Abdul-'azīz b. Marwān. During his governorship of twenty years (685–705/65–85) a fundamental change in the organization of the province was quietly and successfully carried out. Previously all the Arabs had been stationed at the garrison town of Fusṭāṭ with rotating garrisons at Alexandria and Khirbetā. With the conquest of North Africa this system became less relevant. Under the new system the garrison at Fusṭāṭ was disbanded and the Arabs were dispersed around various parts of Egypt, especially

[1] Ṭabarī, II, p. 837. [2] *Ibid.*, pp. 837–8.

along the Mediterranean coast.[1] Thus the security of the province against Byzantine attack was assured, while at the same time the Arabs could keep a closer watch over the activities of the native Egyptian officials.[2] Furthermore, for the first time stipends, *'aṭā'*, were instituted and organized for all the Arab tribesmen in Egypt, the average stipend being probably twenty-five dinārs in addition to the foodstuffs distributed to them.[3] Apparently the number of Arab tribesmen settled in Egypt at that time was between 30,000 and 40,000 men.[4] These tribesmen were now released from the confines of the unnatural life of a garrison town and were transformed into a proper army of occupation. They were made responsible for the security and stability of the province and were adequately paid for their services. Their leaders were, naturally, made responsible for the proper administration of their districts and Arab rule effectively reached the grass roots in the whole province.

In Iraq, the lack of reliable forces hampered Ḥajjāj's attempt to establish a similar system, even on a limited scale. His province was much bigger than Egypt, and Kūfa and Baṣra were far more developed than Fusṭāṭ which had never progressed beyond the strict limitations of a garrison town at that stage. The revolt of Muṭarrif b. al-Mughīra convinced Ḥajjāj of the futility of relying on forces from within to control the province. Such an attempt had simply failed and Syrians had to be brought in to save the situation. Now that a Syrian army occupied Iraq, Ḥajjāj had an opportunity to establish firm control over the administration of the province and its dependent territories. Again, sub-governors were appointed to the various districts, only this time their full powers were backed by the all-powerful governor and the Syrian troops if necessary. The governor himself was completely under the control of 'Abdulmalik and faithfully carried out his explicit instructions. A chain of authority, emanating from the increasingly powerful office of the *Amīr al-Mu'minīn* and reaching down to the local district level, was effectively in control of most of the empire.

In Damascus the infant administration created by Mu'āwiya was gradually expanded to cope with and co-ordinate the activi-

[1] The governor himself set the example by moving his administration from Fusṭāṭ to Ḥilwān (Kindī, *Governors*, p. 49).
[2] *Ibid.*, pp. 59, 94. [3] *Ibid.*, pp. 45, 49, 50. [4] *Ibid.*, 42.

ties of the numerous members of this new imperial structure. Thus, the *dīwān al-khātam*, bureau of the signet, of Mu'āwiya was enlarged into a fully fledged department of state archives in Damascus.[1] In the same manner the provincial administrations were also expanded, although they remained strictly under the control of the governors. It was too early yet to attempt the complete integration of the bureacracies of the central government and the provinces. However, there seem to have been attempts to standardize the offices of the provincial administrations. This was most evident from the fact that the language of the public records, which until then had been Coptic, Greek or Pahlavi, was changed to Arabic. Of course this helped to increase the hold of provincial governors over the local administrations and to open the bureaucracy to Arabs. Similarly the central government gained a firmer control of the economy by issuing for the first time a standardized Arabic coinage. Previously Sāsānian silver dirhams and Byzantine gold dinārs had been the only coins in circulation, and even the few new coins issued from time to time had always been imitations of them only distinguishable by the occasional Islamic superscription. It was clearly unsatisfactory to be partly dependent upon the enemy for money supply. The new coins were successful in their object, and in particular those coined by Ḥajjāj, since they had less precious metal in them than the Byzantine and Sāsānian coinages.[2] On the principle that a bad coinage drives out the good, the new coins drove the Byzantine and Sāsānian out of circulation, which was what 'Abdulmalik intended.

More important in implementing 'Abdulmalik's policies was the actual power structure composed of the Syrian army, the *muqātila*, the governors and the Marwānid family. Under the circumstances, the Syrian army was the most important of these. It was gradually transformed from a regional militia, concerned only with its region's frontiers, into an imperial force to control the whole empire. Instead of making short summer forays into Byzantine territory, they were now asked to go as far as North Africa to suppress the Berber revolt. More demanding and certainly less rewarding was the fact that they were required to provide a garrison to control Iraq. Naturally these new activities

[1] Ṭabarī, II, pp. 285–6; Mas'ūdī, *Murūj*, p. 239.
[2] Balādhurī, *Futūḥ*, pp. 466, 488.

would have a profound effect on their, hitherto, almost normal way of life and they had to be compensated accordingly. ʿAbdulmalik had no choice but to extend the institution of stipends to all members of the Syrian army in exchange for their increasingly indispensable services. The Syrian *jund* became a standing army to be called upon when needed, but not necessarily a full-time army. The garrison at Wāsiṭ was composed not of Syrians permanently settled there but of Syrians sent there on a rotating basis. It remains to be said that although Jazīra was now a separate governorship, the tribesmen there who supported ʿAbdulmalik were treated for all practical purposes as part of the Syrian army. Stipends were issued to those who accepted military duty, and in fact Arabs from Iraq were encouraged to move to Mawṣil and enrol in the army,[1] probably indicating that some of the tribesmen of Jazīra were not sufficiently enthusiastic to join the army. The *muqātila* were those tribesmen of Iraq and the eastern regions who supported the regime and its expansionist policy. In exchange for their loyalty and support they received the normal stipends and share of booty and, just as important, they were often given a major part in ruling the countryside through the appointment of their leaders to sub-governorships. This, needless to say, opened to the sub-governor a gratifying vista of political patronage and personal gain, by means of the customary "gifts" presented to the Arab ruler in accordance with an old Sāsānian tradition.[2] The *muqātila* rapidly transformed itself into a privileged caste; they became in a way a respectable Marwānid version of the *qurrā*'.

The governors and the Marwānid house slightly overlap for the simple reason that so many of the Marwānids were governors. To take the ordinary governors first. By the end of this reign they were nearly all pupils and protégés of Ḥajjāj. He had hand-picked and trained them. The youth lucky and able enough to be spotted by Ḥajjāj had a glowing future before him, for ʿAbdulmalik had implicit trust in Ḥajjāj's ability to detect talent and loyalty. Already in 705/86 his pupils were doing him credit with the full support of Damascus behind them. Particularly notable and devoted among them was Qutayba b. Muslim, who at that time was advancing the government's expansionist programme in Central Asia with an

[1] Ṭabarī, II, p. 893; Yaʿqūbī, *Tārīkh*, vol. II, p. 272.

[2] Ibn ʿAbdilḥakam, Abū Muḥammad ʿAbdullah, *Sīrat ʿUmar b. ʿAbdilʿazīz*, Cairo, 1927, p. 166.

exceptional enthusiasm and great success. Members of the Marwānid house held most of the other governorships. They were generally speaking given the easier, less exacting provinces in all but the most extreme situations. In the eastern provinces the chances of failure were too high for the comfort of a family which greatly valued its prestige. The dangerous provinces like Iraq and the East were, as we have seen, usually assigned to such as Ḥajjāj and his protégés, men whose acts redounded to the credit of the ruling family when successful, and to their own discredit when failures. In brief, by the end of his reign ʿAbdulmalik had a fast developing bureaucracy at his disposal and governors whom he could trust.

The importance of the Marwānid family in the regime is worthy of emphasis. It will have been noticed that throughout this chapter we have always said Marwānid rather than Umayyad. The difference is important, for the direct Sufyānid line ends with Muʿāwiya II. From then onwards Marwān and his descendants held the supreme power. This is no mere genealogical quibble for in political terms there is a great difference between the cautious rule of the Sufyānids and the authoritarianism of the Marwānids. Also the Marwānid family as a unit was of unusual importance. One of the most characteristic aspects of Marwānid politics was the emphasis on the collective rights of the ruling family. Unlike the Sufyānids, the Marwānids increased and multiplied with some vigour, which was no doubt a great advantage in their rise to power. They then capitalized on their large families by creating what can only be called collective rule. The *Amīr al-Mu'minīn* kept his almost absolute authority in theory, but in practice he had to share his power with the family, because it was to it as a whole rather than to the individual ruler that the crucial loyalty of the Syrian troops was directed. Thus the very choice of the *Amīr al-Mu'minīn* depended upon the agreement of the family, and when in power he had to see that the family was suitably rewarded, consulted and employed. The suitable employment we have already described. We have only to add here that appointing Marwānids to governorships had the advantage, besides all the others, of training the family's future leaders.

Such was the power structure of the regime, and it was all in the service of an *Amīr al-Mu'minīn* who made no claims to religious authority, but whom circumstances and his own pragmatic policies had forced into a position of almost absolute secular authority. By the end of 'Abdulmalik's reign this power structure had become strong and efficient, as the remarkable calm and stability of his successor's reign shows. 'Abdulmalik was succeeded by his son Walīd, who in turn was to be succeeded by a second son, Sulaymān. Walīd I's reign (705–15/86–96) was in every way a direct continuation of his father's and was unruffled. Ḥajjāj remained in power, in fact he became more powerful, and the same policies were followed. The only difference was that the tranquillity of these years allowed Walīd to develop further the internal implications of the 'Abdulmalik–Ḥajjāj policy.

A combination of Marwānids and Ḥajjājites continued to rule the empire. Sulaymān, the heir-apparent, was receiving his training as governor of Palestine, while his brother Maslama was establishing his military reputation on the Byzantine borders. 'Umar b. 'Abdil'azīz, Walīd's cousin, governed Madīna for the next seven years, but his history showed that Ḥajjāj had become too powerful for even a Marwānid to be safe in his position. He was dismissed in 712/93 in favour of a Ḥajjāj protégé, not because of incompetence but because he carried his well known disapproval of Ḥajjāj's policies to the lengths of welcoming and protecting the latter's Iraqi political opponents in Madīna.[1]

The wars of conquest continued in full spate in North Africa and Central Asia. Ḥajjāj even opened a new front into India through that part of the Indus valley now known as Balūchistān. More interesting and novel was Walīd's social and economic policy. The period is notable for a remarkable increase in government spending on public works of every kind, and on what would appear to be an extraordinarily enlightened welfare policy. This was not completely novel, for 'Abdulmalik had shown some interest in public building – it was he who built the Dome of the Rock – but to nothing like as great an extent as his son. Ḥajjāj had also spent considerable public funds on restoring and extending the Iraqi irrigation system, particularly in the south, and he continued to do so. Ḥajjāj's reasons for these public works are clear enough; he had to restore a sophisticated agricultural system which had been damaged during long years of war, and extend it to provide employment for the demilitarized populations of Kūfa and Baṣra. But Walīd I's projects,

[1] Ṭabarī, II, p. 1254.

mainly in Syria and Ḥijāz, were altogether more elaborate and it is rather more difficult to see the rationale behind them.

The most plausible approach is to consider the general economic situation of the time. The empire under Walīd I inherited two things from 'Abdulmalik – enormous wealth from the new conquests and what was in effect a debased coinage. At the same time the cities of the empire were growing at a far faster rate than the trade and industry that should have provided employment for the new urban masses. Moreover, the regime was prodigally generous in grants of lands and money to the ruling house, Arab leaders, poets and even to its ancestral enemy, the family of the Prophet. In short, all the ingredients were there for social unrest. Walīd therefore applied some of the treasury's immense wealth to the improvement of urban conditions. In fact all of this money was spent in the towns. Numerous mosques of magnificent proportions, notably the Umayyad mosque in Damascus, hospitals and roads were constructed. These buildings did indeed have some utilitarian purpose, but in many cases they were built on a more lavish scale than was necessary in order to provide the urban unemployed with work.[1] These projects were planned mostly for the benefit of the non-Arab populations of Syria whose skills could be usefully put to such work; the unskilled could certainly provide the cheap labour. Although one cannot consider these plans as of long-term economic importance, they were a step in the right direction. For the first time the Arab rulers were thinking in terms of the relief of the problems of the subject population, at least that of Syria. Undoubtedly, those involved were of the lower class; one cannot talk of a middle class at this period. In the imperial scheme of ideas there were only two social classes: the ruling Arab class, and the subjected indigenous population.

Although naturally the upper class was well taken care of, nevertheless there were poor elements within it, such as the lepers, the chronically sick and the blind. For the benefit of these Walīd I devised what can best be described as a special state subsidy to the ruling class. One must not forget that this was a strongly patriarchal society in which the unfortunates were the ultimate responsibility of their more fortunate kin. True, the Qur'ān had clearly intended the alms for the poor Muslims but the system of alms collection had changed since the time of 'Uthmān. The original

[1] *Ibid.*, pp. 1193–6; Dhahabī, *Tārīkh*, vol. IV, p. 46.

system had been that alms due on any kind of riches were assessed, collected and delivered to the public treasury by an official appointed for this purpose, *'āmil al-ṣadaqa*. The change of direction from trade to conquests had brought enormous wealth, which had rendered alms irrelevant. The payment of alms was left to the conscience of the individual, except for those alms due on lands held by Muslims. This Muslim land tax continued to be paid to the tax-collectors, just like any other land tax.[1] The state collected these alms in the form of tithes on the produce of the land and accordingly the welfare of the poor became one of its special responsibilities. Walīd I saw this responsibility as extending only to Arab Muslims, and he therefore allocated pensions to them only. He even went further and gave the blind, of whom there were many, slaves to guide their steps.[2] The new conquests had brought a great number of war captives as part of the fifth of the booty. As a result slave prices were greatly reduced and the cost to the treasury was comparatively low, but the satisfaction of the ruling Arabs was more assured.[3] In this light the "welfare programme" of Walīd I can be easily understood as no more than a "gigantic system of relief for the ruling class".

Ḥajjāj died in 714/95, almost a year before Walīd I's own death, a fortunate occurrence for he himself was perfectly aware of the humiliation he would be subject to under Sulaymān.[4] It was no secret that Sulaymān would follow completely different policies but nothing could be done about it. 'Abdulmalik's wish that Sulaymān should succeed Walīd I was absolutely clear and had been accepted by all members of his family before his death. It might be thought surprising that the validity of a policy which had worked so smoothly for at least fifteen years should now be questioned. This policy, however, had had a profound effect on the lives of all the population of the empire. It had devoted supporters but it had also provoked strong opposition. In modern times such a division on public questions would take the form of political parties. Thirteen centuries ago such sophisticated machinery did not exist, yet there were important public issues on which people took a stand. Reports on the history of this period are full of the names of groups united in a cause. These names can

[1] Ibn Sallām, *Amwāl*, pp. 568, 573; Al-Suyūṭī, *Tārīkh al-Khulafā'*, Cairo, n.d., p. 164.
[2] Ṭabarī, II, p. 1271; Dhahabī, *Tārīkh*, vol. IV, p. 67.
[3] Dhahabī, *Tārīkh*, vol. IV, p. 62.
[4] Ṭabarī, II, p. 1272.

be as easy to explain as the *shī'a* or as complicated to trace as the *qurrā'*. It is the responsibility of the historian to find out the real issues which united people in a particular cause. At the same time he must be careful not to be misled by a superficial interpretation.

The continuation of the 'Abdulmalik–Ḥajjāj policies remained a major controversial issue, not only during their lives but for the rest of the Umayyad era. One central theme of their policies was expansion, with all its implications for the peoples involved all over the empire. Those who supported these policies came to be called Qays–Muḍar; those opposed were known as Yaman. Unfortunately these terms have been understood to indicate ordinary tribal factions. Certainly these words are the names of actual tribal groupings, but in this context they were used to indicate Arab groups who had a common interest which had nothing to do with tribal divisions. It should not be surprising that these names were put to such usage at that time. These were times when arbitrary or even artificial tribal names were imposed on various Arab groups for the purpose of town planning, army organization and the distribution of stipends. The meticulous genealogical tables provided by later Arab genealogists fail to tell us the exact tribal affiliations of many important clans such as Bajīla which played an important role in the conquest of Iraq.[1] They are not even certain whether the influential Syrian clans of Quḍā'a belong to the so-called Qays or Yaman divisions.[2]

It is significant that this conflict between Yaman and Qays–Muḍar existed only in the period under discussion. There was nothing of this nature in pre-Islamic times, in the *ridda* wars, in the wars of conquest and in all the disputes and fighting of the first civil war. After the fall of the Umayyads and the establishment of the 'Abbāsids, this conflict soon came to an end. It is absurd to interpret this conflict as simply a tribal squabble. It is equally absurd to see it as a conflict between so-called Northern and Southern Arabs. These interpretations do violence to the facts and sadly underrate Arabs' ability to grasp issues more relevant than those of tribal rivalries and jealousies. Indeed, important issues were at stake in this conflict, whether in the heart of the empire, in Syria and Iraq, or in the far away regions of

[1] *Ibid.*, pp. 2183–200.

[2] Balādhurī, *Ansāb al-Ashrāf*, vol. I, ed. M. Hamidullah, Cairo, 1959, pp. 15–16; Al-Isfāhanī, *Aghānī*, vol. VIII, p. 90; Ibn Ḥazm, *Jamhara*, pp. 8, 440, 445.

Khurāsān and North Africa. And whenever conflict existed between these two groups, anywhere in the empire, men of the clans of Qays–Muḍar were to be found on the Yaman side and vice versa.[1]

At first, conflicts between these two groups occurred as isolated incidents and thus the basic factor, common to them all, was blurred. Naturally the group in power, the Qays–Muḍar, was aggressive, articulate and able to put forward positive policies, while the opposition, the Yaman, was disorganized and uncertain of its own mind. In fact at the beginning no fundamental disagreement was apparent between the two factions. It was the cumulative effect of the expansionist policy, added to their determination not to allow any change, that drove the Yaman into a more pronounced opposition. The final break-down of the Marwānid regime was due to the failure of these two groups to unite against the more radical supporters of the 'Abbāsid revolution.

There is a curious, though exact, analogy of the conflict between Qays–Muḍar and Yaman in the history of the Whigs and Tories of seventeenth-century England. It would be interesting to see what conclusions a modern historian would come to, if he followed the literal interpretations of the terms Whig and Tory. To interpret English history on the basis of a conflict between Scottish mare-drivers and Irish robbers would not be different from interpreting Islamic history on the basis of the tribal jealousies of Qays–Muḍar and Yaman.

The greatest weakness of the 'Abdulmalik–Ḥajjāj system was that it relied overmuch on wars of conquest as the universal panacea for all the empire's ills. It took no account of the assimilation which was beginning to take deep roots among the Arabs themselves in their new environment. Thus, the most important social development of the period was either ignored or opposed. This was an increasingly serious problem, because the more settled and assimilated tribesmen became, the more they were inconvenienced by and opposed to the policy of perpetual war. The result was that the movement towards assimilation eventually turned against the Marwānids, and, being a living force, destroyed them. The Yaman dimly understood the significance of this development and fastened on to it as their alternative to the Qays

[1] Shaban, *The 'Abbāsid Revolution*, pp. 93–4.

system. This was by far their most telling criticism of the policies of 'Abdulmalik and Walīd I, because in their own times the movement towards the assimilation of interest, of culture, of religion and of race, was visibly under way.

In Khurāsān during the second civil war there were no campaigns for fourteen years. Naturally the Arab immigrants began to acquire a taste for the settled life, and an interest in the trade and agriculture of the region. Thus began an integration of interests between the Arabs and the Iranians. Even Qutayba, the devoted pupil of Ḥajjāj, helped the movement forward for the best of Ḥajjājite reasons – he needed the soldiers. So eager was he to win new conquests that he even raised non-Muslim levies. Naturally he spared himself the expense of paying them stipends but they received a share of the booty. The results were greater than he bargained for. Arab and Iranian soldiers fighting side by side got used to each other, and began to establish new common interests. In fact they finally co-operated to depose Qutayba himself in order to return to their homes from his endless campaigns.[1]

In Jazīra many of the tribesmen who came there after the second civil war decided to settle down rather than go on continual raids into Armenia and Adherbayjān. Before long they too began to be assimilated to the native population.[2] The same is true of the Iraqi tribesmen after the demilitarization of Kūfa and Baṣra.

The Berber tribesmen are a striking example of immediate assimilation. Although they tried to take advantage of the second civil war to drive out the Arab conquerors, 'Abdulmalik's Syrian troops soon put an end to their revolt. Apparently they were offered very good peace terms because they were converted to Islam in great numbers. These new Berber converts were treated in exactly the same way as the Arab Muslims. Most important, they were recruited into the Arab army and were given stipends.[3] It is no wonder that they showed such enthusiasm in the conquest of Spain. However, once they had served their purpose, the Arab authorities tried to stop the process of assimilation. The result was smouldering discontent which would eventually have burst into another rebellion had it not been for the timely intervention of 'Umar II.[4]

1 *Ibid.*, pp. 73–4.

2 Balādhurī, *Futūḥ*, p. 333.

3 See above p. 101.

4 Ya'qūbī, *Tārīkh*, vol. II, p. 313; Ibn 'Abdilḥakam, *Sīrat 'Umar*, pp. 34, 156; Ibn Khaldūn, *'Ibar*, vol. VI, p. 110.

In Egypt, too, during the long governorship of ʻAbdulʻazīz (685–705/65–85), the father of ʻUmar II, we see a remarkable drawing together of interests, although assimilation of religion, culture and race had not yet taken place. As we have mentioned before, ʻAbdulʻazīz disbanded the garrison at Fusṭāṭ and dispersed the Arabs around various parts of the country.[1] Fusṭāṭ began to shrink visibly while Alexandria steadily expanded. ʻAbdulʻazīz himself set the fashion by removing his residence to Ḥilwān a few miles south of Fusṭāṭ. The more influential Arab leaders were given properties in newly reclaimed areas. In short, the Arabs were beginning to live side by side with the native population, and their interests began to converge. We even have occasional records of native Egyptians helping Arabs to fight off Byzantine raids.[2] But the most impressive example of this confluence of interests was the Egyptian navy. The Syrians had a small navy of their own but for all important naval battles they relied heavily upon the very much larger Egyptian navy, especially during the sieges of Constantinople. Nevertheless all its sailors, helmsmen and oarsmen were Egyptian Christians, hired for the duration of each campaign and receiving a share of the booty.[3] This navy was the classic justification of the Yaman argument for making concessions to conquered populations.[4] It is the only clear case in this period of a very large number of non-Muslims and non-Arabs being allowed to perform a task of paramount importance in the empire's defence, and they performed it very well.

The arguments of the Yaman had considerable force because concessions to the subject peoples proved to be useful even in the pursuit of the policy of expansion. But while the Yaman were willing to pay the price of gaining the full co-operation of these peoples, the Qays adamantly refused to share their privileges with them and at the same time exploited them whenever possible. Qutayba, a notorious leader of Qays, pushed this exploitation of local populations, in Khurāsān and the East, to the extreme. At the same time he took all measures to put into effect the complete segregation of Arabs and Iranians, in order to stop any process of assimilation. Although he achieved new conquests, the result of his strict application of the Qays policies was disastrous.

1 See above p. 112.
2 Kindī, *Governors*, p. 70.
3 Ṭabarī, II, p. 1346; Dhahabī, *Tārīkh*, vol. III, p. 331; also see above p. 82.
4 See below p. 157.

He himself was killed by the men he had so victoriously led in battle. His masters' policies received a severe setback in that the process of assimilation was accelerated in Khurāsān. The Arab tribesmen there began to show great reluctance to join any expeditions and a revolutionary movement was born amongst them.[1]

It was this very danger that the Yaman had foreseen, but the tide was against them and their advice went unheeded until it was too late. They saw that the 'Abdulmalik–Ḥajjāj policy, supported by Qays, had many serious shortcomings. Admittedly this policy worked well enough for a time, but most of the major social forces were moving away from its implicit assumptions. The Yaman advocated practical measures to meet rapidly changing social conditions which endangered the very power structure of the empire. They realized that the political base of the regime was not only narrow but was also steadily losing ground to the forces of assimilation. Each of the components of this base, the Marwānids, Ḥajjāj's following, the Syrian army and the *muqātila*, was in itself a minority. There were many other important families whose prestige was as great as the Marwānids', notably the branches of the Hāshimites. Besides, the scramble of the Marwānids to acquire lands had tarnished their reputation. 'Abdulmalik and his son, Walīd I, had extended the principle of *ṣawāfī* to appropriate the lands reclaimed at public expense from desert, marshes or sea, and granted much of it to members of their family.[2] It was also a dangerous practice to restrict all major appointments to the Marwānid family and Ḥajjāj's protégés. Although the appointees were on the whole efficient and loyal, this policy excluded many other responsible men from high office. The *muqātila* were increasingly outnumbered by their more peaceable fellow tribesmen. Furthermore, they were emerging as a privileged class and were aggressively trying to maintain their privileges. As we shall see, this was particularly serious in Khurāsān.[3]

The Syrian army, the strongest component of the Marwānid power base, was in fact its weakest point. The Syrians supported Mu'āwiya in defence of their interests and they helped Marwān to restore an Umayyad regime for the same reasons. But for them to be used as a force to police the whole empire was a different

[1] Shaban, *The 'Abbāsid Revolution*, p. 103.
[2] Ibn 'Abdilḥakam, *Sīrat 'Umar*, pp. 152–3.
[3] See below pp. 141,178.

matter. While it is true that the Syrian army was reasonably efficient and sufficiently loyal there was a limit to both its efficiency and its loyalty. First, because of the restrictions on immigration into Syria, there were simply not enough Syrians to take such responsibility. The tribesmen of Iraq alone far outnumbered the Syrians, and Iraq was only one trouble spot where the Syrian presence was required to help enforce the authority of the central government. Second, it was this very presence that aroused the fiercest resentment against both the Syrians and the central government. The revolt of Muṭarrif b. al-Mughīra was the first sign of this resentment. The stationing of a permanent Syrian occupation force at Wāsiṭ was too great a humiliation to be endured for long by the Iraqis. As we shall see, the revolt of Yazīd b. al-Muhallab in Baṣra, only five years after the death of Ḥajjāj, was a clear demonstration of this bitter resentment. The fact that part of the Syrian garrison in Iraq joined this revolt is the strongest evidence of the third and most important factor in this situation.[1]

The resentment the Syrians aroused was doubly unfortunate in that many of them were innocent of the wish to dominate other provinces. Syria had always been an exceptionally stable and contented province. Had it not been for its close connection with the ruling house Syria would have preferred a policy of non-involvement. In fact this was the Syrians' request to 'Alī at Ṣiffīn. But the exigencies of Marwānid politics forced them into a position of involvement and there is no doubt that this position was disagreeable to many Syrians.

Particularly relevant is the case of Rajā' b. Ḥaywa, one of the leaders of the district of Jordan.[2] We recall that the Syrians of this district were the only group who stood fast by the side of Marwān during the perilous years of the second civil war.[3] They were directly responsible for his accession to power. It is significant that Rajā' b. Ḥaywa rose to high office under 'Abdulmalik and Walīd I,[4] but his rise to even higher office under their immediate successors, Sulaymān and 'Umar II, indicates that he was out of sympathy with Ḥajjāj's policy.[5] He had supported the Marwānids during the second civil war in the hope of restoring the com-

[1] See below p. 136.
[2] Ibn 'Abdilḥakam, *Sīrat 'Umar*, p. 143.
[3] See above p. 93
[4] Ṭabarī, II, pp. 1341–5; Ibn 'Abdirabbih, Aḥmad b. Muḥammad, *al-'Iqd al-Farīd*, Beirut, 1951–4, vol. XVI, p. 24; vol. XVIII, p. 74.
[5] Ṭabarī, II, p. 838.

paratively peaceful and modest regime of Mu'āwiya and Yazīd I. He and the men he represented had no objections to the summer campaigns against the Byzantines. They considered this a primary duty ultimately involving the safety of their own homes. However, now that the new policy of 'Abdulmalik imposed on them prolonged garrison duty in Iraq and endless campaigns in North Africa and elsewhere, completely revolutionizing their lives and meaning virtual exile for some, they began to have second thoughts. There were, of course, some who were happy to offer their services in exchange for the newly established stipends; but others, like Rajā' and especially those who joined the revolt of Yazīd b. al-Muhallab, came to hate these new conditions and did their best to modify them.[1] There was obviously something amiss when the policemen of the regime were not particularly contented with their new role. The Marwānid political base was not only too narrow and too unpopular, but also insecure in its one essential support, the power and the will of the Syrian troops to enforce the absolute authority of their *Amīr al-Mu'minīn*.

With the death of Walīd I and the accession to power of men with a glimpse of a different method of governing, the 'Abdulmalik–Ḥajjāj policy was gradually discredited. It was now the responsibility of the new *Amīr al-Mu'minīn*, Sulaymān, to devise an alternative successful policy for the empire.

[1] For subsequent actions of Rajā', see below p. 131.

7

MODERATE REFORM, RADICAL REFORM AND REACTION: THE REIGNS OF SULAYMĀN, 'UMAR II AND YAZĪD II

As we have shown in the last chapter the Qays system had its weaknesses which were quickly seized upon by an increasingly strong opposition. This opposition had only to wait for a new and more sympathetic *Amīr al-Mu'minīn* for their hopes to be realized. With the accession of Sulaymān their time came. Sulaymān and 'Umar II reigned for only a short time – a mere five years – but in terms of intensity of political activity and change these five years are as important as the thirty years of 'Abdulmalik and Walīd I. Particularly fascinating in this period is the swift acceleration of change, going far beyond the thinking of the Yaman in their years of opposition. The development of Sulaymān's cautious moderation into 'Umar II's decided radicalism was swift, and strikingly similar to that of the great European revolutions of the last two centuries. But there was one crucial difference: this "revolution" was always so firmly directed from the top that the radical forces it unleashed were easily brought under control when the top changed its politics. It was a revolution which never got past the initial stage.

Sulaymān moved so cautiously that his politics are difficult to categorize. Our sources show their uncertainty about him by emphasizing his gluttony and hinting at lechery, while still praising his reversal of Ḥajjāj's policies and his appointment of 'Umar II as his successor.[1] In fact they are not at all sure about the significance of his very short reign. Yet there is no doubt that this marked a decided breakaway from the 'Abdulmalik–Ḥajjāj policies. Certainly his first action leaves no doubt about this – namely the dismissal of all Ḥajjāj's protégés in favour of the more liberal and moderate Yamanites.[2] Yazīd b. al Muhallab b. Abī Ṣufra,

[1] Ṭabarī, II, pp. 1273, 1309, 1337.

[2] Ibn Khayyāṭ, *Tārīkh*, vol. I, pp. 323–5.

for example, supplanted a Ḥajjāj protégé as governor of Iraq. He was an able man but a well-known leader of the Yaman, and for this reason Ḥajjāj had blighted his career in 704/84 by persuading 'Abdulmalik to dismiss him after only two years as governor of Khurāsān. The appointment of this man, a well-known opponent and victim of the Qaysites, as Sulaymān's own "Ḥajjāj" was clearly politically significant. All the Qays governors yielded power without a fight, with one important exception, Qutayba b. Muslim, governor of Khurāsān. He had been one of Ḥajjāj's favourite protégés and since 705/86 had loyally deputized for his master in Khurāsān. It was in fact he who had eventually supplanted Yazīd. When he heard of Walīd I's death he immediately realized that this meant the end of his political usefulness, and he therefore tried to raise a rebellion in spite of the fact that he was on campaign at the time. In this he was unduly ambitious since his support in Khurāsān was much less than he imagined. As soon as Qutayba's intentions became clear the Arab tribesmen and their new allies, the *mawālī*, turned against him, murdered him and returned to their homes. Weary of Qutayba's endless campaigns, they saw no reason to join forces with him against a government expected to be much more pacific.[1] This revolt against revolt in Khurāsān was one of the most telling arguments in favour of Yamanite policies. All this no doubt appeared satisfactory to Sulaymān, but when the tribesmen of Khurāsān proceeded to elect a provisional governor from their own leaders he became seriously alarmed at the prospects of disorder that this opened up. He therefore instructed Yazīd to move his headquarters to Khurāsān and appoint representatives in Kūfa, Baṣra and Wāsiṭ. He also decided to keep the fiscal affairs of Iraq under his own control, appointing a personal representative in the province with special responsibility for taxation. His choice for this exacting post fell upon Ṣāliḥ b. 'Abdilraḥman, a client of Tamīm long experienced in Iraqi administration.[2]

If Sulaymān's first action indicates a complete break with the policies of Ḥajjāj, his subsequent foreign policy was slow and cautious. In some respects it seemed to be an intensification of previous policies. In Khurāsān, Sulaymān was much less pacific than the rebels against Qutayba had expected. He appreciated that

[1] Shaban, *The 'Abbāsid Revolution*, pp. 72–5.

[2] Ṭabarī, II, pp. 1304–14.

this was not going to be popular and therefore reinforced Yazīd with a large contingent from the Syrians stationed at Wāsiṭ.[1] This was almost an extension of Ḥajjāj's policy into Khurāsān, but once Yazīd arrived there his policy differed from Qutayba's. It certainly involved frequent campaigns, but these were campaigns of consolidation rather than conquest. Yazīd concentrated on the mountainous Caspian provinces of Gurgān and Ṭabaristān, which had theoretically long been part of the empire but had never been properly subdued. However invincible Arab tactics had been elsewhere they had almost always proved themselves painfully inadequate when fighting in mountains. This time Arab arms met with greater success. A major factor in this success was the greater manpower Yazīd was able to bring to bear on the problem. In accordance with the Yaman policy of winning the voluntary co-operation of the conquered peoples, he had recruited large numbers of local non-Arab volunteers.[2] Although he was no more able than his predecessors to make any impression on the upper slopes, he was able to subdue the lower. The booty was considerable, enough to cause a damaging amount of disagreement about its distribution.[3]

Sulaymān's policy on the Byzantine front, though it was ruthlessly clear and simple in itself, is equally unhelpful in determining his political line. To end the ceaseless and exhausting campaigning along the Byzantine front, Sulaymān decided to crush the Byzantine empire itself by a siege of Constantinople, meticulously planned and massively strong. The general of the grand combination of Syrian army and Egyptian navy was his brother, the redoubtable Maslama. This project was not as wildly ambitious as might be imagined; Muʿāwiya himself had very nearly succeeded in the two previous sieges of the city (669/49 and 674–80/54–60). The siege began in 716/98 and very soon the Byzantines were in an extremely parlous position. Fortunately for them, the year 717/99 saw the succession of Leo the Isaurian to the Byzantine throne, a man, ironically enough, of Syrian origin. He was a very cunning tactician and soon outmanœuvred Maslama. This, combined with the unexpected death of Sulaymān in the same year, forced the Arabs to raise the siege and withdraw.[4]

[1] *Ibid.*, p. 1327. [2] *Ibid.*, pp. 1318, 1327, 1329.
[3] *Ibid.*, pp. 1318–35; Yaʿqūbī, *Tārīkh*, vol. II, p. 355; Balādhurī, *Futūḥ*, pp. 335–8.
[4] Ṭabarī, II, pp. 1314–17; Dhahabī, *Tārīkh*, vol. III, p. 331.

Throughout his reign Sulaymān clearly opposed the Qays and encouraged the Yaman leaders. On balance, he continued the same imperial policy as his immediate predecessors, only softening it by trying to bring in the non-Arabs into this structure. His reign was very short and will permit more than one interpretation. This is why he is such an ambiguous figure for the historian. Yet his choice of 'Umar II as his heir strongly tempts us to view him as a very cautious Yaman supporter. He must have known that 'Umar, who had long been one of his closest advisers, was far more radical than the Yaman. Indeed he must have approved of this radicalism for otherwise 'Umar would never have been chosen as his successor. The significance of this choice cannot be over-emphasized. It defied accepted convention, and the transition of power was planned with extraordinary care and ingenuity. There had been a general understanding among the Marwānids that the office of *Amīr al-Mu'minīn* should be limited to the sons of 'Abdulmalik. 'Abdulmalik had fathered no less than sixteen sons, including three who had died in infancy and seven born to non-Arab concubines. Since the lack of pure Arab blood ruled out these last, even including the formidable Maslama, four eligible sons were left after the deaths of Walīd I and Sulaymān. 'Abdulmalik himself had named only his two adult sons as his immediate heirs, but it was assumed that he intended Yazīd and his younger brothers to succeed in due course.[1] Sulaymān could not, therefore, claim that there were no more sons, but he chose to ignore his father's clear, though not explicit, intentions on the pretext that allegiance had never been paid to Yazīd. He went, instead, outside the circle of 'Abdulmalik's sons, and selected the patriarch's nephew, his cousin 'Umar b. 'Abdil'azīz b. Marwān, as the man most sympathetic to his policies.[2]

It is clear that Sulaymān did not trust his own family to carry out his intentions. The will in which he designated 'Umar as his successor was drawn up in great secrecy at Dābiq, a frontier post as near to the Byzantine expedition as he dared to go. Although he was surrounded by his relations at Dābiq, he selected Rajā' b. Ḥaywa al-Kindī as his executor rather than any member of his own family. The choice of Rajā' was again of great significance.

[1] Dhahabī, *Tārīkh*, vol. IV, 168; *al-'Uyūn wa al-Ḥadā'iq fī Akhbār al-Ḥaqā'iq*, anon., ed. M. J. de Goeje, Leiden, 1869, p. 29.

[2] Ṭabarī, II, pp. 1317–41.

We have already mentioned Rajā' at some length as one of the most important Syrian opponents of the 'Abdulmalik–Ḥajjāj policy. His presence here at this time rather than with the main Syrian forces at Byzantium implies that Sulaymān had chosen his *jund*, that of Jordan, to accompany him on the minor expeditions around Dābiq. This was to be expected; it was quite logical for the *Amīr al-Mu'minīn* to choose the most loyal of all the Syrian troops to surround him. As events proved, Rajā' was a very good choice as executor of Sulaymān's will, for he not only strongly sympathized with 'Umar's policies but also had the military strength to enforce the latter's accession. The political characters of the man Sulaymān chose as his successor and of the men who were to enforce this succession show Sulaymān as a rather more radical figure than do other acts of his reign.

On Sulaymān's death, Rajā' was in a very strong position to see his master's intentions carried out. Before the assembled Marwānids he proclaimed himself the executor of the late *Amīr al-Mu'minīn*'s will, making them all pay allegiance to an undisclosed name. The terms of the will were then disclosed and when some of the family protested at this flouting of their rights, Rajā' threatened to use force. The Marwānids appreciated the point of this threat and eventually a compromise was arrived at. 'Umar II should succeed in accordance with Sulaymān's will, but after his death the succession should go to Yazīd in accordance with 'Abdulmalik's intentions. Rajā' gave in to this without much ado – he was not to know that 'Umar would disappoint his hopes by dying in his prime. For the time being it seemed as if Rajā' had accomplished a virtual *coup d'état*.[1]

Where Sulaymān's policies had been cautious and ambiguous, 'Umar II's were clear and radical. Sulaymān had continued with the campaigns; 'Umar stopped every one of them. No sooner was he firmly in power than he recalled the expedition besieging Constantinople, and ordered a retreat from all the advanced outposts established within the Byzantine territories.[2] Similarly, he called a complete halt to every expedition on the eastern front, even ordering a general withdrawal from Transoxiana.[3] In comparison with the boldness of these moves, the foreign policy of the Yamanites under Sulaymān was almost Ḥajjājite.

[1] *Ibid.*, pp. 1340–5. [2] *Ibid.*, p. 1346; Balādhurī, *Futūḥ*, p. 165.
[3] Ṭabarī, II, p. 1365; Ya'qūbī, *Tārīkh*, vol. II, pp. 55–6.

But 'Umar II's most important work was in internal policy, in which he left the vague policies of the Yaman far behind. In this, he must not be seen as an 'Abbāsid born into the wrong dynasty. He was very much a Marwānid, but he was first and foremost a Muslim ruler who saw no conflict between the claims of Islam and the Marwānid house. He felt that the Marwānids had to live up to the high responsibilities of their position. For himself, he behaved throughout his reign with exemplary simplicity and asceticism despite his previous and just reputation as a *bon viveur*.[1] He also tried to see that his relations behaved fittingly and to that end anulled all the *ṣawāfī* land grants to the Marwānids, together with various other privileges like the public payment of their private guards.[2] Most important of all, he felt that his house should govern in a Muslim way. This was no mere religious fanaticism but realistic politics. He had the insight to realize that Mu'āwiya's moderation had degenerated under 'Abdulmalik into a narrowly Arab authoritarianism and that the regime he had inherited was too narrowly based to last much longer. 'Umar II was convinced that an ideology and not a Syrian police force should and could keep the empire together. In Islam such an ideology was at hand, professed throughout the empire, and all he had to do was to apply its principles without discrimination to establish a society of equal rights in exchange for equal responsibilities. This implied the assimilation of all Muslims, Arabs and non-Arabs, into one Muslim community and it was such a development that 'Umar II proceeded to encourage.

This new policy did not involve any surrender of authority by the central government. In fact 'Umar II supervised every action of his governors to an unprecedented degree. Unlike his three immediate predecessors, he dispensed with powerful viceroys like Ḥajjāj and Yazīd. Instead of relying on the discretion of trusted lieutenants, 'Umar II only demanded of his governors that they carry out his detailed instructions. In these circumstances the political views of individual governors mattered less than under the seemingly less centralized regime of Sulaymān. 'Umar required efficiency and implicit obedience, and he was prepared to appoint Ḥajjāj protégés if they had these qualities. One of his first actions was to dismiss Yazīd ibn al-Muhallab, Sulaymān's trusted viceroy in the East, and then to split up this huge domain

[1] Ibn 'Abdilḥakam, *Sīrat 'Umar*, pp. 20–1. [2] *Ibid.*, pp. 50–1, 56–7, 152–3.

into three governorships – Kūfa, Baṣra and Khurāsān – so as to have it more firmly under his own control.[1] Furthermore, he ordered Yazīd to be arrested on the grounds that he had failed to pay Damascus its proper share of the booty from Gurgān, but it seems more likely that ʿUmar II had stronger reasons for such a measure. As we have seen, Yazīd was totally committed to Sulaymān's policies which stopped far short of ʿUmar II's plans. Although Yazīd was an acknowledged leader of the Yaman, there was a danger that he might not support the more radical new policies. As his history shows, he could muster enough support to raise serious problems for ʿUmar II. His arrest was a precautionary measure, as well as a significant declaration, on ʿUmar II's part, of a complete departure from his predecessors' policies.

There is an unprecedented mass of detailed instruction to provincial governors to be found in our sources for this reign. Nothing was too unimportant to escape ʿUmar's attention. For example, and any Egyptian would appreciate this, he forbade the planting of trees along the Nile banks since it would interfere with the towing of boats upstream.[2] This is only one example of his meticulous attention to detail and shows his great knowledge and concern for conditions throughout the provinces. The tenor of these instructions, when viewed as a whole, indicates a completely new approach to governing the empire. It was at once more and less authoritarian than ʿAbdulmalik's; more authoritarian because of the greater degree of central control, and less in the sense that he no longer relied on brute force to carry out his policies. He withdrew most of the Syrian garrisons from Iraq and Khurāsān and tried to gain stability through a rebalancing of the political forces in each province.[3] To do this he recognized and encouraged the assimilation of Arab and non-Arab far more than Sulaymān had done. The solutions to all the minor local problems he concerned himself with show an insistence on the principle of equal rights and equal responsibilities for every Muslim, whether Arab or not. The cumulative effect of this mass of detailed instruction meant a major change in the internal policy of the provinces, sweeping away anomalies and setting up guide-lines for an assimilated society. Nor did he confine himself to minor matters

[1] Ṭabarī, II, p. 1346. [2] Ibn ʿAbdilḥakam, *Sīrat ʿUmar*, p. 67.
[3] Ibn Aʿtham, *Futūḥ*, vol. II, pp. 167–8; Shaban, *The ʿAbbāsid Revolution*, pp. 90–2.

in his insistence on the Muslim rather than Arab character of the empire. The most celebrated of his major measures, the Fiscal Rescript, is the best example of this. This document, circulated among all his governors, concerned itself with routine abuses for most of the time, but one of its clauses entailed a revolution in all the empire's habits. This clause ordered that stipends should be paid to every Muslim who accepted his military obligations, regardless of whether he was an Arab or not.[1] This was revolutionary enough, but even more far-reaching was the insistence throughout the document that all converts to Islam should pay exactly the same taxes as all Arabs in similar occupations.[2]

There were also rather more specific encouragements towards assimilation. In North Africa, as we have already noted, there had been a very early assimilation of Arab and Berber. Clearly this went somewhat against the Marwānid grain, but the arrangement was of necessity continued until Spain was securely conquered in Walīd I's reign. When the Berbers had performed their essential role, Walīd I and his Ḥajjājite governors proceeded to rescind their previous agreement, forbidding any further assimilation between Arab and Berber. The Berbers did not take kindly to this degradation, and since Sulaymān did nothing to redress their grievances they were on the point of rebellion when 'Umar II succeeded to the throne. 'Umar II simply reaffirmed the old policy of no discrimination, and the Berbers were once more satisfied and obedient. Needless to say, when the Qaysites returned to power after 'Umar's death the new governor, Yazīd b. Abī Muslim, returned to the policies of his mentor Ḥajjāj. The result was his murder (720/102) and a growing revolt throughout North Africa and Spain.[3]

In Egypt, 'Umar II developed and intensified the policies of his father 'Abdul'azīz. We have already commented on the remarkable co-operation of the Egyptians in the navy. The situation was extremely favourable to 'Umar II's policy of equal rights for equal responsibilities for all Muslims. In his reign 5,000 new stipends were added to the Egyptian *dīwān*.[4] Since there was no new

[1] Ibn 'Abdilḥakam, *Sīrat 'Umar*, p. 95; H. A. R. Gibb, "The Fiscal Rescript of 'Umar II", *Arabica*, vol. II, January 1955, pp. 3, 9.

[2] Gibb, "Fiscal Rescript", p. 16.

[3] Ibn 'Abdilḥakam, *Sīrat 'Umar*, pp. 34, 156; Ya'qūbī, *Tārīkh*, vol. II, p. 313; Ibn Khaldūn, *'Ibar*, vol. VI, p. 110; Ṭabarī, II, p. 1435.

[4] Kindī, *Governors*, p. 68.

immigration into Egypt at this time, these new stipends can only have been for native Egyptians, and in all probability for members of the navy. Needless to say again, ʿUmar's successors deprived these men of their stipends.[1] The folly of this action was graphically demonstrated twenty-five years later, when they themselves instituted a similar scheme.[2] But by then it was too late to win the confidence and gratitude of native Egyptians.

This uniquely promising experiment was brought to an untimely end by ʿUmar's tragically early death. The two years of his reign were far too short for his reforms to become firmly entrenched, indeed too short for them to have any major effect. Worst of all it was too short a time to change the political habits of the men clustered around the other Marwānids. When Rajā' compromised with the Marwānids he had gambled on ʿUmar's longevity and that, given time, Yazīd II could always be elbowed out of the way. But time was not given and Rajā' lost his gamble. Yazīd II succeeded to the supreme office and the Qaysites returned to power embittered and reactionary after their five years in the wilderness. They had less than thirty years of power left, after which they were to collapse before a revolution urging policies remarkably similar to ʿUmar II's. It is often implied, if not said directly, that their policies were more realistic than those of the idealistic and fanatical ʿUmar. It is hard to see how anyone can arrive at such a conclusion. If success is the true criterion of realism, then by that token Yazīd II and the Qaysites were unrealistic. Whatever their religious justification ʿUmar's policies made remarkably good political sense. He appreciated that the two rising forces in the empire were assimilation and a desire for peace, and he framed his policies accordingly. The result was that he was able to do something no other Marwānid could do: he governed the empire, and even increased his power, without the machinery of repression evolved by ʿAbdulmalik and Ḥajjāj. In short, he succeeded in governing the empire by consent, which no ruler had done since Muʿāwiya. His policies worked and would have worked better as time passed. That some should call them unrealistic can only be attributed to a misunderstanding of the history of this era.

Meanwhile Yazīd II succeeded to the office of *Amīr al-Mu'minīn* and in his wake the Qaysites returned to power.[3] As for Rajā', he

[1] *Ibid.*, p. 70. [2] *Ibid.*, p. 84. [3] Ibn Khayyāṭ, *Tārīkh*, vol. II, pp. 340–4.

retired into pensioned obscurity. It was a time of fierce political feeling. The Qaysites had lost power, held for twenty years, once and they had no intention of losing it again. Their feelings were all the more bitter because of the humiliations suffered at the hands of Sulaymān, 'Umar II and the Yamanites. Not only had they seen the policies sanctified by 'Abdulmalik and Ḥajjāj openly scorned and flouted, but they had been scorned and flouted themselves. One of their greatest leaders, Maslama, had been snubbed by 'Umar II and sent into inglorious retirement. These humiliations increased the bitterness of the party strife which then commenced. For, unlike Rajā', not all the Yamanites meekly accepted the return of the diehard expansionists. Yazīd b. al-Muhallab had admittedly fallen from the high position held under Sulaymān. Indeed 'Umar II had imprisoned him throughout his reign but this had not altered Yazīd's devotion to the principles upheld by Sulaymān. On hearing of Yazīd II's accession he simply walked out of prison and raised a revolt in Baṣra.[1] In contrast to Sulaymān and 'Umar II, who were in a position to pursue their opposition to the 'Abdulmalik–Ḥajjāj policy by legitimate means, Yazīd b. al-Muhallab had no alternative but to resort to armed revolt. His declared purpose was that "the policy of Ḥajjāj must not be re-imposed on us".[2]

It is wrong to interpret this revolt as a mere tribal struggle between Yaman and Qays and certainly this interpretation is not borne out by our sources. While Yazīd b. al-Muhallab was joined by tribesmen from all clans, his own fellow tribesmen of Azd sided against him.[3] Most significant as a portent for later developments, some of the Syrian troops in Iraq supported Yazīd b. al-Muhallab, although his slogan was to "prevent the Syrian troops from stepping on our lands".[4]

The revolt gained momentum after Yazīd's capture of Baṣra and its governor, but the central government acted quickly and vigorously. The renowned Maslama was placed at the head of a great Syrian army and soon nothing could "prevent the Syrian troops from stepping on our lands". Yazīd b. al-Muhallab's army fell apart and scattered, leaving its leader dead on the battlefield. Maslama was appointed governor of Iraq and the East and proceeded to stamp out every remaining centre of resistance, to

[1] Ṭabarī, II, pp. 1359–61.
[2] *Ibid.*, p. 1398.
[3] *Ibid.*, pp. 1381, 1390.
[4] *Ibid.*, pp. 1382–3, 1398.

eject every Yamanite from office and reverse his every decision.[1] By the time he handed over a subdued and crushed Iraq to his successor, ʿUmar b. Hubayra, it was as if the reigns of Sulaymān and ʿUmar II had never happened. In the short reign of Yazīd II (720–4/101–5), the Syrians were back in Wāsiṭ, the Berbers were slighted and insulted, the Egyptians lost their stipends, the Fiscal Rescript was ignored, the wars of conquest recommenced. The triumph of the Qaysites was complete, but it was gained at the expense of the Marwānids' chance of avoiding disaster. It was not the Qaysite policies but ʿUmar II's which were remembered and eventually came to govern the empire. It was the Qaysites whom every ʿAbbāsid historian declared damnable and accursed, while a complex legend gathered around ʿUmar II, making him more formidable in death than in life, the only righteous Marwānid.

[1] *Ibid.*, pp. 1416–18.

8

HISHĀM: SURVIVAL OF THE EMPIRE

Hishām, the fourth son of 'Abdulmalik to become *Amīr al-Mu'minīn*, promptly succeeded his brother Yazīd II. This smooth succession strongly indicates the complete victory of the expansionists and their determination to continue the 'Abdulmalik–Ḥajjāj policies which had been successfully reimposed during the reign of Yazīd II. There is no doubt that this was Hishām's intention, although the circumstances of his reign forced him, at times, to deviate from these particular policies, and yield to the forces of assimilation. However, this deviation was only temporary, and once the impending danger receded Hishām dutifully reverted to implementing the expansionist policies to the full. It is a measure of his ability and dexterity as a statesman that he was able to survive as long as he did. In his long reign (724–43/105–25), Hishām was faced with the most serious threats on all frontiers of the empire. Internally, he ruled over a people with conflicting interests long divided against itself. While these internal conflicts were simmering, he had to use every resource at his command to save the empire itself from being torn apart by its external enemies. In this task he succeeded, but not even an absolute ruler, as capable as Hishām, could resist the tremendous pressure brought to bear on him by powerful sections of his subjects whose support he badly needed. He was able, to some extent, to contain these pressures throughout his reign, but after his death the deluge was inevitable.

His first problem, and indeed the most serious threat to the empire, materialized on the far eastern frontier. The resumption of wars of expansion in Central Asia under Yazīd II in 723/104 met with stubborn resistance from the rising power of the Turgesh nomads. Under the Khan Sü-Lü (716–38) the Turgesh tribes were able to assert their independence and win the hegemony of the western Turks. With the help of the Chinese they established a new kingdom in the Ili basin. In 724/106 they dealt the Arabs of

Khurāsān a disastrous defeat known as the Day of Thirst. This was the first time the Arabs had met the Turgesh armies in their full strength and from that time onwards, for about fifteen years, the Arabs were on the defensive and were gradually driven back across the Oxus. To repel this dangerous enemy and restore Arab prestige in Khurāsān became Hishām's responsibility. He began by dismissing Yazīd II's governor of Iraq and the East, 'Umar b. Hubayra, and appointing in his stead Khālid b. 'Abdillah al-Qasrī. This was no mere change of personnel to satisfy a whim of Hishām; it was a clear indication of a major change of policy in this part of the empire. 'Umar b. Hubayra was a well-tried and loyal servant of the Marwānids but he was also a faithful disciple of Ḥajjāj and a leading Qaysite figure. On the other hand Khālid al-Qasrī, though a man of insignificant tribal standing, was the acknowledged leader of the Yamanites in the empire. His appointment was the clearest possible declaration of a change from the harsh unbending Qaysite policy to the moderate and flexible Yamanite approach, at least in Iraq and the East. Hishām knew that he did not have enough Syrians willing and ready to be dispatched to Khurāsān to meet the Turgesh threat. He realized that the manpower needed for this purpose would have to be raised from the eastern provinces themselves. To this end he needed the full co-operation of the populations of these provinces, Arabs and non-Arabs alike. The Yamanite Khālid was eminently suited for this particular task and upon his appointment he entrusted the co-ordination and application of his policies in the East to his own brother, Asad.

Asad arrived in Khurāsān without an army but with a plan which ultimately proved successful. This plan was to ensure the co-operation of the Hephthalites against their traditional enemy, the Turgesh. These Hephthalites formed the majority of the local population of the Principalities of Ṭukhāristān to the east of the old Sāsānian borders.[1] They had finally been brought under Arab control during Qutayba's governorship (705–15/86–96), and were organized in what can best be described as protectorates, keeping their autonomy under their own princes.[2] These princes were in

[1] M. A. Shaban, "The Political Geography of Khurāsān and the East at the time of the Arab Conquest", *Minorsky's Memorial Volume,* ed. C. E. Bosworth and J. Aubin, London, forthcoming.

[2] Shaban, *The 'Abbāsid Revolution*, pp. 66–7.

fact military lords who, if united, could put together a considerable army. Asad's first attempts to strike an alliance with the Hephthalites against the Turgesh were not successful. The Arabs, it seems, were not an attractive ally against the Turgesh who had just dealt them a severe defeat. Besides, the Arabs of Khurāsān themselves were not completely united in their determination to fight the Turgesh attackers. On the one hand some of the *muqātila* were becoming increasingly reluctant to join military expeditions, particularly against such a formidable enemy as the Turgesh who until then had confined their attacks to Soghdiana. On the other hand, those who were ready to join the fight were not enthusiastic about the projected alliance with the Hephthalites. They realized that such an alliance would ultimately result in the loss of their own power and prestige. Their fears were probably increased by Asad's Yamanite overtures towards the local populations of the East. His attempts to incorporate local administrations into the Arab structure represented an added threat to the *muqātila*, who saw these measures as concessions to the local populations. Although Asad's policy ultimately proved useful in checking the Turgesh threat and maintaining Arab rule in Soghdiana, it was fiercely resisted by a strong section of the *muqātila*. Alarmed by this threatening division in a embattled region, Hishām ordered Asad to be recalled and a new governor was sent to the East in 727/109, at the head of a small Syrian contingent to help enforce his authority.[1]

Nevertheless, the Arab position *vis-à-vis* the Turgesh steadily deteriorated and the reversal of Asad's policy drove the Soghdians to side openly with the enemy. Finally, Hishām decided on a radical reorganization of the Arab army in Khurāsān, which at this time numbered about 30,000 men. In 732/113 he instructed his governor to limit the number of enlisted men to only 15,000 and drop the rest from the *dīwān*. Since they were unwilling to fulfil their military duty they had forfeited their right to any stipends. To fill the vacuum created by this drastic cut in the army of Khurāsān, Hishām dispatched a new army of 20,000 newly recruited tribesmen from Iraq who arrived at Khurāsān in the same year.

It should be realized that Hishām had decided to yield to the assimilation movement in the region, thus allowing a consider-

[1] *Ibid.*, pp. 107–9.

able number of the Arabs in Khurāsān to settle down to a more peaceful way of life. To prevent any further loss of Arabs to the army, and at the same time to break the hegemony of the old *muqātila* over the region, Hishām decided that the newcomers should be kept close to the governor in Merv to serve as a ready striking force, while the original *muqātila* of Khurāsān should be divided into garrisons to be settled permanently on frontier posts to guard Khurāsān against Turgesh attacks. In 734/116, 4,000 of these tribesmen stationed at Andkhūy in Gūzgān, in the heart of Hephthalite territory, revolted under the leadership of al-Ḥārith b. Surayj. These rebels represented a serious threat from within, particularly as their fellow Arabs did not want to fight them. The Hephthalites, fishing in troubled waters, sided with the rebels probably hoping to establish an Arab principality in Khurāsān under their domination. Negotiations and fighting did not resolve the situation and Hishām in 735/117 had to fall back on Asad to save the East.

Asad, making use of his personal relationship with the leaders of the newcomers from Iraq, was able to persuade them to fight the rebel al-Ḥārith, who was finally defeated and fled to join the Turgesh enemy. By now much stronger, Asad was finally able to persuade the Hepthalites to join the Arabs against their common enemy and in 737/119 they decisively defeated the Turgesh. This Battle of Kharīstān was the signal for the disintegration of the Turgesh power and the turning-point of Arab fortunes in Central Asia.

When Asad died shortly afterwards, in 738/120, the Arabs of Khurāsān were rid of the Turgesh threat but divided amongst themselves into four distinct parties. In modern terms there was the extreme right, a minority represented by al-Ḥārith, who preferred to take refuge with the Turgesh rather than risk any loss of their privileges as conquerors of the province. The second party was right wing, best represented by Naṣr b. Sayyār, an old warrior of Khurāsān about whom we shall hear more later. These were tribesmen reared in the imperial policy of Ḥajjāj who were hopeful that they had enough power to restore the balance in the province in their favour. They are referred to in our sources as the Muḍar group. To the left of these were the Yaman group, the moderate party. These were the newcomers under the leadership of Juday' b. 'Alī al-Kirmānī, a man who was in full agreement with

Asad's policy. The left was composed of the assimilated Arabs who preferred to settle down and who were soon to be the revolutionaries. The Iranian population of this vast region was divided into many groups which varied in attitude from complete animosity to the Arab rulers, like the landowners of Soghdia, to complete co-operation, like the local nobility of the Merv oasis.[1]

In Iraq itself Khālid was clearly successful, as is evident from the remarkable stability of the region throughout his rule. He completed many irrigation projects and reclaimed much cultivable land at the expense of the treasury. While he personally grew extremely rich, the region as a whole must have benefited from this productive spending by the treasury. Furthermore, Hishām allowed most of the revenue from the region to be reinvested there.[2] Khālid needed all the manpower available for these agricultural projects, and accordingly he was in complete agreement with the continued demilitarization of Iraq. The 20,000 men sent from Iraq to Khurāsān in 732/113 must have been a drain on the manpower he badly needed, but many of them probably came from the dependencies of Iraq, as we can see from the name of Juday' al-Kirmānī. In fact we are told of some "*khawārij*" rebels in Iraq at that time whose complaint was that they were refused enlistment in the *dīwān* to be sent on expeditions.[3]

In accordance with the general Yamanite policy, Khālid was very lenient with the indigenous population of Iraq, Muslims or non-Muslims. This liberal attitude, added to the fact that his mother was Christian and had never been converted, opened the door for exaggerated attacks against him by his enemies. He must have been a very devoted son because he went to the length of building a church for his mother. In 737/119 a small group from the army of neighbouring Jazīra started their own "*khawārij*" rebellion with the specific purpose of killing Khālid, who so favoured the non-Muslims.[4] About the same time al-Mughīra b. Sa'īd and Bayān b. Sam'ān, two agitators in the name of extreme forms of Shī'ism,[5] were arrested and executed in Kūfa on Khālid's orders. Obviously they did not have much of a following, but their unnecessary execution shows the extreme nervousness of the authorities over such agitation. They must have realized how delicately the balance was held and accordingly felt they had

[1] *Ibid.*, pp. 95–9. [2] Ṭabarī, II, pp. 1642, 1655, 1658. [3] *Ibid.*, p. 1633.
[4] *Ibid.*, p. 1623; Athīr, *Kāmil*, vol. V, p. 167. [5] Ṭabarī, II, pp. 1619–21.

to clamp down severely to secure the new stability in Iraq. Hishām himself had to deal with two other agitators in the same way. Al-Ja'd b. Dirham and Ghaylān al-Dimashqī were seized for preaching heretical doctrines and were also executed. These men may have been executed as scapegoats for popular discontent and the charges of heresy concocted to generate public support for the regime. The executions indicate a new trend with regard to the authority of the *Amīr al-Mu'minīn*. Hitherto, he had assumed only the authority to punish political crimes with the death penalty. Now as a self-appointed guardian of the faith he was beginning to claim some religious authority, at least with regard to the suppression of heresy.[1]

Once the Turgesh threat was over Hishām made a most serious mistake with regard to Iraq and the East. He appointed Naṣr b. Sayyār, a confirmed imperialist from the right-wing Muḍar, as governor of the East. To Iraq he appointed Yūsuf b. 'Umar of Thaqīf, a cousin and disciple of al-Ḥajjāj, and a leading figure of the Qaysites, to replace Khālid the Yamanite. This general swing to the right could not have been more pronounced and its motives are open to conjecture. Hishām probably overestimated the strength of the Muḍarites in Khurāsān and thought that after the disappearance of the Turgesh threat the stability of the province could best be served by a renewal of the expansionist policy.[2] He also needed money to finance campaigns on other fronts and therefore hoped that new conquests would bring new revenues. His appointment of Yūsuf b. 'Umar to Iraq is a confirmation of this particular purpose. In contrast to Khālid, Yūsuf was not in the least lenient to his subjects, extracting as much in taxes as he possibly could. He also stopped any expenditure on agricultural projects and thus was more able to meet the demands of the central treasury.[3]

In the East there was not much trouble, at least until the death of Hishām, but in Iraq there was a subsequent armed revolt in Kūfa. This revolt was led by Zayd, a grandson of Ḥusayn. Naturally it was a Shī'ite movement, although it was not supported by all the *shī'a* of Kūfa who were beginning to formulate hopes for a descendant of the Prophet to be the *Imām–Amīr al-Mu'minīn*. Zayd apparently did not promise as much as his rival

[1] *Ibid.*, p. 1733; Athīr, *Kāmil*, vol. v, p. 197; Dhahabī, *Tārīkh*, vol. iv, p. 289.
[2] Ṭabarī, ii, pp. 1659–63.
[3] *Ibid.*, pp. 1778–9.

cousins and was more practical in outlook,[1] but his practicality did not serve him well. He grossly overestimated the extent of his support in Kūfa, and when he rose in revolt he had exactly 218 supporters.[2] The governor had previous knowledge of his moves, and the task of the Syrian troops was easy. Zayd was killed, and his son Yaḥyā fled to the East where he was also easily killed. Although this revolt was of no serious consequence to the government, it underlined the precarious condition of Iraq and the restiveness of subjects and rulers alike.

The situation in Syria and Jazīra was very much connected with the other serious external danger, the Khazar attacks on the Ādherbayjān and Armenian frontier. In 722/104 the Arab army on this front was badly defeated but was promptly reinforced from Syria and was able to repel the Khazar attack.[3] This front had been mainly the responsibility of the relatively small army of Jazīra, whilst the Byzantine front was the responsibility of the much bigger Syrian army. Now that the Byzantine front was not as active as before, especially after the failure of the Arab attack on Constantinople in 717/98, the Khazar front had become the major Arab field of activity. When the Khazar reacted violently, this in turn provoked a stronger Arab reaction, and the Syrians were sent to that front. Hishām sent more Syrians under his brother the formidable Maslama against the Khazar. Whether because Maslama, who was never in robust health, was getting too ill for this kind of task, or because the Syrians did not have their hearts in the fight, the Arab position did not improve. A major campaign planned for 730/112 under a new commander-in-chief met with absolute disaster and the Khazar threatened the heart of Jazīra itself not far from Mawṣil. The Khazar attacks lasted throughout the following winter and spring 732/113 and the Arabs were hardly able to resist.[4]

Hishām was badly in need of new troops to repel the Khazar. In 732/114 he entrusted the whole region of Jazīra, Armenia and Ādherbayjān to his cousin Marwān b. Muḥammad who had been long acquainted with the problems of the region and was also a good military commander. Hishām gave him a free hand to re-

[1] *Ibid.*, p. 1700. [2] *Ibid.*, pp. 1698–9, 1702.

[3] Athīr, *Kāmil*, vol. v, pp. 79, 83–5; Ibn Aʿtham, *Futūḥ*, vol. II, pp. 179A, 184B, 185A, 193A.

[4] Ṭabarī, II, pp. 1506, 1530–1, 1560; Athīr, *Kāmil*, vol. v, pp. 94, 100, 102, 117–20, 129–30; Ibn Khayyāṭ, *Tārīkh*, vol. II, pp. 352, 353, 354, 357, 358.

cruit and enlist in the *dīwān* as many men as possible from Jazīra.[1] This move was also meant to solve a new problem peculiar to this region, that of over-population. As has been already observed, immigration into Jazīra was accelerated by the suppression of the various uprisings and the demilitarization of Iraq.[2] Although our sources do not give a clear description of the manner of this immigration, at this time there were vast numbers of Arabs in Jazīra. Of course there were Arabs there before Islam. The Taghlib who, though they had continued to be Christian at the time of the conquest, were fast being converted to Islam at that time, were certainly part of the Arab population of what came to be known as Diyār Rabī'a. This region had its centre in Mawṣil and formed by far the greatest part of the province. It was this part of Jazīra which had previously been part of the Sāsānian empire and was, for the most part, the battlefield against the Byzantines. After the Arab conquest of this region and adjacent Ādherbayjān, it offered vast opportunities for the Arab immigrants. The Arab garrisons in Ardabīl in Ādherbayjān and in Mawṣil were never of any considerable size because Armenia offered them protection from any outside attacks from the north. As a result the Arabs who moved in there were allowed to settle down to a life of agriculture and cattle raising in this rich region.[3] These Arabs were by no means exclusively from clans of Rabī'a, because we know for certain that there were Azdites among them.[4] However, since they formed the largest group – Taghlib is a Rabī'a sub-tribe – and since tribesmen from Rabī'a clans moved there, the region probably for convenience became known as Diyār, the abodes of, Rabī'a. Their peaceful life and relative prosperity in this region naturally helped to swell their numbers.

The northern part of the province, known as Diyār Bakr, centred around Āmid and was constituted partly from previously held Byzantine territory in addition to some small areas of southern Armenia. The Arab–Byzantine frontier to the north-west of this region fluctuated according to the strength of the Arab yearly forays and the Byzantine resistance. The Arab tribesmen who settled there were from the clans of Bakr, another branch of

1 Athīr, *Kāmil*, vol. v, p. 132; Ibn A'tham, *Futūḥ*, vol. II, p. 193 B.
2 See above p. 115.
3 Ibn Khayyāṭ, *Tārīkh*, vol. II, p. 397; Balādhurī, *Futūḥ*, p. 329.
4 Ya'qūbī, *Tārīkh*, vol. II, p. 272; Athīr, *Kāmil*, vol. v, p. 58; Al-Azdī, Abū Zakariyā, *Tārīkh al-Mawṣil*, vol. 2, ed. A. Ḥabība, Cairo, 1967, p. 10.

Rabīʿa. They were mostly not members of the *dīwān*, though they joined in the summer expeditions in the hope of booty. In some of the former Byzantine strongholds, small garrisons of members of the *dīwān* were stationed to hold these positions for the following campaigns.[1]

Diyār Muḍar was the south-western part of Jazīra which was the former Byzantine eastern frontier region. Many of the towns of this region had been fortified strongholds and under the Arabs continued to be so. Raqqa and later Ḥarrān were the central points of this region. The Arab tribesmen here were mostly from Qays and other related clans of Muḍar. The majority were from the original conquerors of the region and were the bulk of the army of Jazīra and of course members of the *dīwān*.[2] Their military activities consisted mainly of going on yearly campaigns in the Caucasus, after which they returned to their flourishing towns where trade was fast increasing. This arrangement was to their satisfaction and after their initial objection to the Ummayads for opening up their region to further immigration, they became staunch supporters of the Marwānids. They certainly supported their imperial policy and undoubtedly became the true representatives of the Arab military class, the *muqātila*, in the province. It was from them that the Qays–Muḍar party took its name. Nevertheless they had minor problems; they also suffered from over-population. They were eventually joined by fellow clansmen from Ḥijāz, but significantly enough these new arrivals were not taken into the army. They were not even allowed to settle in the towns and instead settled in the adjacent Iraqi–Syrian desert. In 727/109 Hishām ordered that some of these tribesmen should be re-settled in Egypt. To begin with, 400 families were settled in Bilbays, to the east of the Nile delta. They were granted stipends from the *dīwān* of Egypt in addition to grants of reclaimed lands and pasture grounds. Furthermore they were subsidised by tax revenues from the treasury of Egypt to help them re-settle. They were soon joined by others from their clansmen and by the end of Hishām's reign at least three thousand families had been re-settled in Bilbays. Ironically they eventually became a major source of trouble for the government of Egypt. Meanwhile they prospered tremendously and were engaged in raising horses and transporting foodstuffs to the Red Sea which, we are told, gave a man the considerable

[1] Balādhurī, *Futūḥ*, pp. 183–5, 188.

[2] *Ibid.*, pp. 172, 175, 176, 177, 178.

income of ten dinārs a month.[1] This is an outstanding example of the extent of over-population in Jazīra and the substantial measures which the central government was ready to take to relieve these pressures.

Marwān b. Muḥammad had little trouble in raising a larger army from all the regions of Jazīra, and by 737/119 the powerful Khazar were completely defeated and driven out of Armenia and Ādherbayjān.[2] Hishām also had to give attention to the Byzantines who had taken advantage of the Khazar attacks to increase pressure on their frontier with the Arabs. In 731/113, at the height of the Khazar danger, the Byzantines were able to deal the Arabs a considerable defeat.[3] Hishām retaliated by mounting two summer campaigns, instead of the customary one, into Byzantine territory. One campaign, the responsibility of the Syrian army and led by two of Hishām's sons, Mu'āwiya and Muḥammad, was to advance along the Mediterranean coast.[4] The other was to advance from Jazīra north-west into the eastern region of the Byzantine lands and was led by Hishām's son Sulaymān.[5] This is the more important of the two campaigns because of the structure of its army. As we know, all the available Arabs in Jazīra had been dispatched to meet the Khazar threat, yet this army was grouped together in Raqqa where Sulaymān had charge. To arouse enthusiasm for this army Hishām himself marched into Raqqa brandishing his sword.[6] We know from Sulaymān's later activities, only a few years later after the death of his father Hishām, that he had a following of about 5,000 men who remained faithful to him personally during the events of these troubled years. They are referred to, in our sources, as the Dhakwāniyya, followers of Dhakwān, a *mawlā* of Sulaymān, and these followers were also *mawālī*.[7] The obvious conclusion is that Hishām, in his desperate efforts to meet the Khazar and Byzantine threats, had allowed the recruiting of converts from the local population of Jazīra to form what amounted

[1] Azdī, *Mawṣil*, p. 31; Kindī, *Governors*, pp. 76–7.

[2] Athīr, *Kāmil*, vol. v, pp. 132, 137, 160, 180; Ibn A'tham, *Futūḥ*, vol. II, pp. 193B, 197B.

[3] Dhahabī, *Tārīkh*, vol. IV, p. 227.

[4] Ṭabarī, II, pp. 1560, 1562, 1564, 1573, 1588, 1728; Ibn Khayyāṭ, *Tārīkh*, vol. II, pp. 364, 369; Athīr, *Kāmil*, vol. v, pp. 137, 145.

[5] Ṭabarī, II, pp. 1561, 1573, 1588, 1635, 1727, Ibn Khayyāṭ, *Tārīkh*, vol. II, pp. 360, 364, 365, 367, 369.

[6] Azdī, *Mawṣil*, pp. 40, 43; Balādhurī, *Futūḥ*, p. 186.

[7] Azdī, *Mawṣil*, p. 70; Ṭabarī, II, pp. 1870, 1892, 1909.

to a private army. They probably were not registered in the *dīwān* as such but were paid on the basis of a private arrangement with Sulaymān, though indirectly from the government treasury.[1] It was to help recruit these *mawālī* that Hishām took his unusual and melodramatic step in Raqqa.

Another significant step with regard to the non-Arab population took place in Mawṣil, which was specifically excluded from Marwān's governorship of Armenia, Ādherbayjān and Jazīra. A brother-in-law of Hishām was appointed governor of this growing urban centre in 724/106, although Marwān himself had been governor until two years earlier. The main occupation of Mawṣil's new governor was nothing less than the construction of a major water supply project through the town. This project consisted of the digging of a canal, branching off from the Tigris and flowing into the town, where eighteen water mills were constructed at a cost of eight million dirhams. The project was finally accomplished after fifteen years in 739/121 and it is reported that as many as 5,000 men were engaged on it at the same time.[2] The importance attached to this project is emphasized by the fact that it was carried out at a time when the treasury was under great pressure to meet external threats. Hishām, however, must have realized the effects of over-population in this area and tried to amend the situation with a long-term productive project which improved the employment prospects of at least the local population.

In Syria, the demands on the army were limited to the summer campaign on the Mediterranean coast and the rotating garrison in Iraq. When the governor of Sind on the Indian frontier asked for support in 737/119, there were only 600 Syrians who could be dispatched there, reluctantly and unwillingly.[3] Of course there were some Syrian troops in North Africa and Spain but this region was soon to become a major field of activity for the Syrian army. Let us take Egypt first. Although it was the quietest part of the empire, signs of unrest were already becoming visible there during Hishām's reign. The country as a whole was densely populated and, apart from some small pockets of under-population

[1] Before 'Umar II it was the practice to pay members of the Marwānid house for their private guards: see Ibn 'Abdilḥakam, *Sīrat 'Umar*, p. 152.

[2] Azdī, *Mawṣil*, pp. 18, 24, 26, 32, 43.

[3] Ṭabarī, II, p. 1624, Athīr, *Kāmil*, vol. V, p. 156.

like Bilbays, there was an actual demand for land. As a result of this demand, in 725/107 Hishām's permission was sought to build on the lands reclaimed when the Nile receded at the mouth of the eastern branch of the delta.[1] In the same year we hear about the first revolt by local Egyptians since the conquest as a result of a 5 per cent increase on all taxes advised by the governor of Egypt and his financial director. The Copts of Dimyāṭ particularly objected and additional troops had to be sent there to suppress an uprising which lasted for three months.[2] Another move which did not appeal to the Arab population was the introduction of a new grain measure which resulted in a decrease in the amount of grain allotted to the Arabs along with their stipends. They simply refused to use the new measures and broke them. Hishām retorted by ordering an outright decrease for such grain, from twelve to ten *irdabbs*. This created such objections that in 742/124 Hishām had to order the whole amount to be restored to them.[3]

In Hishām's reign the Egyptian navy was still active, though not as it had been before. We only hear about a defeat inflicted by the Byzantines, probably in the eastern Mediterranean in 736/118.[4] It was surprisingly in the western Mediterranean that the North African navy had become actively engaged against Sicily and Sardinia in successive raids (734–40/116–22).[5] Although some of these naval operations were an outstanding success, they point to a new field of military activity and an expensive one at that. As is well known the Arabs reached their farthest limit in Europe in 732/114 when they were defeated by Charles Martel at the Battle of Poitiers. As always, the mountains proved to be a real obstacle in the path of Arab armies and the Pyrenees were no exception. It should be noted that the Berbers formed the great majority of the Arab armies which crossed to Spain in 711/94 and in their first campaign they indeed destroyed the main forces of the Visigoths. In the following year an Arab Syrian army followed and practically finished the conquest of the whole peninsula.[6]

The Berber troops tended to settle in the conquered areas and enjoy the fruits of their conquests. Although they were soon joined by great numbers of their kinsmen, very few traces of them

[1] Kindī, *Governors*, p. 74.
[2] *Ibid.*, pp. 73–4.
[3] *Ibid.*, pp. 78, 82.
[4] *Ibid.*, p. 79; Ṭabarī, II, p. 1495, 1526.
[5] Athīr, *Kāmil*, pp. 137, 141.
[6] Ṭabarī, II, pp. 1235, 1253, 1267, 1271; Athīr, *Kāmil*, vol. IV, p. 447; Ibn 'Abdil-ḥakam, *Futūḥ Miṣr*, pp. 204–10.

occur in the later campaigns. These were carried out mainly by Syrian troops who thought of themselves as on a long extended expedition. Their frequent attempts to establish a foothold across the Pyrenees, starting from 718/100 to the defeat of 732/114, were unsuccessful. It was only after this decisive turn of events that the central government began to think in terms of settling Syrian troops in Spain. The frequent succession of Syrian generals as governors and sub-governors in Spain indicates a continuous rotation of Syrian troops there.[1] It is important to remember that the Berbers were increasingly settling in the conquered territories as their original conquerors and of course in the best locations. If any settlement of the Syrians was contemplated, there were two major difficulties. The first was where to settle them and the second was how to stop the influx of Berbers into Spain. The first issue, though difficult and creating a great deal of friction between Syrians and Berbers, was not as serious in its immediate results as the second issue. When in 739/122 the sub-governor of Tangiers tried to stop the Berbers crossing into Spain, an instantaneous revolt took place which spread like wildfire through the whole of North Africa and very seriously threatened the Arab position there.[2] Naturally there must have been long-standing reasons for discontent among the Berbers for such a revolt to spread so quickly. It should be remembered that from the very beginning of the conquest the Berbers, in contrast to all other conquered people, were granted equal status with the Arab tribesmen as long as they accepted Islam and joined the Arab armies. Attempts to deprive them of some of the privileges accorded to them forced 'Umar II to interfere on their behalf and also resulted in the murder of the Arab governor in the reign of Walīd II.[3] The considerable expenses of naval operations from North Africa led to attempts to extract more taxes from the local Berbers to alleviate the strain on the treasury. Now came this attempt to deprive them of the benefits of their own conquests in favour of their fellow Muslims, the Syrians in Spain. Their revolt was of such magnitude that in 740/123 Hishām had to send all the available Syrian troops to rescue the whole region.[4]

It was a period of near chaos in North Africa and Spain. The

[1] Athīr, *Kāmil*, vol. v, 373–4.
[2] *Ibid.*, p. 122; Ibn 'Abdilḥakam, *Futūḥ Miṣr*, pp. 217–18.
[3] See above p. 134.
[4] Ibn Khaldūn, *'Ibar*, vol. VI, pp. 110–11.

Berbers' revolt developed into a separatist movement under the banner of Khārijism and they even had their own Berber *Amīr al-Mu'minīn*.[1] This purely Berber *khawārij* movement was completely non-Arab and was the first of its nature in the empire. Although it was given the name Ibāḍiyya, it had nothing whatsoever to do with the *khawārij* movement bearing the same name in eastern Arabia. Any attempts to relate the two movements are completely unfounded and are not borne out by our sources. The evidence of the so-called Ibāḍī sources, of many centuries later, is not to be taken seriously because these sources are clearly an exaggerated romanticization of the history of an insignificant sect.[2] Indeed, its very insignificance has been the only reason for its survival in isolated areas until now. The Ibāḍiyya of eastern Arabia were remnants of the neo-*khawārij* rebellion during the second civil war. It is not surprising that after the suppression of the neo-*khawārij* revolt they found it prudent to be quietists, *qa'ada*, i.e. self-declared non-rebels. Accordingly, the central government tolerated their existence in the remote corner of the peninsula, without going to the trouble of crushing them altogether.[3] Apparently they eventually succeeded in reviving their ancient trade across the Indian Ocean and this would probably explain their contacts with Baṣra. But it is certainly absurd to suggest any relation between them and the Berbers at this stage.

Since this is the case, an explanation has to be found for this particular Berber movement being called Ibāḍiyya. As Muslim rebels against the central government it is understandable that these Berbers should be considered *khawārij* by their contemporaries. They themselves would accept and even encourage this because it implied their equality with their fellow Arab Muslims, the main purpose of their revolt. The only *khawārij* movement in existence at that time which had escaped the complete control of the central government was the Ibāḍiyya of eastern Arabia. It is not difficult to see that the terms *khawārij* and *ibāḍiyya* had become synonymous, at least from the Berber point of view. Therefore, in calling themselves Ibāḍiyya the Berber rebels were in fact clearly equating their cause with the cause of other Arab Muslim rebels.

But if the Ibāḍiyya of eastern Arabia were quietist, those of

[1] Athīr, *Kāmil*, vol. v, p. 142; Ibn 'Abdilḥakam, *Futūḥ Miṣr*, p. 218.

[2] For an opposite point of view, see T. Lewicki, "al-Ibāḍiyya", *Enc. of Islam*, new edition, Leiden, 1954– .

[3] See above p. 104.

North Africa were unequivocally activist. They practically drove all the Arabs out of North Africa, some withdrawing to Spain where they were badly needed to support their fellow Arabs against the Berbers there.[1] When the revolt was contained, the Arabs in Spain split as usual into Muḍar and Yaman factions. Some of them favoured settling in Spain and establishing some *modus vivendi* with the Berbers. These, of course, were the Yaman faction. On the other hand, the Qays faction were clamouring to return to Syria and wanted no part in settling or co-operating with the Berbers. Finally, after the temporary suppression of the Berber revolt, the Arabs reached a tentative agreement amongst themselves to settle in Spain. The way in which they were settled reflects very well the composition of the Syrian army in Spain at that time. The contingent of Damascus was settled in the district of Elvira, that of Qinnasrīn in the district of Jaen, that of Ḥimṣ in Seville and that of Palestine in Madina Sidonia and Algeciras.[2]

By the end of Hishām's reign in 743/125 the situation in North Africa and Spain, and for that matter all over the empire, was that of uneasy internal peace. However, it is no small achievement that he succeeded in defeating all the formidable external threats.

1 Athīr, *Kāmil*, vol. v, pp. 143–4; Ibn 'Abdilḥakam, *Futūḥ Miṣr*, pp. 218–25.

2 Athīr, *Kāmil*, vol. v, pp. 374–6; Ibn 'Abdilḥakam, *Futūḥ Miṣr*, p. 223.

9

THE COLLAPSE OF THE MARWĀNIDS

Hishām was succeeded by his nephew Walīd II. Our sources give the impression that Walīd's succession had been pre-arranged twenty years earlier by his father Yazīd II, Hishām's predecessor. Although this is possible, a closer study of the situation indicates that it was not that simple. There is no doubt that Hishām himself was not completely satisfied with this arrangement. Within his close circle, opposition to Walīd's succession was voiced by as prominent a scholar as al-Zuhrī.[1] It is also reported that Hishām tried to change the succession in favour of one of his sons, Maslama, who, oddly enough, was not as active or prominent as his brothers during their father's long reign.[2] If this is true, it would seem that Hishām was, in effect, trying to promote a compromise candidate. Subsequent events clearly show that members of the Marwānid family were deeply divided on the question of Walīd's succession. Naturally, disagreements must have arisen before within the family, but this time the disagreement was most serious and it heralded the disintegration of one of the pillars of the regime, the unity of the Marwānid family itself.

It may easily be surmised that those members of the family who favoured Walīd's succession were in fact urging the continued implementation of the expansionist policies vigorously reimposed during the reign of his father, Yazīd II. Later events show that those opposed to Walīd favoured the reversal of these policies. Hishām must have realized that this division existed within his family, hence his attempt to offer a compromise candidate. When this failed and as he himself inclined more towards the expansionist policies, the members of the family supporting Walīd won the day and his succession was assured.

Walīd II is portrayed, in our sources, as a self-indulgent man concerned only with his pleasures,[3] but such accusations are

[1] Ṭabarī, II, p. 1811.
[2] *Ibid.*, pp. 1741–3.
[3] *Ibid.*, pp. 1741, 1775.

simply one example of exaggeration by these sources of his failings. Indeed these accusations may have been no more than rumours propagated by his many enemies and dutifully reported. Walīd's major failing was that he did not comprehend the effects of the heavy burdens imposed on the limited strength of the Syrian army. He also did not realize that the recruiting of a new army from Jazīra had brought into being an alternative power base for a new regime in the empire. Of course from Walīd II's point of view such an army would serve the interests of the empire if deployed in new wars of expansion.

Walīd II, in his short reign, seems to have favoured more militant Qaysite expansionist policies than Hishām. This is best indicated by his attitude towards Khālid al-Qasrī, the leader of the Yamanites. After his dismissal from office as governor of Iraq and the East, Khālid took up residence in Damascus and is reported to have joined the summer campaigns into Byzantine territories. For almost six years he tried to stay out of the political struggle, but he was nevertheless accused of continued opposition and of conspiring against Qaysite policies. Walīd II ordered him to be arrested and handed over to his arch-enemy Yūsuf b. 'Umar, governor of Iraq and leader of the Qaysites. Yūsuf, in turn, ordered him to be tortured, and as a result Khālid died in prison in 743/126.[1] This action against the acknowledged leader of the Yamanites is a clear indication of Walīd II's total commitment to the Qaysites. He also took another very harsh and most unusual measure against a prominent member of the Marwānid family: he ordered Sulaymān b. Hishām to be beaten and banished to 'Umān where he was imprisoned.[2] As we know, Sulaymān had been very active during his father's reign and had led many summer expeditions against Byzantium. Of more significance, he had recruited his own private army from the non-Arab population of Jazīra.[3] With such an army, and in view of the division within the Marwānids, Sulaymān represented a powerful threat to Walīd II, and it is not surprising that the latter should have taken such an unprecedented action against his own cousin.

Turning to the Syrian army, Walīd II knew perfectly well that he could not afford to recall those sent to North Africa to hold down the Berbers. Instead, he turned to the long forgotten island

[1] *Ibid.*, pp. 1812–22.

[2] *Ibid.*, p. 1776.

[3] See above p. 147.

of Cyprus, which had been captured from the Byzantines as early as 649/24, during Mu'āwiya's governorship of Syria, and was subsequently settled by Arabs from Syria.[1] Walīd II sent a naval force there, in 743/125, to recall these settlers and to force them to join expeditions against Byzantium.[2] As for the remaining troops in Syria, he sought their firmer allegiance by ordering an increase in their stipends. In addition, relying on the comfortable surplus in the central treasury, he announced the resumption of the practice of granting pensions and giving slaves to the blind and the chronically ill.[3] This practice, as we suggested before, was meant as a subsidy for the Arabs of Syria and had apparently been suspended by Hishām.[4] But all these inducements were to no avail. The Syrians, disgruntled with policies which had entailed constant campaigning in all parts of the empire, turned against Walīd II. The generals of the Syrian army, in co-operation with members of the Marwānid family, engineered a successful *coup d'état*, and scarcely a year had passed when Walīd II's reign was brought to an end.[5] He himself was murdered by the hitherto most loyal subjects of the Umayyad house, the Syrian *jund*. Our sources refer to them as Yamanites for two reasons.[6] First, regardless of their nominal tribal affiliations, they were rebelling against the pronounced Qaysite policies of Walīd II. Second, the nomenclature, Yamanite, was the opposite of Qaysite, which at that time meant the army of Jazīra. Significantly enough, the latter stayed out of this upheaval in Syria but, as we shall see, it was very soon to be used to control Syria itself.[7] In fact the *coup d'état* against Walīd II was, for all practical purposes, the end of the Marwānid regime. The very basis of its rule was destroyed when it lost the support of the Syrian army.

Yazīd III was the choice of the Syrian generals to succeed his cousin Walīd II in 744/126. Surprisingly, his first act was to abolish the increase of the stipends to the Syrian troops granted by his predecessor.[8] This was not a sign of ingratitude to those who had put him in power, but the first indication that under the new regime the Syrians would not be asked to perform any tasks

[1] Balādhurī, *Futūḥ*, p. 153
[2] Ṭabarī, II, p. 1769; Athīr, *Kāmil*, vol. V, p. 206.
[3] Ṭabarī, II, p. 1754; Ya'qūbī, *Tārīkh*, vol. II, p. 336.
[4] See above p. 119.
[5] Ṭabarī, II, pp. 1755, 1777–810.
[6] *Ibid.*, pp. 1755, 1778, 1784.
[7] *Ibid.*, pp. 1785, 1850, 1870–3.
[8] *Ibid.*, p. 1825.

beyond those required from the rest of the *muqātila* in the empire. In effect, Yazīd III was promising to keep the Syrian troops in Syria and to rule the empire without relying on them to police other provinces. This was but one step of many he announced which meant a complete reversal of the imperial Qaysite policies. In a widely publicized inaugural speech reported in all our sources, he gave the outline of what can best be described as the manifesto of the Yamanites. He promised that, (*a*) an end would be put to all construction of unnecessary monumental works; (*b*) no more agricultural projects would be undertaken at public expense for the reclamation of lands to be granted to members of his family; (*c*) the revenues of each region would be spent on the needs of its inhabitants and only the surplus would be used for the needs of adjacent regions; (*d*) no long expeditions would be undertaken which would keep men away from their homes; (*e*) subject peoples would be fairly treated in matters of taxation so that they would not have to abandon their lands or be distressed in any way; (*f*) all Muslims, i.e. Arabs and non-Arabs, in all parts of the empire would receive equal stipends; (*g*) finally, he renounced all claims to absolute authority and promised to allow himself to be deposed if he did not fulfil these promises.[1]

This last point is of special importance because it probably throws some light on the political attitude of a little-known early Islamic sect, the *qadariyya*. Although we are uncertain about the theological doctrines of this sect, especially at this formative stage, its political views are important because of its apparent connection with the opposition to the Marwānid regime. We recall that Ghaylān al-Dimashqī was executed on Hishām's orders because of unspecified "heretical" views, which are only described as Qadarite.[2] Yazīd III is reported to have been a Qadarite and a Ghaylānite at the same time,[3] and one may assume, therefore, that either they both held the same views or that both names were used for the same groups. Ghaylān's view, which probably cost him his life, seems to have been the advocacy of certain limitations to the authority of the *Amīr al-Mu'minīn*.[4] Naturally he could not afford to be as explicit about this issue as Yazīd III in his inaugural

[1] *Ibid.*, pp. 1834–5; Ibn Khayyāṭ, *Tārīkh*, vol. II, pp. 382–3; Azdī, *Mawṣil*, pp. 50–1; Dhahabī, *Tārīkh*, vol. v, p. 189.
[2] See above p. 143; Dhahabī, *Tārīkh*, vol. IV, p. 289.
[3] Ṭabarī, II, pp. 1828, 1837, 1869, 1874, 1891.
[4] Al-Nawbakhtī, al-Ḥaṣan b. Mūsā, *Firaq al-Shī'a*, ed. H. Ritter, Leipzig, 1931, p. 9.

speech. There is no doubt that the Qadarites held the view that the *Amīr al-Mu'minīn* must not have absolute power; and that his limited secular authority must be subject to the approval of the community, which would have the right to depose him if he abused his powers of office. Of course there was no question of any religious authority being accorded to the *Amīr al-Mu'minīn*. Ghaylān, the Qadarites and Yazīd III were not against the Marwānids; they were against the Marwānid conception of the office they held.

Although the great majority of the Syrian army supported Yazīd III, some of the *jund* of Ḥimṣ and Palestine, who had probably not been involved in the *coup d'état*, objected to the murder of their legitimate ruler. However, their objections were not very serious and were easily overcome. In this respect, Sulaymān b. Hishām, who had been imprisoned on the orders of Walīd II and who was released by Yazīd III, played a significant role. With his private army, the Dhakwāniyya, he was able to convince the objectors of the new regime's point of view.[1] Marwān b. Muḥammad, governor of Armenia, Ādherbayjān and Jazīra and commander of the considerable Qaysite army of Jazīra, was placated by having the rich populous region of Mawṣil included in his governorship.[2] Obviously Yazīd III was moving cautiously to accommodate this powerful group in the hope that he could eventually convince them of the futility of the outdated policies of his predecessors.

In Egypt the situation was advantageous for the full implementation of Yazīd's new policies. Although there had been some minor unrest in Hishām's reign, this had been easily overcome. The Egyptian population was basically co-operative towards the Arabs as is evident from their long-established participation in the operations of the Arab Egyptian navy.[3] It was clear that with minor concessions the Egyptians could be completely won over and serve better the Arab interests, and the governor of Egypt was instructed to grant stipends to as many as 30,000 Egyptians at the rate of twenty to twenty-five dinārs per annum. These new members of the *dīwān* of Egypt are specifically referred to in our sources as the *maqāmiṣa* and *mawālī*.[4] The *maqāmiṣa* were the Egyptians who had been serving in the navy as sailors, rowers, helmsmen,

[1] Ṭabarī, II, pp. 1826–33.
[2] *Ibid.*, p. 1873.
[3] See above p. 123.
[4] Kindī, *Governors*, p. 84.

and so on who had been paid wages for the duration of the annual campaigns. It should be noticed that the Arab navy was an imitation of the Byzantine model. The fighting unit was a galley with a minimum of a hundred rowers in addition to other professional staff. Although these were all armed, there was on each ship a fighting force who took up positions on the upper deck. This fighting force was probably Arab although the main manpower of each ship was Egyptian. The number of Egyptians involved in the naval operations must have been very large because we know that the number of fighting units was close to a thousand ships.[1] Since this navy closely imitated the Byzantine model, it is no wonder that the Greek term *machimos*, i.e. fighting man, was used by the Arabs in the corrupted (plural) form *maqāmiṣa* to denote the Egyptians serving in the Arab navy.[2] Yazīd III was now offering these men the opportunity to enlist on a permanent basis, provided, of course, that they would accept Islam. The specific reference to the *mawālī* in addition to the *maqāmiṣa* confirms this condition. It may also mean that Yazīd III was planning to raise an Egyptian force to be used in connection with the navy to relieve the pressure on the Syrians in North Africa and Spain.

The situation in these regions was getting completely out of control as a result of the continued differences among the Arabs in Spain in their attitude towards the Berbers. Although the Berber revolt had been contained by the fresh Syrian troops sent to North Africa during Hishām's reign, disagreement among the Arabs in both North Africa and Spain became the major threat to the precarious stability of these regions. In 743/125 Ḥanẓala b. Ṣafwān, the Syrian general and governor, sent a contingent of his troops to restore order in Spain. The result was chaos not only in Spain but also its dissemination to North Africa itself. Some of the Arabs in Spain crossed to North Africa and took matters into their own hands. In 745/127 Ḥanẓala was compelled to withdraw with his troops to Syria and to leave North Africa in the hands of the Arab rebels, who were led by ʿAbdulraḥman b. Ḥabīb, grandson of ʿUqba b. Nāfiʿ, the celebrated leader of the first Arab conquests in the region. While chaos prevailed in Spain until the establishment

[1] As early as 648/27 the ships numbered over two hundred: Ibn ʿAbdilḥakam, *Futūḥ Miṣr*, p. 190.

[2] The Greek word *nautēs* was also used in the Arabic form *nūtī* meaning sailor on the Nile: Ibn ʿAbdilḥakam, *Sīrat ʿUmar*, p. 67.

of the Umayyads there in 756/138, North Africa remained under the control of the rebels who had to contend with the resumed Berber revolt until the region was reconquered by the 'Abbāsids in 763/146.[1]

As for Iraq, Yazīd III dismissed the Qaysite governor Yūsuf b. 'Umar in favour of Manṣūr b. Jumhūr al-Kalbī, the chief conspirator of the Yamanites who had engineered the *coup d'état*.[2] His task, the most significant of the short reign of Yazīd III, was to reconstruct the Iraqi army, the central treasury helping to pay the stipends of the new recruits.[3] The Iraqis would normally have welcomed such a step, but Manṣūr's approach was not acceptable to them. He seems to have favoured the Syrian troops stationed in Iraq or to have demurred at their complete integration into the new army. After only three months, when it became apparent that as a Syrian general he could not have the full trust of the Iraqis, regardless of his role in the successful *coup d'état*,[4] he was replaced by a new governor, who significantly was not a Syrian general, but who had the distinction of a glamorous name, 'Abdullah the son of 'Umar II. To the Iraqis the appeal of this name lay in the fact that it represented to them a revival of his father's policy – to put an end to the Syrian domination of Iraq. The new governor proceeded to reconstruct the Iraqi army in which he proposed to integrate the Syrian troops in Iraq. Manṣūr, the previous governor and the Syrian general, was to be one of the generals of this new army.[5]

During his short governorship of Iraq and the East, Manṣūr b. Jumhūr appointed his brother Manẓūr as his lieutenant in the East. Although Manẓūr himself never arrived in Khurāsān, the news of his appointment caused great excitement there, particularly among the Yamanites. To them it meant the end of the power of the right wing Muḍarite governor, Naṣr b. Sayyār, and the expectation that a more moderate Yamanite policy would be applied by Manẓūr. However, Naṣr himself refused to recognize this appointment and proceeded to take measures against the leaders of the Yamanites in Khurāsān to secure his position.[6] These measures led to the eventual unity of all his opponents and this

[1] Athīr, *Kāmil*, vol. v, pp. 204–5, 235–6, 375–6.
[2] Ṭabarī, II, pp. 1778, 1794, 1803–4, 1836–7.
[3] Ya'qūbī, *Tārīkh*, vol. II, p. 336.
[4] Ṭabarī, II, pp. 1836–7.
[5] *Ibid.*, pp. 1854–5.
[6] *Ibid.*, pp. 1845, 1847, 1859.

unity was a major factor in the success of the 'Abbāsid revolution in Khurāsān.

Unfortunately, Yazīd III died suddenly at the end of 744/126 after ruling for no more than six months. His brother, Ibrāhīm, who succeeded him for four months, was not acknowledged by all factions as *Amīr al-Mu'minīn*. Factionalism spread among the Syrian army in Syria itself and the situation deteriorated into complete chaos in almost all the empire.[1]

Marwān b. Muḥammad was now sitting comfortably in Jazīra at the head of the most powerful force in the empire. He himself came to Ḥarrān from the Armenian frontier and consolidated the strength of his army by recruiting new men and by appealing to the old guard of Jazīra.[2] The last of the Syrian troops in his army, a group from the *jund* of Palestine, threatened a mutiny if they were not allowed to return to their homes and Marwān was forced to accept their demand.[3] Another group of dissidents on his own doorstep in Jazīra consisted mainly of the settled Arabs in Diyār Rabī'a who either did not want to join Marwān's army at all or wanted to leave the army and stay at home.[4] Significantly they were supported by a group of the recently converted Muslims from Taghlib who had settled in Adherbayjān.[5] Their most prominent leader was al-Ḍaḥḥāk b. Qays of Shaybān from Rabī'a. They are celebrated in our sources as a *khawārij* sect, the *ṣufriyya*.[6] They were essentially a group of assimilated Arabs who refused to support the Umayyad regime in any form any longer. They also saw no reason for involvement with the so-far unsuccessful Shī'ite uprisings. Their basic tenets cannot be more precisely defined for they are described to us as *qa'ada*, literally sitters. As such they were diametrically opposed to any adventurous policies. If al-Ḥārith b. Surayj represented the extreme right wing in Khurāsān, al-Ḍaḥḥāk b. Qays would have represented the extreme left wing in the heart of the empire. Knowing that in Jazīra they would be an easy prey to Marwān, these quietist *khawārij* swiftly moved down on Kūfa.[7] There, 'Abdullah b. 'Umar was still busy reconstructing the army of Iraq. After some initial objection from the Syrian troops stationed in Iraq, he had been able to

[1] *Ibid.*, p. 1875.
[2] *Ibid.*, pp. 1873, 1876; Azdī, *Mawṣil*, p. 61.
[3] Ṭabarī, II, pp. 1871–3; Azdī, *Mawṣil*, p. 66.
[4] Ṭabarī, II, pp. 1897–9; Azdī, *Mawṣil*, p. 60.
[5] Ibn Khayyāṭ, *Tārīkh*, vol. II, p. 395.
[6] Ṭabarī, II, p. 1900.
[7] *Ibid.*, pp. 189–9; Ibn Khayyāṭ, *Tārīkh*, vol. II, p. 396.

enlist a sizable force and with the help of the Kūfan treasury the stipends for this force were assured.[1]

Meanwhile Marwān entered Damascus where, in 744/127, he proclaimed himself the new *Amīr al-Mu'minīn*.[2] There was some opposition from the *jund* of Ḥimṣ and Palestine, but it was soon overcome.[3] Another group opposed to Marwān II gathered around Sulaymān b. Hishām and his *mawālī* private army, the Dhakwāniyya, but it was also overcome and Sulaymān fled with his army to join the *khawārij* converging on Kūfa.[4] Marwān II, now in control of the situation in Syria, sent his new governor, al-Naḍr b. Sa'īd, to Iraq at the head of a contingent of the army of Jazīra.[5] Although 'Abdullah b. 'Umar was acceptable to a section of the population in Iraq, he was still a Marwānid appointee and a Marwānid himself. While he refused to recognize Marwān II, he did not repudiate Marwānid rule. The anti-Umayyad forces in Kūfa could not be expected to accept this situation without taking advantage of this lapse of Marwānid power and another pseudo-Shī'ite movement sprang up there. The only reason it is described as Shī'ite is that it was led by 'Abdullah b. Mu'āwiya, a great-grandson of a brother of 'Alī. This was the first time such a movement was openly proclaimed in the name of a person who was not a direct descendent of 'Alī. It only shows that the notion of the right of members of the House of the Prophet to rule was gaining wider acceptance and accordingly was being broadly applied to include all cousins of the Prophet. It is not surprising that other cousins, the 'Abbāsids, were also at that time actively engaged in furthering their own claims to the supreme office. However, 'Abdullah b. Mu'āwiya was not able to raise enough support in Kūfa to resist the new army of 'Abdullah b. 'Umar.[6] When he was driven out of Kūfa, he went to Madā'in whence he established himself in western Iran. Although his success was short-lived, his appeal to the local *mawālī* seems to have been considerable.[7] It must be noted that this was the first time that these *mawālī* had taken part on a large scale in the chronic upheavals in the empire. This indicates that Islam had begun to strike deeper roots in western Iran and that the new converts

1 Ṭabarī, II, pp. 1854–5.
2 *Ibid.*, pp. 1890–2.
3 *Ibid.*, pp. 1892–3, 1912.
4 *Ibid.*, pp. 1877–8, 1897, 1908–12; Azdī, *Mawṣil*, p. 61.
5 Ṭabarī, II, p. 1899.
6 *Ibid.*, pp. 1879–87.
7 *Ibid.*, pp. 1880–1, 1976–7.

were increasingly affected by the movement towards assimilation. Since the Marwānid regime, which was completely identified with the opposition to this movement, was showing unmistakable signs of imminent disintegration, these *mawālī* had no hesitation in supporting the revolt of ʿAbdullah b. Muʿāwiya. But their support should not be overestimated since it melted away at the first sight of Marwān II's troops.

Meanwhile, in Kūfa a most confused struggle was going on between three different groups. The first was the new army of Iraq, including the Syrian garrison and all led by ʿAbdullah b. ʿUmar, the ex-governor of Iraq of Yazīd III. Our sources refer to this group as Yaman.[1] The second group, referred to as Muḍar, was a contingent of the army of Jazīra under the leadership of Naḍr b. Saʿīd, the new governor of Iraq appointed by Marwān II.[2] These two groups were temporarily united only to fight the third group, the *khawārij* of Ḍaḥḥāk, now attacking Kūfa.[3] The latter captured Kūfa where they were joined by the Syrians previously with the former governor ʿAbdullah b. ʿUmar.[4] The remaining united forces of Yaman and Muḍar withdrew to Wāsiṭ, where they fought against each other, only to be united once more when the *khawārij* attacked their town.[5] Notwithstanding, the alliance between the Muḍar and the Yaman soon dissolved. While the Muḍar withdrew with Naḍr b. Saʿīd to Syria, the Yaman and ʿAbdullah b. ʿUmar joined the *khawārij*.[6] Soon these rebel forces gained more strength when they were joined by yet another leading member of the Marwānid family, Sulaymān b. Hishām and his private army, the Dhakwāniyya.[7] These combined forces attacked Mawṣil and occupied it. Having consolidated his position in Syria, Marwān II wasted no time and quickly marched on Mawṣil. In the ensuing battle (746/128), the rebel forces were shattered and their leader Ḍaḥḥāk was killed.[8] Any rebels who fled to, or had remained in, Iraq were vigorously pursued and soon this province in addition to Jazīra and Syria was under the complete control of Marwān II.

At this point, Marwān II does not seem to have been unduly

[1] *Ibid.*, pp. 1898, 1899, 1900, 1905. [2] *Loc. cit.*
[3] Ṭabarī, II, pp. 1898–1900.
[4] Athīr, *Kāmil*, vol. v, p. 255; Ṭabarī, II, p. 1899.
[5] Ṭabarī, II, pp. 1902, 1905. [6] *Ibid.*, pp. 1913–14.
[7] *Ibid.*, pp. 1914, 1939–41; Azdī, *Mawṣil*, p. 70.
[8] Ṭabarī, II, pp. 1940–1.

worried about the situation in Khurāsān. He had promptly confirmed Naṣr b. Sayyār, who had defied Yazīd III, in his governorship.[1] To Marwān II, this open and successful defiance was sufficient proof that Naṣr could muster enough support to hold the province. While it is true that there were reports about conflicts among the Arabs in Khurāsān and strong rumours about an impending local uprising, Marwān II could not have anticipated the unthinkable outcome of this situation. Furthermore, there were more pressing matters at hand. The revolt of ʿAbdullah b. Muʿāwiya was rampant in western Iran and was gathering more momentum and support from the remnants of the rebels of Iraq and Jazīra. Sulaymān b. Hishām, his *mawālī*, Manṣūr b. Jumhūr, and his Syrian followers fled only to join his forces.[2] More significant, albeit less important in terms of strength, Muʿāwiya was also joined by three leading members of the ʿAbbāsid family, one of whom was no less than Abū Jaʿfar, better known as al-Manṣūr.[3]

The pseudo-Shīʿite movement of ʿAbdullah b. Muʿāwiya had come to be a Shīʿite–Khārijite–Marwānid–ʿAbbāsid movement. To try to find any ideological basis for this conglomeration is to defy logic. Indeed the lack of ideology was a fundamental weakness of this revolt, in addition to its absolute lack of organization. The participants, whether Syrians, Iraqis, Jazīrans, Arabs or non-Arabs, were certainly dissatisfied with the Marwānid regime but this in itself was not enough to unite them against the formidable forces of Marwān II. This revolt lasted two years only because he was busy elsewhere, but once he turned his attention to it, the rebels had no hope of success. At the first encounter the rebels again dispersed in all directions and simply waited to join in the next inevitable uprising. Their leaders fled to remote corners of the empire; Manṣūr b. Jumhūr to India; and ʿAbdullah b. Muʿāwiya to Khurāsān where he was murdered in 746/129 at the instigation of a fellow Shīʿite rebel, Abū Muslim.[4] The ʿAbbāsids Abū Jaʿfar and his two uncles, quietly returned to their homes in Palestine whence they would soon come to Kūfa to assume the leadership of a better organized revolution.

In Egypt, Marwān II's governor cancelled the stipends ordered by Yazīd III to the new recruits for the army and the navy. They mutinied and re-installed Yazīd III's governor who

[1] *Ibid.*, p. 1917.
[2] *Ibid.*, p. 1947.
[3] *Ibid.*, p. 1977.
[4] *Ibid.*, pp. 1979–80.

they presumably hoped would re-issue their stipends.[1] Marwān II sent an army which was able to restore order to the province, but once this army was withdrawn uprisings erupted again.[2] The would-be recruits, who were well entrenched in Alexandria and other coastal towns, resumed their mutiny.[3] Minor but numerous uprisings spread to all districts. A local Coptic peasant revolt occurred in the heart of the delta and another two were reported to have taken place in Upper Egypt.[4] The Arabs of Egypt were hardly able to maintain their control of the province. To add to the complexity of the situation, a mutiny erupted among the Arabs themselves. Those involved were the tribesmen from Jazīra settled in Bilbays during the reign of Hishām. They were ordered to be stationed on the Egyptian borders in Sinai to prevent any possible attacks from outside rebels. Although as members of the *dīwān* they were required to take part in military duties, they objected to this and their mutiny added to the general unrest in the province. The central government, however, was too occupied with developments in the east to send another army to help regain control of Egypt.[5]

Yaman was another province where unrest had long fermented because of the attempts of the central treasury to extract more taxes from the Arabs there.[6] Another *khawārij* uprising spread quickly in this region. It would probably have been left alone had the rebels not moved on Ḥijāz and occupied Madīna itself in 748/130 after the bloody Battle of Qudayd where many Qurayshites were killed. If only for prestige Marwān II had to take strong action, and an army was sent which drove the rebels out of Madīna and pursued them into Yaman. The revolt was suppressed and its leaders were killed.[7]

It was under these circumstances that another group of revolutionaries in Khurāsān decided that the time was ripe to carry out their well-organized plan to bring down Umayyad rule.

[1] Kindī, *Governors*, pp. 85–7.
[2] *Ibid.*, pp. 88–92.
[3] *Ibid.*, p. 96.
[4] *Ibid.*, pp. 94, 95.
[5] *Ibid.*, pp. 90, 94, 95.
[6] Ibn 'Abdilḥakam, *Sīrat 'Umar*, p. 65; Ibn Khayyāṭ, *Tārīkh*, vol. II, p. 408.
[7] Ṭabarī, II, pp. 2006–15.

10

THE END OF AN ERA

If military ability and power were needed to save the Marwānids and restore order in the empire, Marwān II undoubtedly had both. He had spent the greater part of his life leading expeditions on the Armenian frontier where he had earned himself a well-deserved military reputation. Furthermore, he had assembled a powerful army which had enabled him to defeat the formidable Khazar. As we have seen he now proceeded to re-conquer the empire, but in spite of his success in Syria, Iraq and western Iran his efforts were doomed to failure. His regime was bound to arouse more opposition throughout the empire because in fact it was a more pronouncedly Qaysite regime than that of his predecessors. He himself was certainly a strong advocate of expansionist policies. In contrast to his predecessors who had the waning support of the Syrian army, Marwān II had the willing and solid support of the army of Jazīra, his own creation. These Jazīrans were indeed the hard core of the Qaysites and, now revitalized and reorganized by Marwān II, they were ready to take over more forcefully the role of the Syrians under the previous regime. But even such a well-organized group, which by its very nature was clearly a minority, could not give new life to bankrupt policies. Their stubborn attempt to re-impose their will on the rest of the empire was but a last stand. Indeed, it provoked their opponents to take the more decisive action which destroyed the Marwānid regime.

So far the Arabs had failed to solve the social and political problems of the empire they had so easily won. The Madīnan regime was so hopelessly unprepared to cope with these problems that it soon dissolved into civil war which nobody really wanted. With the exception of the *qurrā'*, the interests of the various Arab groups were not yet too far apart to prevent a compromise. This compromise was personified in Mu'āwiya whose extremely shrewd balancing acts were successful as long as he lived. In his long reign of twenty years, he did not and could not offer profound solutions to the existing problems. He simply offered the rival groups a chance to co-exist in the hope that their contradictory interests would be brought closer together. But this respite merely gave the rival groups the opportunity to consolidate their strength and perhaps to drift further apart. Soon after his death the civil war was resumed on a devastating scale.

The failure of Ibn al-Zubayr, the rival *Amīr al-Mu'minīn* of Makka, to offer a viable alternative system threatened the dismemberment of the empire. To preserve it 'Abdulmalik was forced to use the power of the Syrian army, but the price of his success was too great for the future of Islamic politics. The use of military power became the main basis of government and armed revolt the only means of opposition. This was the result of the failure of the Arabs to develop their political institutions in response to new circumstances.

Abū Bakr was selected on the basis of slightly modified Arab tradition to cope with purely Arab problems. Although he was given the vague title of *Khalīfa*, the powers of his office were as limited as those of an Arab chief and his success is significant. After the conquests, the Arabs basically wanted an Arab chief to preside over a confederation of conquered provinces. These provinces were conceived of as autonomous territories practically owned and ruled by their respective original conquerors. According to well-established Arab tradition they were willing to concede to their chief, the *Amīr al-Mu'minīn* in Madīna, a small share of their gains, but it was unthinkable that they should concede to him any authority over themselves or over the territories they had conquered. The autonomy of the provinces was enhanced by the fact that the Arabs retained the existing social and administrative structures of the conquered territories. Under the circumstances and because of the complete lack of any administrative apparatus in Madīna, the *Amīr al-Mu'minīn* had no control over developments in the provinces. Important decisions were taken by the leaders on the spot in each province and obviously such decisions could only be enforced if they were in accordance with the interest of the conquerors of the particular province. The *Amīr al-Mu'minīn* was merely informed of these decisions and perhaps could act as an arbitrator if a specific dispute were brought to his attention. Neither Arab tradition nor Islam itself could offer any guidance to the Arabs on the subject of the proper powers to be granted to the head of their empire. Perhaps the most unfortunate factor in this situation was the speed with which these developments took place, thus making it virtually impossible for the Arabs to develop their limited political institutions to meet a most unexpected new situation. It goes without saying that the Arabs, even had they wanted, could not have copied the Byzantine or Sāsānian imperial structures at this early stage.

It did not take long for the Arabs to realize that they would not be able to preserve their empire if they could not rule it, and the question of extending the powers of the *Amīr al-Mu'minīn* acquired a certain urgency. Eventually two points of view emerged and these could best be described as Arab and Islamic respectively. The Arab was first expressed and put into practice by 'Uthmān. During his reign, he tried to increase the secular powers of his office. In other words he favoured strengthening the powers of the *Amīr al-Mu'minīn* as an Arab chief. The Islamic point of view was first advocated by 'Alī, who made it a condition of his acceptance of the office after 'Umar's assassination that he should be given religious interpretative powers. Although both 'Uthmān and 'Alī failed in their attempts to extend the powers of the *Amīr al-Mu'minīn*, their points of view continued to represent the main trends within Islamic society concerning the functions of this office. Two centuries later, we find, on the one hand, a profound intellectual like al-Jāḥiẓ, propagating the 'Uthmāniyya point of view. On the other hand the *shī'a* of 'Alī became even more articulate in their demands for more religious power for the *Imām–Amīr al-Mu'minīn*.

It is significant that the *khawārij*, who were most opposed to both 'Uthmān and 'Alī, conceived of their *Amīr al-Mu'minīn* as no more than an Arab chief, i.e. a leader with neither secular nor religious authority. At the same time, Mu'āwiya's compromise did not include granting him any religious authority, although it tacitly consented to giving him more secular power. Yet Mu'āwiya was astute enough to recognize the growing strength of the Arab leaders in the provinces and to allow them a share in the government of their respective provinces. This was also a shrewd step towards weaving the new provincial tribal structure into the nascent imperial government. It was essentially an Arab solution to the problem and it is not surprising that it was a variant of 'Uthmān's solution. Evidently it had some success and indeed it could have been the best answer because in effect it would have allowed Arab political institutions to adjust to the political problems arising from the conquests. But there were other social problems in the empire demanding immediate solutions and unfortunately Mu'āwiya did not pay enough attention to them. Alternatively, he may have been unable to devise another ingenious compromise because of the conflicting interests of the various groups in the provinces. His only solution was further expansion, but this could be no more than a temporary measure and in the long run it added to, rather than solved, these social problems. Indeed the failure of the Arabs to find a cure for the social ills of the empire was the main reason why 'Abdulmalik had to use naked military power to maintain his rule. But neither the continuous suppression of social grievances nor the temporary relief of wars of expansion brought about internal social stability. This, the basic objective of any system of government, eluded the Marwānids, and the short-lived attempts at reform by 'Umar II and Yazīd III had no effect other than to arouse more despair among the discontented. The Marwānids had to rely more and more on naked power to sustain their rule, which came to be regarded as absolute tyranny by their opponents. Moreover, this tyranny was supported by the socially privileged groups and naturally this added to the bitterness and vehemence of the opposition. The revolt of the Syrian army against the Marwānids offered the opportunity for the Marwānid regime to be brought down. Yet Marwān II sought to re-establish this hated regime on exactly the same lines. Social discontent, however, proved a more powerful force than his well-organized army.

This social discontent was again caused by the failure of the Arab conquerors to allow for social mobility in the empire they had conquered and subsequently settled. Islam could have provided the framework for a new social structure in the empire, but it was Arab traditions and the Arabs themselves who were to blame for this failure. Before they realized that their conquests were permanent accomplishments, they had been willing to welcome into their ranks any converts from the conquered populations. They had even been ready to accept the co-operation of those who retained their own religions to fight their formidable antagonists, the Byzantines and the Sāsānians. But once they realized their strength and their extraordinary achievements this spontaneous process of assimilation was stopped. With the exception of Syria, where a good part of the indigenous population were Arabs who accepted Islam, the Arabs set themselves apart from the conquered populations and tried to limit their settling to the garrison towns built for this purpose. This social segregation served as a cohesive force to unite the conquerors and to strengthen their identification with what they considered their own by right of conquest. Their strong common interest was to take full advantage of their conquests where they were intent on settling permanently. As an army of occupation, there was no pressure on them to integrate into the social structure of the conquered territories, but as settlers the situation was drastically different. If they were to be integrated, their relatively small numbers would soon be assimilated into the vast conquered populations, and inevitably they would lose not only their identity but the rewards of their conquests. It is not surprising, then, that they decided in favour of segregating themselves and remaining outside the social structure of the conquered populations. This was a convenient arrangement for conquerors and conquered alike, but very soon pressures from both sides began to build up dissipating its initial success.

On the one hand new Arab immigrants poured into the garrison towns and their arrival signalled the beginning of a long struggle among the Arabs themselves. Although the clamour of the newcomers for a more equitable share in the rewards of the conquests was swiftly channelled into new conquests, this only multiplied the problems of the garrison towns. These towns were quickly losing their military character and changing into booming urban centres. The accumulated wealth of their inhabitants opened up dazzling prospects for traders to supply goods for consumption and for merchants to engage in the vast operations of exchange and banking required in the distribution of stipends and the transfer of the fifth of all booty to the central treasury. Although the Makkans were the first to exploit such opportunities, other Arabs soon followed in their steps and discovered that these commercial activities were even more lucrative than their stipends or shares of the booty. As a result, there developed among the Arabs of the garrison towns an increasing reluctance to join military expeditions. Of course, there were also others who were not able to enrol in the *dīwān* or simply refrained from doing so, preferring to keep their freedom of action. In short, there were elements among the Arabs of the garrison towns who were losing their zest for military activities and gradually turning to a more civilian way of life. It is to be expected that these elements would have a different attitude towards the conquered populations than that of their fellow Arabs who saw themselves only as conquerors.

The influx of people into the garrison towns was not by any means restricted to the new Arab immigrants. Many non-Arabs from the surrounding areas flocked to these rapidly expanding urban centres to take advantage of the new economic opportunities. Whether they were craftsmen, skilled or unskilled labourers, their services were in demand and probably well paid for by the affluent Arabs. Flourishing trade would also attract many indigenous merchants from other trade centres. Furthermore, the ravages of the Arab civil wars and numerous uprisings had driven many of the peasants from the land into the expanding towns in search of safety and employment. These other non-Arab civilian populations contributed much to the change of character of the garrison towns. Their living in close proximity to the Arabs helped to bring down the barriers between Arabs and non-Arabs which had in effect been the main purpose in building these garrison towns. The process of assimilation was begun in the citadels of segregation and in no more than two generations even Ḥajjāj had to concede its success and declare Kūfa and Baṣra demilitarized.

The importance of the assimilation movement lies not so much in its impact on the non-Arab population, as in its effects on the Arabs themselves. Although it was a living social force, it was also a slow process and in this case it affected the lives of only a minority of non-Arabs. By and large this minority stayed out of the political struggle taking place among the Arabs and it is important to emphasize that the participation of these non-Arabs in the various uprisings of this period was absolutely minimal, if it existed at all. The picture which has so often been painted of an inveterate struggle taking place between Arabs and non-Arabs in the empire is not correct. The struggle was between the Arabs themselves over the attitude that should be adopted towards the non-Arab subjects and the issue of assimilation. The Qaysites, a powerful and articulate group, saw this movement as a threat to the position of the Arab conquerors and stubbornly resisted any policies which would lead to more assimilation. The Yamanites thought it better to take advantage of this movement and channel its energies for the good of the empire and all its peoples. Therefore they accepted, and sometimes encouraged, steps in this direction. Since assimilation in effect encouraged conversion of non-Arabs to Islam, it is possible to conclude that those in favour of it were seeking an essentially Islamic solution to the social problems of the empire as opposed to the primarily Arab–Qaysite solution. Here again, as in the case of the controversial powers of the *Amīr al-Mu'minīn*, there were two discernible attitudes at variance, one clearly Arab and the other basically Islamic. This dichotomy of views on two main issues inevitably led to the polarization of general political attitudes; that of conservative Arab in contrast to progressive Islamic. Needless to say, 'Umar II was the epitome of the latter.

Although assimilation had struck roots in all corners of the empire, its progress and opposition to it varied from one region to the other. In this respect and particularly in view of the 'Abbāsid revolution, Khurāsān has a special position in the history of this period. The details of the situation in this region have been explained elsewhere, and it will be sufficient, for the purposes of this book, to point out its salient features.[1] The first to be considered here is the political geography of Khurāsān and the East, al-Mashriq, at the time of the Arab conquest. The Murghāb River formed the easternmost frontier of the Sāsānian empire and thus Khurāsān was a little province of no more than the districts of Nīshāpūr and the immediate vicinities of the frontier towns of Merv and Merv-ar-Rūd. To the east of Khurāsān were extensive territories with considerable populations. First, the Principalities of Ṭukhāristān extended along the Oxus basin to the northern slopes of the Hindū-Kūsh. These were numerous principalities, each governed by a military lord and all subject to the nominal suzerainty of the *jabghū*, ruler of the Principalities of Ṭukhāristān. The populations of these principalities were nomadic, semi-nomadic or settled communities, mostly of Hephthalite, *hayāṭila*, origin. Scholars disagree as to whether these people were of Turkish or Iranian origin. In the absence of agreement or of any conclusive evidence in support of either origin, and in the light of their traditional animosity to the Turks of Central Asia, we are inclined to consider them Iranian. Perhaps more important is the fact that they were predominantly Buddhists.

[1] For details and sources see Shaban, *The 'Abbāsid Revolution.*

On the southern slopes of the Hindū-Kūsh there was another branch of the Hephthalites known to us as the Zābulites. Their territory was called the Kingdom of Zābulistān ruled over by a king called Zunbīl. Again, Buddhism was the main religion of this mountainous region. To the north of the Principalities of Ṭukhāristān lay Soghdiana, the land of the Soghd, a people certainly of Iranian origin. In the rich lands of the Zarafshān valley the Soghd were divided into city-states, each ruled by a prince. Besides being agricultural centres, these city-states, particularly Samarqand, Kish and Paykand, served as centres for the east–west Chinese trade. Among the Soghd, Zoroastrianism existed alongside Christianity and Manichaeism. The common feature of all these peoples to the east of the Sāsānian empire was that, although they were probably influenced by Sāsānian culture, they had different social, political and economic institutions.

After the collapse of the Sāsānian central government in the west, the Arab task of conquering Khurāsān was a relatively easy one. The swift Arab campaign of 651/31 successfully carried Arab arms to the eastern Sāsānian borders and the surrender of the citadel of Merv was the crowning reward of this effort. Deprived of the support of a central government, the helpless local leaders of the districts and towns of Khurāsān found it expedient to conclude separate peace treaties with the conquerors. Accordingly, the Arabs received an annual tribute and in return undertook not to interfere in any way with the existing administrative, social and economic structure of the area. In Khurāsān this meant the maintenance of the Sāsānian system according to which the local nobility, *dahāqīn*, had the greatest advantages. They owned most of the lands and their principal function was the allocation and collection of taxes. They, as well as the civil servants and the priests, were exempt from the poll-tax, which had to be paid by the peasantry and craftsmen. Indeed, the burden of taxes fell heavily on the peasantry to the advantage of the *dahāqīn*. Thus, from the beginning there was a tacit alliance between the Arab conquerors and the privileged classes who continued to rule these newly created "protectorates" with Arab support.

In contrast to Kirmān, where Arab settlement coincided with the conquest, there was no Arab settlement in Khurāsān at the time. After conquering practically the whole of the Sāsānian empire the Arabs seem to have decided to pause before embarking on new adventures in new territories. Their plan was to leave behind a garrison of 4,000 men after each annual campaign to hold the province until the arrival of the following expedition from Baṣra. Significantly, the treaty of Merv provided for the housing of this garrison in the houses of the inhabitants of the villages around Merv.

In the following two years (652–3/32–3), the Arab expeditions completed the conquest of all Sāsānian possessions and raided Hephthalite territories, again leaving behind a garrison to secure the province for their return. However, in the last uneasy years of 'Uthmān's rule and then during the first civil war, Arab expeditions were not sent to Khurāsān although the garrison was regularly replaced by fresh troops from Baṣra. During this period minor revolts occurred but the garrison of Merv was able to hold the province. It was not until 667/47 that vigorous campaigning was resumed in Khurāsān, primarily to relieve the pressures of immigration into Baṣra. As a result the Arabs succeeded in the following four years in making substantial inroads into Hephthalite territory and including some of the principalities in their protectorates. However, no Arabs had been settled anywhere in Khurāsān until Ziyād b. Abī Sufyān finished the reorganization of Kūfa and Baṣra. In 671/51 he organized the biggest mass migration movement of the time and re-settled 50,000 families from these two garrison towns in the villages of the Merv oasis. The stipulation of the treaty of Merv that the inhabitants of these villages should provide housing for the Arabs was stretched to cover housing for the new arrivals, at least temporarily until they built their own houses. The importance of this move cannot be over-emphasized because it probably had the most far-reaching effects on the development of Islamic society. No garrison town was built for this new army of Khurāsān, perhaps because garrison towns had proved to be a problem from the central government's point of view. It was a unique new experiment the results of which could not have been realized or anticipated by those who took part in it. Of course, the government's objective was to secure the conquests already made and to provide the forces for their further extension. As members of the *dīwān* receiving stipends, the Arabs of Khurāsān were duty bound to join the annual expeditions for the greater part of the year and return to their homes only for the winter months; sometimes they even spent the winter campaigning. These regular expeditions conquered most of the Principalities of Ṭukhāristān and penetrated deep into Soghdiana bringing considerable booty to the Arabs. Although new Arab protectorates were created in the conquered territories, no Arabs were settled there.

The second civil war interrupted this process and for fourteen years (684–96/64–77) no campaigns were undertaken. The conflict in the heart of the empire had its repercussions in Khurāsān and led to internal fighting between the supporters of Ibn al-Zubayr and those of 'Abdulmalik. Ironically, it is during this period of instability that the process of assimilation took root in the Merv oasis between the Arabs and the indigenous population. Some of the Arabs of Khurāsān preferred to stay out of this unrewarding fight which could only threaten the Arab position in this frontier region. During this long period of military inactivity on the frontiers these neutralists did not remain idle and turned to more peaceful activities. Merv was an important trade centre and it offered some of these men profitable opportunities for which their accumulated wealth and wide contacts in the rest of the empire were eminently suited. The local merchants of the market town of Merv found it profitable to use these assets and for the first time Arabs moved in to live in the town itself. Other Arabs who remained in the villages began to invest in agricultural lands. Apparently they were so interested in acquiring such lands that they agreed to pay the taxes imposed on them. These were the land taxes which were supposed to be paid by the original owners and for the allocation and collection of which the *dahāqīn* were responsible according to the treaty of Merv. In effect, this meant that some of the Arab conquerors were now subject to the authority of the local nobility, at least in matters of taxation. This unusual situation is a remarkable proof of the degree of assimilation that was taking place in Merv at this time.

It is instructive to notice that these seeds of assimilation began to take root in a period of complete absence of control and direction from the central government. Once such control was re-established under 'Abdulmalik, the policy of constant campaigning was resumed and the assimilation of the Arabs into the local population of Merv was temporarily checked. Instead, and perhaps in an attempt to reverse the process, in 704/85 the government allowed the enlistment of all Iranian converts in Merv in the *dīwān* and offered them stipends if they joined the *muqātila*, i.e. the Arab army of Khurāsān. This may seem like a move on the government's part to encourage the assimilation of the Iranians into the Arab population, but happening as it did under the direction of Ḥajjāj, this could not have been the case. The purpose of this move was to put an end to any further assimilation. It was no secret that conversion to Islam was not widespread among the Iranians and the number of such converts could not have been much more than the 7,000 men whom we find ten years later in Qutayba's army after this measure had been applied to the whole region.

Indeed in Qutayba's governorship (705–15/86–96) strict measures were taken to stop the process of assimilation altogether. This period was a distinguished one not only from the military but also from the organizational point of view. Qutayba's conquests reached far into Central Asia and his reorganization of the army of Khurāsān had a profound effect on the lives of all concerned. Taking as a model the organization of Baṣra, he divided the Arabs of Khurāsān into five groups on tribal lines. He then segregated the *mawālī*, converts, in a special division of his army instead of allowing them to join the tribes or the clans whose clients they were supposed to be. These measures were meant to allow the governor maximum control over the Arabs and the *mawālī*, and by engaging them continuously on the battlefield it was possible for him to stop any further assimilation. To secure the success of these measures and to continue his policy of endless expansion he also required levies from the non-converted populations in the districts of Khurāsān and the adjacent regions. These levies would join expeditions in the spring and return home for the winter. Not being enlisted in the *dīwān*, they saved Qutayba the expense of having to pay them stipends. In Khurāsān at least this step could not have been achieved without the full co-operation of the *dahāqīn* whose interests were directly involved. It must always be remembered that the Sāsānian social structure according to which these *dahāqīn* enjoyed their privileges had been maintained by the Arabs. Any changes in this social structure represented a powerful threat to their privileged position. The assimilation of a few thousand *mawālī* into the Arab army was not such a threat and it was probably encouraged by the *dahāqīn* as a sign of their co-operation with the Arab rulers.

But the assimilation of the Arabs into the local population, if it continued, would definitely lead to a basic change in the structure of society. The assimilated Arabs could not be kept indefinitely outside this social structure and a suitable place would have to be found for them within it. This would ultimately abolish the *dahāqīn*'s authority over their subjects and put an end to their privileges. Therefore, it was to their advantage to co-operate with Qutayba and encourage the policy of expansion in the hope of keeping the unassimilated Arabs as a fighting force continually engaged on the battlefield. This co-operation was at the expense of the Iranian subjects who had no cause to participate in Arab military glory and whose real interests were completely ignored. Their absence from their homes and from their productive work for the greater part of the year was certainly detrimental to their economic condition and for no apparent gain. Although the wars of Qutayba brought a considerable amount of booty to Khurāsān, it also deprived the countryside of its needed manpower. This situation created a war economy and inflation which in turn caused the price of grain to rise. The levies from Khurāsān were the first to be hurt by this situation and they were also the first to complain. Eventually both the Arabs and the *mawālī* became tired of the successive campaigns and at the first opportunity, while they were actually on an expedition in Farghāna, they co-operated to depose and murder Qutayba in order to return to their homes. This was a turning-point in the history of the Arabs in Khurāsān.

The excessive pursuit of expansionist policies had rebounded against its advocates. It brought about further co-operation between Arabs and Iranians and the resulting murder of Qutayba was an ominous sign to the *dahāqīn* of the resentment and the potential strength of their own subjects. To the Arabs the whole question of assimilation was brought into focus and the issues involved became clearer to all concerned. Inevitably the movement towards assimilation was accelerated.

When 'Umar II came to power in 717/99, Khurāsān provided the ideal circumstances for the implementation of his plans to reconstruct a Muslim empire. There, in Merv and its surrounding villages, a relatively large Arab community had been living in close proximity to the indigenous Iranian population for almost half a century. He could not have been blind to the trend towards assimilation that had been making progress among these Arabs.

Furthermore, this Iranian population had co-operated with the Arabs, and Islam had already struck some roots amongst them. With some encouragement the complete assimilation of the two communities could be brought about and it could serve as a good example for the whole empire. His decision that no more expeditions should be undertaken on this front was a clear concession to those elements opposed to expansion. He went even further and announced the withdrawal of the Arab garrisons stationed in Bukhārā and Samarqand during Quṭayba's governorship. Apparently there was strong resistance to Arab rule among the Soghdians and, realizing this, ʿUmar II was proposing to re-establish a peaceful relationship with them. Of course such a relationship would be to the great advantage of those interested in trade on both sides. In other words he was preparing the ground for the Arabs of Khurāsān to turn completely from military to more peaceful activities. To encourage the assimilation of the Iranians with the Arabs in their midst he offered all Iranian converts complete equality with their fellow Arab Muslims in matters of taxation and stipends. Such measures could not take effect in his short reign, but the important thing is that they gave a great impetus to the assimilation movement and outlined a viable plan for its eventual success. It is not surprising that our sources, perhaps euphemistically, tell us that in the year 718/100 a revolutionary movement began in Merv.

However, revolutionary movements are usually started by a small minority against the stubborn will of the majority and this particular revolution in Merv was no exception. Only a minority of the Arabs there were willing, at this time, to give up their privileges in favour of assimilation. The majority continued to cling to the conqueror's privileges and to perpetuate the unnatural conditions of the conquest. Although this majority had the powerful support of the *dahāqīn*, both parties were fighting a losing battle against the progressive forces of assimilation. Although military expeditions were resumed after the death of ʿUmar II, there was a marked reluctance on the part of some of the Arabs to join them. Even the appearance of the Turgesh threat in Soghdiana did not convince these unwilling fighters of the necessity to join in the effort to repel the enemy, and force had to be used to persuade them. It soon became apparent that it was useless to try to put an end to this trend and Hishām decided to yield to the assimilation movement. He allowed a considerable number of the

Arabs, about 15,000, to withdraw from the army of Khurāsān and settle down to the peaceful life they wanted. At the same time, as explained before, he replaced them in 732/113 with 20,000 new recruits from Iraq. Although this step helped to take care of the Turgesh threat, it did not solve the particular problem of Khurāsān, namely the existence in Merv of two completely opposed Arab groups. The first group, the Muḍarites, were the old guard of the *muqātila* who were continuously losing ground to the forces of assimilation and who were increasingly apprehensive about their position in the province. They favoured the maintenance of the *status quo*, at any price, and were supported by the *dahāqīn* who shared their conviction. The second group consisted of the assimilated Arabs, whom we shall call the Settlers, whose numbers were steadily increasing especially after Hishām's recognition of their existence. They had not only lost their privileges as members of the Arab ruling class but were also forced to accept the authority of the non-Muslim aristocracy of Merv who formed the local administration and continued to enjoy their pre-Islamic status under Arab rule. The social position of these Settlers was in effect the same as that of the peasants at the bottom of the Sāsānian social structure. This exceptionally Sāsānian solution to an Arab problem was in glaring contrast to the essentially Islamic solution which 'Umar II had initiated and which never lost its impact on the Settlers. Between the Muḍarites and the Settlers stood the Yamanite *muqātila* who were the latest comers to Merv. Under the plan of the Yamanite governor, Asad al-Qasrī, they had successfully co-operated with the Hephthalites to defeat the Turgesh. While they represented a threat to the position of the old guard Muḍarites in the province, they had no objection to further co-operation with non-Arab subjects and thus were more inclined to the point of view of the Settlers.

Alarmed by the confusion which prevailed in the heart of the empire after Hishām's death the Muḍarite *muqātila* of Khurāsān, led by the old warrior Naṣr b. Sayyār, took matters into their own hands, even in defiance of the central government during the short reign of Yazīd III (744/126). The failure of all the uprisings against the Marwānids and the re-establishment of their regime under Marwān II convinced the Settlers that a well-organized armed revolt was the only way to throw off the yoke of their oppressors. Meanwhile, the nature of this explosive situation in

Merv and the potential energies it could unleash had been realized by a small group of revolutionaries from Kūfa, the Hāshimiya. For more than a quarter of a century they persevered in preaching their cause among the Settlers in Merv and successfully changed their local revolt into a fully fledged revolution which ended Marwānid rule.

The Hāshimiyya was one of the many Shī'ite movements founded in Kūfa towards the end of the Umayyad period. Although the Kūfans had vigorously demonstrated their objection to Umayyad rule, their support of Shī'ite uprisings had proved utterly unreliable. The failure of the revolt of Zayd b. 'Alī in Kūfa in 740/122 is sufficient proof of this fact and of the ability of the government to control the town. Nonetheless, there was enough discontent and anti-Umayyad feeling to allow Shī'ite activities to take place there. Such underground activities were naturally very limited and generally ineffective, but they resulted in the formation of minor Shī'ite sects. It is unrealistic to try to define the religious doctrines of these various sects at this formative stage and it is unwise to allow ourselves to be misled by the elaborate descriptions of later Muslim heresiographers. It is more useful to analyse any particular information we can gather from reliable historical sources to explain their activities.

All Shī'ite sects were agreed on the necessity of an *Imām* to occupy the office of *Amīr al-Mu'minīn*, i.e. they wanted a leader of the Muslim community who would have both secular and religious powers. They also agreed that such an *Imām* should be a member of the House of the Prophet. Their differences centred around the actual choice of the *Imām*, the method advocated to install him in the office of *Amīr al-Mu'minīn*, and the nature and extent of religious and secular powers to be invested in him. The availability of a member of the House of the Prophet willing to lead a movement or at least to lend his name to it determined each sect's interpretation of the extent to which membership of this house should apply. Thus some sects preached the cause of direct descendants of the Prophet while others had to be content with cousins of varying degrees. But it should be noted that some sects did not find it difficult to change their allegiance from one member of the house to another. The method advocated by each sect to achieve its cause was very much dictated by its own circumstances. Some favoured armed revolt or even the use of terror, while others were for more peaceful means. To all Shī'ites, 'Alī was the exemplary *Imām–Amīr al-Mu'minīn* who proposed to use his knowledge, *'ilm*, to solve the problems of the Muslim community. This knowledge had become a cornerstone of Shī'ite thought and was believed to be inherent in his descendants, or at least, to be passed on from one generation to another. As there were now many descendants and cousins who were claimants to this particular knowledge, the means by which an *Imām* was believed to acquire it differed from one sect to another. Inheritance, intuition, divine guidance or simply the passing on of this knowledge to his chosen successor by an *Imām* were all alleged. Naturally such distinctions would limit or extend the religious powers of the *Imām* concerned and presumably would have some corresponding effect on his claims to secular powers when installed as *Amīr al-Mu'minīn*. But, by and large, the question of these secular powers was deferred until the ultimate success of the movement concerned, though perhaps with the general understanding that these powers would be much less than those of the authoritarian Marwānids.

It is within this general frame of Shī'ite thought that the Hāshimiyya sect was founded in Kūfa sometime between 700/81 and 716/98. It took its name from its acknowledged *Imām*, Abū Hāshim 'Abdullah, son of Muḥammad b. al-Ḥanafiyya, the third son of 'Alī. Muḥammad b. al-Ḥanafiyya (d. 700/81) was proclaimed the *Mahdī*, divinely guided *Imām*, by Mukhtār during his revolt in Kūfa (684–7/64–7). The former only ambiguously consented to lend his name to this revolt and this constituted his only relationship to it. We know too little about Abū Hāshim's activities to enable us to know whether he actively pursued his father's claims, whatever their value, or whether like his father he simply agreed, in some vague way, to lend his name to Shī'ite groups in Kūfa. The fact remains that after his father's death more than one such group proclaimed Abū Hāshim as the rightful *Imām*. Apparently the Hāshimiyya was the only Shī'ite sect in Kūfa that continued to preach his cause while other sects changed their allegiance to other members of the House of the Prophet. Perhaps it should be noted that while other Shī'ite sects in Kūfa were discovered by the authorities, and their leaders executed, the Hāshimiyya maintained its complete secrecy.

In 716/98 Abū Hāshim, who had never lived in Kūfa, went on a visit to Syria. On his way home to Ḥijāz he died in Palestine in the house of ʿAlī b. ʿAbdillah b. ʿAbbās, a third cousin of his father, and a grandson of ʿAbbās the Prophet's uncle. Out of this most unexpected coincidence a new leadership of the Hāshimiyya came forth, because it is reported that Abū Hāshim, before his death, bequeathed his claims to his host's son, Muḥammad b. ʿAlī. Whether this report is true or not is not very important; what is important is that Muḥammad b. ʿAlī took over the claims of Abū Hāshim and with them the secret organization of the Hāshimiyya in Kūfa. Adherents of the sect did not find it difficult to switch their allegiance from one branch of the House of the Prophet to another. The descendants of ʿAbbās, who enjoyed a sound reputation, had so far refrained from involvement with the Shīʿite cause, although they were not on the best terms with the Marwānids. However, by taking up residence in Ḥumayma in Palestine after the second civil war, ʿAlī b. ʿAbdillah b. ʿAbbās was in effect indicating his willingness to live in peace with the new regime. Perhaps he himself was not convinced that his family had any right to be properly considered members of the House of the Prophet, or that such claims on their part would receive any support. Obviously his son Muḥammad had a different opinion, which may explain his readiness to accept Abū Hāshim's bequest in his own father's lifetime.

Muḥammad b. ʿAlī, the new *Imām* of the Hāshimiyya, proceeded to transform this small secret organization into the instrument of the ʿAbbāsid party. Its membership in Kūfa was kept to a minimum and never exceeded thirty men, Arabs and *mawālī*, many of whom were involved in trade between Iraq, Syria, Ḥijāz and Khurāsān. This allowed them to operate in extreme secrecy and helped them to gather valuable information about conditions in all corners of the empire. From their contacts in Merv they realized what the situation was there and accordingly decided that it was the best field for their activities. Once this decision had been taken plans were made to organize a revolutionary base in Merv itself. From about 718/100 Hāshimiyya emissaries from Kūfa were sent there to begin an intensive propaganda campaign. Although some of these agents were discovered and executed in Merv in 736/118, the leaders of the movement were never discouraged and indeed continued to intensify their efforts there.

Shortly afterwards, Bukayr b. Māhān, the leader of the Kūfan organization, was sent to Merv to supervise the setting up of a similar secret organization there. A committee of twelve *naqībs*, leading missionaries, was chosen from among the Arab Settlers in Merv, probably including one *mawlā*. Sulaymān b. Kathīr al-Khuzā'ī was selected to head this new organization. At the same time, fifty-eight *dā'īs*, missionaries, were nominated, forty for Merv itself and eighteen for various localities in Khurāsān. All these missionaries were selected from among the Arab Settlers in Merv and obviously all efforts were concentrated there. Contact with the *Imām* in Ḥumayma was maintained only through Kūfa and his name was kept secret. A few of the leaders of the Merv organization had the opportunity of meeting him in the pilgrimage season in Ḥijāz when they presented him with contributions from their followers. Bukayr continued to be the *Imām*'s emissary to Merv until 743/125 when on his last visit he brought the news of the *Imām*'s death and the succession of his son, Ibrāhīm b. Muḥammad, to the leadership of the movement.

The succession of the new *Imām*, Ibrāhīm, coincided with the breakdown of the Marwānid regime after the death of Hishām. The partisans in Merv agitated for immediate action to take advantage of this situation but the leadership in Kufa advised patience. Abū Salama al-Khallāl, the new leader in Kūfa following the death of Bukayr b. Māhān, came to Merv in 744/126 to control the situation there. He was also accompanied by a young follower whose name was Abū Muslim. After four months in Merv, they both returned to Kūfa leaving Sulaymān b. Kathīr in charge of the organization there. But events in the heart of the empire were moving fast and the leadership of the movement decided that the time had come for an open revolt. In 746/128 Abū Muslim once again arrived at Merv as a personal representative of the *Imām* to take charge of the intended revolution. Sulaymān b. Kathīr objected but was quickly overruled by his colleagues who were in favour of Abū Muslim.

Before we move on to discuss the stage of open revolt, perhaps it is better to pause to emphasize the elaborate propaganda campaign which was meticulously planned to take advantage of every aspect of the situation. It is a tribute to the abilities of the leaders of the movement, particularly Abū Salama, that the stage was so perfectly set for the success of the revolution, not only in

Merv but also in the rest of the empire. Every possible sign in the eschatological prophecies of the time was cleverly used to proclaim the approach of the imminent revolution. Black flags had been hoisted by earlier rebels and had already acquired messianic significance. Now they were adopted by the revolution as its own emblem. Legends and prophecies were invented and widely circulated referring to the rise of the black banners in the East and pointing to the end of Umayyad rule. Slogans were provided to propagate the cause and to appeal to all groups in the empire. The continuous emphasis by the various Shī'ite sects on the rights of the members of the House of the Prophet, and the martyrdom of some of them at the hands of the Umayyads, had brought about the identification of their cause with the cause of justice in the minds of many Muslims. Taking advantage of this widespread feeling, the impending revolution was preached in the name of *al-riḍā min āl Muḥammad*, a member of the House of the Prophet who would be acceptable to all. This was a call for the unity of all Shī'ites in the empire to fight for the cause and an indication that an agreement on an acceptable *Imām–Amīr al-Mu'minīn* would not be difficult after success. This implied self-denial on the part of the 'Abbāsid *Imām* must have made some favourable impression on the general Muslim population.

But the most striking and significant move, designed to appeal to all Muslims, Arabs and non-Arabs, was the choice of Abū Muslim to lead the revolution at this crucial and open stage. Certainly, there were men in Merv who would have been quite capable of fulfilling this task and there was a risk in asking them to submit to a total stranger; yet this risk was taken. Furthermore, the origins of this stranger and even his real name were deliberately kept secret to the extent that our sources do not agree on a single detail about his early life. A definite effort was made to present him in a new image and the key to this is his assumed name, Abū Muslim 'Abdulraḥman b. Muslim al-Khurāsānī. This name represents a Muslim who is a son of a Muslim and a father of a Muslim. He related himself only to Khurāsān, and not to a tribe or a clan, either as a member or a *mawlā*, as was the practice at the time. This assumed name was the best possible slogan for the revolution Abū Muslim was sent to lead. He was a living proof that in the new society every member would be regarded only as a Muslim regardless of racial origins or tribal connection. In other words the leaders of the revolution were giving the clearest possible evidence of their total commitment to assimilation.

When Abū Muslim finally and openly raised the black banners in 747/129 in a village of Merv he was immediately joined by about 2,200 men from *ahl al-taqādum*, the Arab Settlers of the surrounding villages. In little over a month the number of the revolutionary army of Abū Muslim rose to 7,000 men whom he ordered to be listed in a new *dīwān* according to their names, their fathers' names and their villages. Thus, complete assimilation was first achieved in this army, of which the members were all now Khurāsāniyya.

The timing of the proclamation of the revolution was an important factor in its eventual success since it occurred when an internal struggle for power among the *muqātila* of Khurāsān had practically exhausted all their factions. When Naṣr b. Sayyār was confirmed as governor of the province by Marwān II in 745/127, there was an immediate rebellion by the Yamanites, led by Juday' b. 'Alī al-Kirmānī, who considered such a confirmation an affront to their successful policies there. Their hopes had been raised by the appointment of the Yamanite Manẓūr b. Jumhūr to the province in the short reign of Yazīd III (744/126) only to be dashed by Naṣr's defiance and usurpation of power. However, the latter had enough strength to contain their revolt, at least temporarily. To increase the enthusiasm of his supporters he appointed their leaders as sub-governors of the various districts of the province. This move had the adverse effect of weakening his military power, because these sub-governors were accompanied to their districts by some of their followers. He also made another move, probably designed to bolster his prestige among his Muḍarite followers, which proved to be a grave mistake. Remembering the long-forgotten Ḥārith b. Surayj, who had taken refuge with the Turgesh over ten years before, Naṣr invited this extreme Muḍarite to come back to Merv in 745/127 in the hope that he would support his efforts. But to Naṣr's disappointment Ḥārith lost no time in taking advantage of the situation in Merv for his own purposes. Soon fighting broke out between the two and the situation was further complicated by the interference of the Yamanites in the fight. Though Ḥārith himself was killed in battle in 746/128, the fighting continued in Merv between the Muḍarites and Yamanites. The latter had already been joined by some of the Arab Settlers before the proclamation of the revolution. Abū Muslim, with a newly organized army at his command, succeeded in manipulating this struggle in Merv to the decisive advantage of the revolution. After some intermittent fighting during which Merv changed hands more than once, Abū Muslim in alliance with the Yamanites emerged, early in 748/130, as the master of the situation. Naṣr b. Sayyār, in spite of his very advanced age, fled to Nīshāpūr where he planned to continue the fight against the revolution. His allies, the *dahāqīn* of Merv with some of their *mawālī*, fled to Balkh where they joined Naṣr's sub-governors of the town and its adjacent districts in an attempt to take a last stand against Abū Muslim and his forces.

After entering Merv, Abū Muslim summoned his followers to pay allegiance to *al-riḍā*, an acceptable member of the House of the Prophet. It is significant that none of the Yamanites were among those who took such an oath. Nevertheless, amidst all these dangers the alliance between the revolutionary army and the Yamanites had to be maintained. In fact, the presence of such powerful allies in his camp enabled Abū Muslim to dispatch the revolutionary army on its main task, the conquest of the rest of the empire. Soon in the same year 748/130 the Khurāsāniyya army, under the generalship of Qaḥṭaba b. Shabīb, a leading member of the Arab Settlers, started its victorious march westwards gathering more support on its way. In less than two years, early in 750/132, it entered Kūfa, defeating no less than three Marwānid armies and capturing all territories on its route. Meanwhile, Abū Muslim, with the help of the Yamanites, was able after some difficulties to clear up all pockets of resistance and firmly establish himself as the sole master of the East. At this point it was not too difficult to get rid of the leaders of the Yamanites and incorporate their forces in his own. He assumed the title of *Amīr āl Muḥammad*, which meant that he expected wider authority in the affairs of the empire than simply a governor of the East. Indeed, he kept in close touch with developments in Kūfa through his agent Abū al-Jahm b. 'Aṭiyya. The latter was appointed by Abū Muslim as a "political commissar" for the advancing revolutionary army and continued to hold this position after the capture of Kūfa.

Entering Kūfa, the victors were received by Abū Salama who was instantly acknowledged as *Wazīr āl Muḥammad* and immediately took charge of the whole situation. There was definitely no mention of any *Imām*, nor was there any questioning of Abū Salama's assumption of power. The latter's responsibilities amounted to those of a provisional head of state in a revolutionary phase. Nevertheless, the army was not completely under his control; the real control stayed with Abū Muslim's agent, Abū al-Jahm. In other words, the latter represented the military power of the revolution, while Abū Salama directed the civilian organization of the Hāshimiyya in Kūfa, and so far the two were in complete co-operation. The urgent problem was presumably to select the member of the House of the Prophet acceptable to all to be installed as *Amīr al-Mu'minīn*. Although the name of the *Imām* of the Hāshimiyya, Ibrāhīm, was by now circulating among the revolutionaries, it was perhaps only as a possible candidate for the supreme office. Unfortunately the Marwānid authorities belatedly discovered the connection between Ibrāhīm and the revolution. He was promptly arrested in Ḥumayma and was murdered in prison in Ḥarrān in 749/132. The rest of the 'Abbāsids came to Kūfa soon after the arrival of the Khurāsāniyya but Abū Salama ordered them to remain in hiding and even refused to pay them urgently needed expenses. At the same time he did not inform Abū al-Jahm of their presence in Kūfa though amongst them was Abū al-'Abbās 'Abdullah b. Muḥammad, brother of the murdered *Imām* Ibrāhim and supposedly his appointed heir before his death. Thus, it seems that there was a latent disagreement between the revolutionaries about the question of the new *Amīr al-Mu'minīn*. To Abū Salama the term *al-riḍā* implied that the whole question was open and subject to the agreement of all concerned. To the Khurāsāniyya, the question was not necessarily so open, because they were inclined to favour an 'Abbāsid member of the House of the Prophet, and their opinion carried considerable weight.

Abū Salama, a responsible statesman, was undoubtedly more aware of the various trends in Shī'ism and all their practical implications for the powers of the *Imām–Amīr al-Mu'minīn*, especially in a place like Kūfa. He was also aware of the wishes of the Khurāsāniyya on the subject. His problem was to reconcile all these opinions and present the revolutionaries with the member of the House of the Prophet who would command the widest possible allegiance. He was probably convinced that an 'Abbāsid would not be the desired choice. Consequently he corresponded with the other prominent members of the House of the Prophet, Ja'far al-Ṣādiq, 'Abdullah b. al-Ḥasan and 'Umar b. 'Alī b. al-Ḥasan who were all direct descendants of the Prophet and all living in Ḥijāz. Presumably Abū Salama offered them the high office on certain conditions, because they all refused. After more than two months, the Khurāsāniyya took matters in their hands and forced their own choice on their own conditions. This was accomplished through the manipulation of Abū al-Jahm and thus it must have had Abū Muslim's consent. Abū Salama had no choice but to accept the *fait accompli*.

The new *Amīr al-Mu'minīn* was Abū al-'Abbās 'Abdullah b. Muḥammad, who accepted the office on the terms of the Khurāsāniyya. He agreed that Abū Salama should continue in the office of *wazīr* which could only mean the greatest restriction on his own secular power. He did not assume the title *Imām* which indicates that he was not to have the kind of religious powers advocated by all Shī'ites for their *Imām–Amīr al-Mu'minīn*. In other words the Khurāsāniyya, who accepted without any dispute the institution of the office of a *wazīr* who would hold the secular powers, envisaged an *Amīr al-Mu'minīn* with very limited religious and no secular powers. Of course, it can be argued that they were trying to win the support of other Muslims who did not believe in the Shī'ite concept of *Imām–Amīr al-Mu'minīn*. But having discarded this concept the Khurāsāniyya could not consent to invest the new *Amīr al-Mu'minīn* with secular powers either, since this would mean carrying on Marwānid tradition and only changing the holder of the office. This difficult dilemma was resolved by the decision to continue the office of *wazīr*, which was in effect the creation of a new office complementary to that of the *Amīr al-Mu'minīn*.

It will be recalled that Mukhtār, in his earlier revolt in Kūfa, had announced himself the *wazīr* of his proclaimed *Mahdī*, Muḥammad b. al-Ḥanafiyya. The reluctance of the latter to agree to this arrangement and the failure of the revolt did not allow these two positions to acquire any reality at the time. Now the new revolution, while casting aside the notion of *Mahdī*, took up and gave meaning to the notion of *wazīr*. This vague idea conceived by Mukhtār under completely different circumstances was developed into a clearly defined office with definite functions in a new political structure. This principle of the division of power between the

Amīr al-Mu'minīn and the *wazīr* was an innovation of the revolution and its solution to the problem of the political institutions of the empire. Although this solution was not based on the development of existing institutions, either Arab or Islamic, it could have provided the framework for the development of viable governing institutions had the Khurāsāniyya wanted to relinquish power themselves. But by keeping military power in their own hands they emptied these institutions of any moral or material authority. By depriving the *wazīr* of the control of the army they in fact created an administrative official who could only act with their approval. When Abū Salama found it difficult to continue with such an arrangement, he had to go. His execution soon afterwards in 750/132 was carried out with the consent of both the revolutionaries and the powerless *Amīr al-Mu'minīn*, and it is significant that Abū al-Jahm took over his responsibilities. However this did not mean the end of the office of *wazīr*. The controversy about its existence and its powers continued to be a major issue for centuries to come.

The selection of Abū al-'Abbās for the office of *Amīr al-Mu'minīn* is a further proof of the intention of the Khurāsāniyya to allow no real power to the holder of this office. There is no doubt that in his reign of four years (749–54/132–6) he was not a particularly powerful ruler. His selection is generally attributed to the fact that his mother was an Arab woman, whilst the mother of his elder brother, Abū Ja'far 'Abdullah b. Muḥammad, was a Berber slave. It is, however, illogical to believe that the revolutionaries would behave in such a way in this celebrated and exemplary case after risking their lives to achieve complete assimilation. It seems likely that Abū Ja'far was passed over because he was the more powerful personality of the two brothers, and his history shows that he believed in a stronger *Amīr al-Mu'minīn*. Five years later, in 754/137, Abū Ja'far had to carry out a counter-revolution to re-establish his powers as the new *Amīr al-Mu'minīn* al-Manṣūr on very much the same lines as any Marwānid ruler. His execution of Abū Muslim brought the military power of the Khurāsāniyya under his own control and thereafter he exercised full secular powers without any claims to the religious powers of an *Imām*.

It is now clear that from the very beginning both the victorious revolutionaries and the 'Abbāsids had set themselves apart from the rest of the Shī'ites by deviating from the cardinal precept of the latter, that of *Imām–Amīr al-Mu'minīn*. The very serious Shī'ite revolts, especially in the reign of Abū Ja'far, clearly indicate their disappointment in the Hāshimiyya–'Abbāsid revolution. This revolution decisively achieved one of its principal aims, the assimilation of all members of the Muslim community. This Islamic solution for the social problems of the empire greatly helped to spread Islam itself among the non-Arab subjects and created what could be truly described as a growing Islamic society. Unfortunately, the revolution failed to establish a suitable political institution to govern this new society; a failure which impeded its stability.

The year 750/132 saw the final destruction of the remaining forces of Marwān II. Five months after its arrival at Kūfa, early in the same year, the revolutionary army proceeded to finish its principal task. The main army of Marwān II, which was well entrenched in Jazīra, was utterly defeated in the Battle of the Zāb, which took place on the bank of a tributary of the Tigris known by that name. Marwān II himself fled to Syria and Palestine where, understandably, he could not muster any support. He eventually reached Egypt where, only seven months after the Battle of the Zāb, he was captured and slain. Three years after the rise of the revolutionaries in Merv, Marwānid rule was brought to a definite end.

WORKS CITED

SOURCES

ibn ʿAbdilḥakam, Abū Muḥammad ʿAbdullah, *Futūḥ Miṣr*, ed. V. V. Torrey, New Haven, 1922.

Sīrat ʿUmar b. ʿAbdilʿazīz, Cairo, 1927.

ibn ʿAbdirabbih, Aḥmad b. Muḥammad, *al-ʿIqd al-Farīd*, Beirut, 1951–4. 31 vols.

Akhbār al-ʿAbbās wa Waladihi, anon., manuscript in the library of the Institute of Higher Islamic Studies, Baghdad.

ibn ʿAsākir, *Tārīkh Dimashq*, vol. I, ed. S. El-Munajjid, Damascus, 1951.

ibn Aʿtham al-Kūfī, Abū Muḥammad Aḥmad, *Kitāb al-Futūḥ*, Istanbul manuscript, Library of Ahmet III, no. 2956. 2 vols.

ibn al-Athīr, ʿIzz al-Dīn, *al-Kāmil fī al-Tārīkh*, ed. C. J. Tornberg, Leiden, 1866–71. 14 vols.

al-Azdī, Abū Zakariyyā, *Tārīkh al-Mawṣil*, vol. II, ed. A. Ḥabība, Cairo, 1967.

al-Balādhurī, Aḥmad b. Yaḥyā, *Ansāb al-Ashrāf*, Istanbul manuscript, Süleymaniye Kütüphanesi, Reisulkuttap, no. 597–8, 2 vols.; vol. I, ed. M. Hamidullah, Cairo, 1959; vol. IV B, ed. M. Schloessinger, Jerusalem, 1938; vol. V, ed. S. D. Goitein, Jerusalem, 1936; vol. XI (*Anonyme Arabische Chronik*), ed. W. Ahlwardt, Greifswald, 1883.

Futūḥ al-Buldān, ed. M. J. de Goeje, Leiden, 1866.

al-Dhahabī, Muḥammad b. Aḥmad, *Tārīkh al-Islām*, Cairo, 1367–9. 5 vols.

al-Farazdaq, *Dīwān*, ed. R. Boucher, Paris, 1870, 2 vols.

Greek Papyri in the British Museum, vol. IV, *The Aphrodito Papyri*, ed. H. I. Bell, London, 1910.

ibn Ḥazm, ʿAlī b. Muḥammad, *Jamharat Ansāb al-ʿArab*, ed. A. M. Hārūn, Cairo, 1962.

al-Iṣfahānī, Abū al-Faraj, *al-Aghānī*: vols. I–XX, Cairo, A.H. 1285; vol. XXI, ed. R. E. Brünnow, Leiden, 1888.

ibn Khaldūn, *Kitāb al-ʿIbar*, Cairo, A.H. 1284.

ibn Khayyāṭ, Khalīfa, *Tārīkh*, ed. A.. D al-ʿUmary, Najaf, 1967. 2 vols.

al-Kindī, *Governors and Judges of Egypt*, ed. R. Guest, Gibb Memorial Series, vol. XIX, London, 1912.
al-Manīnī, Aḥmad, *Sharḥ al-Yamīnī 'alā Tārīkh al-'Utbī*, Cairo, A.H. 1286.
al-Maqrīzī, Aḥmad b. 'Alī, *al-Khiṭaṭ*, ed. G. Wiet, Cairo, 1911–22.
al-Mas'ūdī, 'Alī b. al-Ḥusayn, *Murūj al-Dhahab*, ed. C. Barbier de Meynard and P. de Courteille, Paris, 1861–77. 9 vols.
al-Mubarrad, Abū al-'Abbās Muḥammad, *al-Kāmil*, ed. W. Wright, Leipzig, 1874–82.
Naṣr b. Muzāḥim, *Waq'at Siffīn*, ed. A. M. Hārūn, Cairo, 1946.
al-Nawbakhtī, al-Ḥasan b. Mūsā, *Firaq al-Shī'a*, ed. H. Ritter, Leipzig, 1931.
ibn Sa'd, Muḥammad, *al-Ṭabaqāt al-Kabīr*, ed. Sachau *et al.*, Leiden, 1905–21. 8 vols.
ibn Sallām, Abū 'Ubayd al-Qāsim, *al-Amwāl*, Cairo, A.H. 1353.
al-Suyūṭī, *Tārīkh al-Khulafā'*. Cairo, n.d.
al-Ṭabarī, Muḥammad b. Jarīr, *Tārīkh al-Rusul wa al-Mulūk*, ed. M. J. de Goeje *et al.*, Leiden, 1879–1901.
ibn Taghry Bardy, *al-Nujūm al-Zāhira*, ed. T. G. Juynboll and B. F. Matthes, Leiden, 1851.
Tārīkh al-Khulafā', anon., ed. P. Griyaznevitch, Moscow, 1967.
al-'Uyūn wa Ḥadā'iq fī Akhbār al-Ḥaqā'iq, anon., ed. M. J. de Goeje, Leiden, 1869.
al-Ya'qūbī, Aḥmad b. Abī-Ya'qūb, *Tārīkh*, Beirut, 1960. 2 vols.
abū Yūsuf, Ya'qūb, *Kitāb al-Kharāj*, Cairo, A.H. 1302.

BOOKS AND ARTICLES

al-'Alī, Ṣāliḥ A., *al-Tanẓīmāt al-Ijtimā'iyya wa al-Iqtiṣādiyya fī al-Baṣra*, Baghdad, 1953.
Belyaev, E. A., *Arabs, Islam and the Arab Caliphate*, tr. Adolphe Gourevitch, London, 1969.
Cahen, Cl., "Djizya", *Enc. of Islam*, new edition, Leiden, 1954– .
Christensen, A., *L'Iran sous les Sassanides*, Copenhagen, 1936.
Dennet, D. C., *Conversion and the Poll-tax in Early Islam*, Cambridge, Mass., 1950.
Eickelman, Dale F., "Musaylima", *Journal of Economic and Social History of the Orient*, 1967, pp. 17–52.

Gibb, H. A. R., "An Interpretation of Islamic History", *Studies on the Civilization of Islam*, London, 1962, pp. 3-33.
"The Fiscal Rescript of 'Umar II", *Arabica*, vol. II, January 1955, pp. 3–16.
Studies on the Civilization of Islam, London, 1962.
Kister, M. J., "Mecca and Tamīm", *Journal of Economic and Social History of the Orient*, 1965, pp. 113–63.
"The Market of the Prophet", *Journal of Economic and Social History of the Orient*, 1965, pp. 272–6.
"Al-Ḥīra", *Arabica*, vol. XV, 1968, pp. 143–69.
Lewicki, T., "al-Ibāḍiyya", *Enc. of Islam*, new edition, Leiden, 1954– .
Løkkegaard, F., *Islamic Taxation in the Classic Period*, Copenhagen, 1950.
Serjeant, R. B., "*Ḥaram* and *Hawṭah*, The Sacred Enclave in Arabia", *Mélanges Taha Husain*, Cairo, 1962, pp. 41–58.
"The Constitution of Madina", *Islamic Quarterly*, vol. VIII, 1964, pp. 3–16.
Shaban, M. A., *The 'Abbāsid Revolution*, Cambridge, 1970.
"The Political Geography of Khurāsān and the East at the time of the Arab Conquest", *Minorsky's Memorial Volume*, ed. C. E. Bosworth and J. Aubin, London, forthcoming.
Watt, W. Montgomery, *Muḥammad at Mecca*, Oxford, 1953.
Muḥammad at Medina, Oxford, 1956.
Muḥammad, Prophet and Statesman, London, 1961.
Islamic Political Thought, Edinburgh, 1968.
Wellhausen, J., *The Arab Kingdom and its Fall*, tr. M. G. Weir, Calcutta, 1927.

INDEX

al-'Abbās, uncle of the Prophet, 18
Abū al-'Abbās 'Abdullah b. Muḥammad, *Amīr al-Mu'minīn*, 186, 187–8
'Abbāsids, 161, 163, 181, 186
'Abdul'azīz b. Marwān, 112, 123
'Abdullah b. 'Āmir, 66, 84, 85
'Abdullah b. al-Ḥasan, 187
'Abdullah b. Mu'āwiya, 161, 163
'Abdullah b. Sa'd b. Abī Sarḥ, 66, 68–9
'Abdullah b. 'Umar, 159, 160–2
'Abdullah b. al-Zubayr, 92–8, 101, 166, 174
'Abdulmalik b. Marwān, 93–117, 166, 168, 174
'Abdulqays, tribe of, 52, 97
'Abdulraḥman b. Ḥabīb, 158
'Abdulraḥman b. Muḥammad b. al-Ash'ath, 107, 110–11
'Abdurabbihi, 104
'Abs, clan of, 40
Abyssinia, 3, 6, 10
Ādherbayjān, 68, 122, 144, 145, 147, 157, 160
ahl al-ayyām, 45, 50–1, 55
ahl al-balā', 45
ahl al-fay', 50
ahl al-Qādisiyya, 45, 50
ahl al-qurā, 23, 29, 51
ahl al-rāya, 36
ahl al-ridda, 45, 50
ahl al-wabar, 29
Ahwāz, 97, 103
'Ā'isha, widow of the Prophet, 71–2
Ajnādayn, battle of, 26, 29, 31, 40, 82
al-Akhṭal, poet, 106
Alexandria, 37, 38, 112, 123, 164
'Alī b. 'Abdillah b. 'Abbās, 181
'Alī b. Abī Ṭālib, 16, 18, 56, 58, 61–2, 71–8, 91, 167, 180
alms, 118–19
Āmid, 145
Amīr al-Mu'minīn, title introduced, 56; interpretation of office, 60, 73, 79–80, 111, 116; *khawārij* version, 76; Arabic and Islamic views of, 167; Shī'ite view of, 179–80; Khurāsāniyya view of, 187–8
'Āmir b. Wāthila, 110
'Ammār b. Yāsir, 58, 69, 72
'Amr b. al-'Ās, 25, 31, 35, 38, 39, 40, 56, 66, 75, 78, 80–1
'Amr b. Sa'īd, 98
Andkhūy, 141
anṣār, 45, 63, 71, 72, 77
'Aqrabā, battle of, 23, 24, 45
Arab traditions: of social organization, 15; of leadership, 16–17, 19, 34, 56; of conquest, 35; of government, compared with Islamic, 167, 171
Arabia, conditions in, 1–15
'arāfa, 53, 87–8
Ardabīl, 145
'arīf, 53, 87
Armenia, 83, 122, 144, 147, 157; mercenaries of, 26
armies: Arab, 34–5, 36, 40–1, 44–6, 52; standing, 105; Syrian, *see* Syrian army
Asad, tribe of, 20, 24, 30
Asad al-Qasrī, 139, 141, 178
al-Ash'ath b. Qays al-Kindī, 21, 27, 30, 54, 67, 68, 72, 75, 77, 89, 109, 111
assimilation, of conquered peoples, 121–4, 133–4, 140, 168–71, 174–8, 184, 189
al-Aswad al-'Ansī, 21
Aws, tribe of, 10, 18
Azāriqa, 96
Azd, tribe of, 52, 97, 98, 136, 145

Baḥrayn, 51, 97
Bajīla, tribe of, 47, 120
Bakr, tribe of, 52
Abū Bakr, *khalīfa*, 16, 18–27, 82, 166
Balī, clan of, 36, 40
Balkh, 185
Balqā', 93
Balūchistān, 117
Banū Qaynuqā', 13
barara, 52
Baṣra: attack on, 97–8; establishment of, 51–5; expeditions from, 66–7; organization of, 87–8, 101–6, 113, 133, 170, 173; people of, 71, 73, 93, 96, 122; revolts in, 111, 136
Bayān b. Sam'ān, 142
bayt, 18, 91
Berber tribesmen, 101, 122, 134, 149–52, 158
Bilbays, 146, 164